# ANGELS
# IN HOBNAIL BOOTS

## Haydn Williams

Published by:
Hafod Books
7 South Close, Bishopston, Swansea SA3 3ER


ISBN 0 9545765 0 0

British Library in Cataloguing in Publication Data:
a catalogue record for this book is available from the British Library.

Design and production:
Country Books, Courtyard Cottage, Little Longstone, Bakewell, Derbyshire DE45 1NN

Printed and bound by Cromwell Press Ltd

## DEDICATION

*For mammy*

# CONTENTS

1 Nearest to heaven 9

2 Malice and spite 18

3 Death, destruction and liberation 24

4 Hitler's done us a favour 36

5 A roof over our heads 50

6 A stranger at my father's funeral 60

7 Go and see your father 66

8 Money and marbles 70

9 Moving on 85

10 Together again 96

11 Starting school 109

12 Friends and neighbours 117

13 Collecting firewood 127

14 The sweet smell of success 152

15 What's in a name 162

16 Work for your keep 170

17 Mario and the cider 196

18 The dark before the dawn 221

19 Growing up                                   242
20 The Yanks arrive                             255
21 Cookies                                      272
22 Love and Welsh cakes                         286
23 Angels in hobnail boots                      301
24 Brammer and the balloon shed                 309
25 More trouble with the law and chickens       319
26 Cub scouts and football                      332
27 The battle won                               348

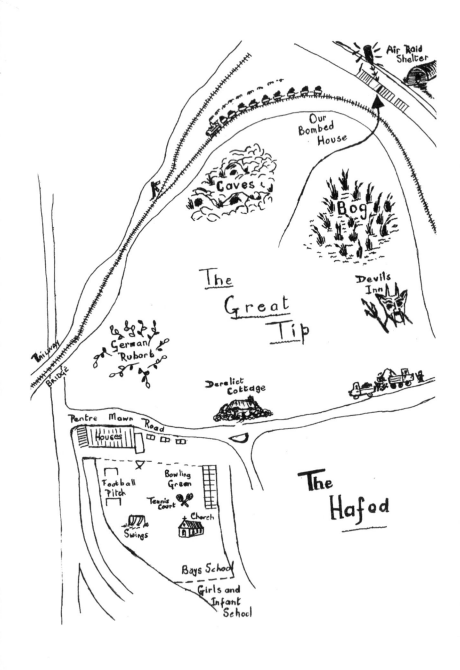

## CHAPTER 1

# NEAREST TO HEAVEN

It was probably the outbreak of World War II in September 1939; and the dramatic effects this terrifying time had on people's lives, that I have the ability to recall events from a very early age. I was three years old when war broke out, and five years old when our family joined the ever-increasing list of casualties. The change from peace to war was a gradual process, the period that was to become known as the phoney war; and things really did not begin to heat up until May 1940, when Hitler made his great and daring push through the Ardennes into Belgium and France. Until then, the war had very little effect on my young life. The necessities for living such as food and clothing were plentiful; and certainly my father's life style did not alter; the beer at the local pub continued to flow.

We lived in a cramped little house, nestling close to the railway bridge, which spanned the main Swansea to Neath road. It was one of six, an odd little group of houses, wedged between the road and the railway embankment: in the curve of the railway line as it snaked across the bridge. My father John Swain had brought my mother Louisa,

Mammy: to this grimy, grubby part of industrial Swansea, one cold dark night in November 1928. A vastly different scene to her home on the family farm, in the rugged yet beautiful Amman Valley; which she had left earlier that day. Mammy was embarking on a perilous journey. Leaving the love and security of her Mam and Dada, to set up home, to live in sin: with my father. It would be seen; as an act of betrayal by her family: and unforgivable by society. But there was no turning back now; she was already several months pregnant, and they would be married at the town's registry office before the year's end. To her staunchly church-going family, this was almost as bad as remaining unmarried; and to make matters worse, my father was Roman Catholic. With time, her Mam did relent, and visited us whenever she could; but her Dada was unforgiving, and never saw or spoke to her again.

I remember frequent visits with my parents, to the town's market on a Friday night, after my father had been paid; when he was in a more sober mood. Everyone got paid on a Friday; and the town, especially the market, was alive with people. Why they chose to take me, I will never know; we were seven children, two girls and five boys. Maggie was the eldest: then Molly, Daniel, Harry, Handel, that's me: then Walter, and the baby, Eddie. Perhaps it made life a little easier for Maggie, who remained at home caring for the others: one less to look after.

Mammy and my father would wear their finest clothes. He, always dressed in a dark suit, and his crowning glory, his bowler hat; and she in a long flowing coat; and hat, held in place with a long pearl decorated hat-pin. Sometimes if the weather was cold, she would also wear her collar of fox furs and tails. Oh! How I wished that they would always be like this, as it was when they first met, here in the town's market place.

That was many years before; when every Saturday, my Grandmother and Mammy, would bring fresh produce to the market from the farm; mainly butter, but any fruit and vegetables that were in season as well. It was during one of these visits, that Mammy had caught my father's eye. She was only just of medium height, but her body was sound and firm; as were her arms and legs; with a strong face and jutting chin, straight nose, and dark brown, almost black eyes: but it was her hair, that was her main attraction, especially to men; coal black hair, touched with the diamond sheen of anthracite.

They would set up their little stall, open for business, and by midday they were usually sold out. My grandmother then, would indulge in a little shopping of her own; and Mammy loved this time of the day as well, as she could wander off and gaze into the windows of the smart ladies dress shops, which were showing all of the latest London fashions. But, it was not by chance that her path crossed with that of the good-looking young widower; several times, on that day they first met. And over the ensuing months, they met as often as they possibly could: but always secretly. Mammy was only too aware, that her Mam and Dada would never approve of her liaison with this workingman from the town. Their moments of love were snatched, in and around the town centre, during that brief hour or so every Saturday; and I dread to think, just where my sister Maggie was conceived.

As a special treat, sometimes, after the shopping had finished; and the carrier bags full of the goods from the market; the three of us would spend the remainder of the early evening at the town's Variety Palace, the Empire Theatre. It cost thruppence each for a seat up in the gods. This was the general slang for the top tier of seats in the theatre, the ones nearest to heaven. It was a venue that I was to visit: often on my own, in later years; and it was here that I was privileged to see the emergence of many entertainers, who were later to become international celebrities: such as Julie Andrews, Harry Secombe, and Morecambe and Wise. But even after outings such as these, there was still no guarantee that the day would end peacefully. There would still be time for my father to visit the pub, after we had arrived home; and all the earlier pleasantries of the day would be wiped out, if the demons of drink were with him when he returned.

The period of the phoney war: that strange time after war was declared, when little or no hostile action occurred, probably helped us to cope with the transition from peace to conflict. Young men of the neighbourhood would suddenly disappear; only to return, to rowdy welcoming parties, dressed in the garb of khaki, blue, or navy-blue. Gas masks were issued: nasty, black, and smelly rubber contraptions. I qualified for one of these, and envied my younger brother Walter, who was issued with a Mickey Mouse mask. My youngest brother Eddie, who was only three weeks old at the outbreak of war, had a special cradle-like container provided, in which he could be placed in the event of a gas attack. I seem to remember, that this came with a special pump attached, which enabled him to receive filtered clean air.

Perhaps the most dramatic and sudden change, were the air raids and bombings, which brought home the full horrifying realities of war. To this day, I still feel instantly cold and shudder with fear, should I hear anything resembling the sound of an air-raid siren. We had many false alarms and practice warnings, during the latter part of 1939 and early 1940; but it still came as an awful shock to the town's population, when we experienced the real thing in the early hours of 27th June 1940. This first air raid by the German Luftwaffe, caused little damage, and thankfully no casualties; but this was only a taste, a prelude of the greater horror and devastation that was to follow.

On the majority of these occasions, the warning siren of an impending raid would occur during the night; which generally meant being snatched from your bed by an older brother or sister, with little or no time to put on your trousers, and rushed out of the house to the nearest shelter. War takes away a person's dignity, it strips you naked, it is felt even by a four or five year old child who is made to stand in a dark and dank air-raid shelter for hours on end wearing only a shirt.

The raids increased in number and ferocity during the months that followed, into the summer then autumn; when the nights were warm and barmy, and the increasing dashes to the air-raid shelter became more tolerable during the short hours of darkness. There were many false alarms, but there were also many raids on the town and the surrounding districts. We would remain quiet and listen for the sound of the German aircraft, the dreaded drone of the Junkers and Heinkel bomber's diesel engines. Then, in the distance, far away from us we prayed; we could hear the strange popping sound as the high-explosive bombs crashed to the ground. Occasionally, the sound would increase in volume to loud bangs, and we shuddered with fear, as we felt the shock vibrations rattle the shelter's foundations. Invariably the tension would be relieved by some wag crying out, "that was a close one"; or Algy the older of the Smith brothers, deriding his younger brother by shouting, "Percy's shit his pants"; and our laughter would ring out to hide the dread and fear that we felt and the tears filling our eyes.

During those first raids the shelter we used was the older, smaller type, divided inside into small compartments.

These proved to be difficult in getting in and out; without lights, and very claustrophobic, with people sometimes, packing these small cubicles like tinned sardines. Because of this, many people were discouraged from using these shelters; preferring to stay in the comfort of their own homes, taking refuge in the confined area under the stairs, which was generally the pantry. My father, in the beginning, tried to persuade Mammy that she too should adopt this practice, but thankfully she listened to wiser heads and insisted that we used the air-raid shelter.

So the authorities decided to build new shelters, much larger than the old ones, with very thick reinforced concrete roofs, and scrapped the idea of compartments. The atmosphere was far better in these taller, much roomier buildings, where families could sit huddled together in their own bit of space. But, the most pleasing feature was probably the introduction of a single electric light bulb, in the centre of the shelter; giving the occupants a feeling of togetherness; instead of standing alone in the dark.

As autumn turned to winter, with its bleak, cold, and often wet nights, we felt the grim horror of war in all its stark reality. The advent of Christmas I remember, still had its same magic, and we enjoyed most of the trappings. We ate well: a chicken dinner, sweets and chocolates, and presents; I had a small battery operated model railway engine, and some lead toy soldiers. This was a wonderful but brief respite from the war; but with the coming of the New Year, so the Luftwaffe returned with its campaign of terror. The raids were getting heavier now; and the death toll and list of casualties was growing longer, as the town and its surrounding districts were remorselessly attacked.

Then came a time of terror and devastation, from which many of the town's people thought that they would never recover. This brief, but horrific time-span, is firmly etched in the memories of all those who lived through it as, "The three nights blitz". There were many false alarms, and some heavy raids during the weeks that followed Christmas up to the beginning of the Blitz; which began on the night of 19th February 1941. Then, for the next three nights, we seemed to spend most of the hours when we should have been asleep, either dashing to, or inside the air-raid shelter.

Although this period was and is still referred to as, "The three nights blitz"; it covered the whole harrowing time, including the days, for it seemed that night and day became one. As the term implies, most of the bombings were carried out at night: sleepless and terror-stricken times for us; of long hours spent in the cold, dank, air-raid shelters.

The area of Swansea where we lived at that time, Landore, came out of this terrible time relatively unscathed, but the centre of the town was completely devastated. Other parts of the town were also heavily bombed, resulting in over 230 people killed, and as many seriously injured. The buildings and infrastructure of the town centre, at the end of the three nights, had been almost completely wiped out.

Even inside the air raid shelter, we could hear the German raiders aircraft; the whistling sounds of the heavy explosive bombs, the thuds as they found their random targets, together with the eerie screeching sounds emitted by the incendiary firebombs. As young as I was, I knew that living through this time, with all the terrible uncertainties; I was a living witness to all the horror that man could inflict upon his fellow man. Listening to the men's talk in the air-raid shelter, I was made aware that the bombers were after certain targets in the town; such as the railways, docks, bridges, and particularly one railway bridge known as the Landore Viaduct.

This bridge, carried all the main line railway traffic from Swansea and West Wales to London and all the other major manufacturing centres of the country. Swansea and West Wales, was at that time, a major producer of metals required for the war effort, such as steel, tinplate and Copper. The docks handled a lot of imported goods from the Commonwealth and America, including tankers carrying crude oil. So the Viaduct became a sort of symbol to us. We believed that as long as it remained intact, the raiders had failed to reach their objective; and we drew a feeling of strength from this show of defiance. It was a time when people got closer together, if only briefly, and it was during this period that even my father accompanied us to the shelter; such was the severity of the bombing.

There are many snatches of pictures in my mind, little cameos of things, memories of what happened at that time. But, there was one moment I still remember, that summed up the whole terrifying experience. On which night of the Blitz it happened, I will never know. Somehow I found myself standing alone in the middle of the road; we had just emerged from the air-raid shelter, and my eyes were drawn in the direction of the town centre. The road here was almost straight for about half a mile, and I had to look through the arches of the two railway bridges that spanned it. In the distance I could see through the haze and smoke, the town-centre; which resembled a spent coal fire of ashes, with a faint red glow at its heart. It seemed like the last dying breath of a beaten man, Swansea Town lay mortally wounded; or to quote the words of Swansea's most famous son, the poet Dylan Thomas, who also witnessed the destruction, "our Swansea is dead".

With the coming of the fourth day and night, the Blitz

was over. The ordeal had ended; the town and its people were spared, and given a little time to recover. There were more raids to come, but nothing like, what had happened during the Blitz. There were also a lot more false alarms. Surprisingly, some people began to take chances again, my father included, staying at home during the raids instead of going to the shelter. Then came the day that was to alter my life and the lives of my family forever.

## CHAPTER 2

# MALICE AND SPITE

March 12th, 1941 started like any other ordinary day. It had been uneventful, and time dragged by as I waited for Daniel and Harry to return home from school. The children's craze in vogue at the time was playing marbles, or arlies, and both of them were caught up in the game. I was eager to know how successful they had been that day; how many had they had won, and what colours were they? If Harry had good day, he was only too glad to show-off and demonstrate just how well he had played; but if he had lost, then I was just as likely to get a smack from him for daring to ask. Today he was totally indifferent and just ignored me. Daniel was easy-going and just shrugged his shoulders if he had lost, but would take great delight in sharing with me if he had won. Today his jacket pocket, was absolutely bulging, he had won 10 more marbles. He took them out and put them on the table; shiny red ones, blue ones, white ones with the red dashes that we called blood arlies; gleaming steel ball-bearings we called baldies, and glass arlies over an inch in diameter known as Pop arlies. To me, they were like jewels in Ali Baba's cave.

Just imagine the delight and astonishment I felt, when he took hold of my hand; and placed in my palm three of the marbles, plus one baldy, and one of the big Pop arlies.

I can still feel the great thrill, the overwhelming excitement, as I clutched the marbles then in both hands; but it was essential if I was to keep this new treasure, that I must find a safe hiding place for them. I knew that if Harry discovered I had them, or where I had hidden them, he would take them from me. The only place I could think of was under the bed that I shared with my brothers; and I was in the bedroom that early evening, when my father returned home from an early drinking session. He was in one of his evil moods. He kicked open the front door, and banged it closed again. Then I heard him ranting and raving downstairs, shouting at Mammy and the rest of the family.

"Right. Louisa, get into the parlour, come on, and the rest of you, get into the parlour now".

I had witnessed similar scenes as this before, but the shock to my nervous system, and the hatred I felt for this man never waned. He had returned home determined to vent his malice on his family, and Mammy would take the brunt of it. Later in life, she tried to explain his fits of brutality; to defend him, by blaming it on beer and the more deadly whisky, and the company he kept. He had a good, and well-paid job as Head Shearer at the local copper works; and envious and jealous men, gripped with malice and spite, would taunt and bait him.

"Comely young wife you have there, John; turning all the men's heads she is. I saw Louisa today, talking to the rent man she was, I do hope you have paid the rent John, have you"?

Remarks like these would fester in his mind, building into rages of jealousy, ending in brutal assaults upon Mammy.

She learned quickly; that appeasement was the best way to defend her-self, and the children that were born during the short but violent marriage. She thought it better that she received the blows, rather than one of her children. He used his fists on Mammy; and the strap, or belt that he wore, on us children. The thick and wide leather belt, with its heavy steel buckle, was an essential part of the workingman's dress in those days. If he was in a particularly malicious mood, then the belt would be folded; and the beating meted out, would include the buckle end.

When these attacks occurred, my sister Maggie; if she could, would run screaming from the house and start banging on the doors of our neighbours' houses; and if Joe Lewis, the one neighbour who was not afraid of my father was in, she would be in luck. He never failed. He always came straight to our aid. Others, afraid to invoke the wrath of my father, would respond by running for the local policeman, Sergeant Clifton.

I knew that it would be useless staying where I was, my father would only come looking for me, and I would be safer joining the family in the parlour now. I got down the stairs as quietly as possible, where I could see Maggie with Mammy, who was carrying the baby; and Molly who was carrying Walter, coming from the kitchen into the passage. My father, who had opened the parlour door, was shouting at them.

"Come-on! Come-on! Get in there".

Then suddenly, Maggie, anticipating what was about to happen tried to make a bolt for the front door; but he was too quick for her, and grabbing her by the hair literally tossed her into the parlour. Mammy was next, and he pushed her, then Molly, into the room, with Daniel and Harry scampering behind. He stood there in the passage, puffing and blowing, and swaying slightly, his brain struggling to register that there was one of his family missing. That was me and I was now standing in his shadow. I did not wait for him to invite me in, as I was likely to be helped by the toe of his boot, or the back of his hand; but shot past him and dived under the small table on which stood Mammy's prized Aspidistra plant.

The parlour where we were all now assembled, was the best-kept room in the house. It was used only on special occasions; such as Christmas, and when we had important visitors. There was a leather couch, with two matching armchairs; the wooden floor was stained brown and highly polished, and in the centre of the room was a square red woollen carpet. The walls were covered with thick and heavily embossed wallpaper, predominantly blue in colour; and there were large gilt picture frames, with portraits of my father's family; his mother, father, and family groups. Apart from the small table under which I was skulking, the one remaining piece of furniture, which was considered to be a great status symbol, was the dark brown gleaming upright piano. And as if to prove my father's dominance over the family, sitting on the top of this, was his black bowler hat.

Mammy sat down in one of the large armchairs, the one furthest away from the door. Molly with Walter on her lap, and Daniel and Harry, sat themselves down on the couch. Maggie, her hair still dishevelled, sat bolt upright in the armchair next to the door. She had her hands clenched tightly in front of her, with a look of righteous defiance on her face. My father, still unsteady on his feet, entered the room and closed the door behind him. He was still breathing heavily; sucking in large gulps of air, trying desperately to retain some dignity; but by now had become completely overwhelmed with rage.

Leaning back against the door to steady himself he pointed his right hand at Mammy, and quietly at first, said, "Haven't I been a good husband to you", then in a louder voice shouted at her, "well haven't I"?

He waited for Mammy's response, "Yes John, you are a good husband", she sighed.

Then raising his voice even louder, and waving his arm around in a semi-circle to include the rest of us, he screamed. "Haven't I been a good father to all of you"?

We remained silent. I still crouched under the table, with my eyes down and half closed most of the time. I had learned from an early age to avoid eye contact with my father, even at the best of times.

He pushed himself away from the door, his shoulders stooped with arms now hanging loosely, and walked unsteadily towards Mammy mouthing and slavering to form his words as he went.

"I work bloody hard for you", he snarled, his right arm shaking and waving about in front of him, trying to point at her.

"There's plenty of food on the table, you have good clothes, you want for nothing,"

The menace in his voice was increasing now as he said, "you do better than most of the women and kids in this cowing dump of a place".

He was standing now almost on top of Mammy, and suddenly, he lurched forward his face only inches away from hers," and what have you been doing all day", he said accusingly.

Like the rest us, apart from Maggie, she avoided eye contact with him, and remained with eyes downcast, gently patting the baby. His hate-filled face, full of menace, was challenging her to look at him, but she refused. Then as he straightened up, he brought his right arm down across her face, striking her first with the palm of his hand, then returning with the back of it, and repeated this action again and again. After the first blow, she had lifted her head to ensure that his hand did not hit the baby. She just looked at him with no anger in her eyes or hate, just sadness. The shock to her system woke the baby, who now began to whimper, then cry, which seemed to bring some sanity back to him. It seems incredible now to think, that the baby had slept through all that noise and commotion.

We knew, but my father was unaware, that while he was attacking Mammy, Maggie had slipped away from the room, and was even now banging on the door of Joe Lewis. She was in luck, he was in; and was soon in our house remonstrating with my father, who was now slumped in the armchair, just vacated by Maggie.

"Take the kids into the kitchen Louisa", he said, "I'll stay with John for a while".

It was only then that I crawled from under the table, and keeping close to Mammy, we all gladly left the room. My father, still huffing and blowing; and holding his head in his hands, remained slumped in the chair, with Joe Lewis his hands on his hips standing over him.

That was the last time I saw my father.

## CHAPTER 3

# DEATH, DESTRUCTION AND LIBERATION

Later that night, as Daniel, Harry, and I, crept past the parlour on our way upstairs to bed; I could still hear my father's heavy snoring, even though the door was closed. He was in another drunken stupor. Joe Lewis had stayed with him, until he was sure that he had fallen into a deep sleep, before leaving. Mammy had warned us to be quiet, not to disturb him, and she had sent Maggie along with us to ensure that we behaved.

The three of us shared a large double bed, and as the youngest I was expected to sleep in the middle. We did not enjoy the luxury of having pyjamas; we just stripped down to the shirt or jersey, we wore that day. I kept as close as I could to Daniel, and as far away from Harry as I possibly could. Apart from getting a kick or a fist in my back or stomach, which was just about tolerable, his biggest problem was that he could not control his bladder. The bed could be flooded at any time during the night, which meant that we would have to lay in the sticky mess until we got up the following morning. To wake Mammy, which meant disturbing my father, would result in dreadful consequences, with Harry getting a beating with the strap.

Thankfully, there was no such problem that night, but greater events were about to overtake us as a family. We hadn't been asleep for any great length of time, when I was being shaken and roughly woken up by Maggie. The air-raid siren was wailing its dreadful warning; we had to get to the air raid shelter; but, by now I had learned to dress quickly at these times, putting on my trousers and boots.

Daniel and Harry had already dressed, and were on their way downstairs. Maggie was waiting for me by the door, shouting. "Hurry up Handel, hurry up".

I was about to join her, when I remembered my marbles; I turned, and avoiding her clutching hands, scrambled under the bed to get them. When I emerged, she was furious, grabbing me, and forcing the marbles from my hand, yelling. "You little bugger, you'll get us all killed".

She then walked across the room and placed my marbles on the mantelpiece above the fireplace; before getting hold of me again by my shirt collar, and dragged me down the stairs where Mammy and the rest of the family were waiting in the passageway. She scolded me,

"You wicked boy Handel, Dere m'llan, come on", she always used her native Welsh when she wanted to emphasise something.

As always, she had the baby wrapped snugly in the shawl, and quickly looking at the rest of us, making a quick mental head count she said. "Right Maggie, open the door and let's get across to the shelter".

There was no sign of my father.

The two wardens, who were in charge of the area, were already at the shelter; and the younger one, who was probably in his late Forties, took his duties seriously, and was always shouting.

"Hurry up, be quiet, and get inside the shelter".

The other, more elderly man had little enthusiasm for the job; probably realising anyway that people would act as they thought necessary to protect themselves, and could do without any prompting from him.

At the entrance to the shelter, Mammy unwrapped the shawl from her body, and wrapping it once more around the baby, handed the little bundle to Maggie.

"Here Maggie", she said, "take them through and settle them down. I'm going back to the house to see your father".

The air-raid siren, which had continued blasting all this time, began to fade, then quickly stopped, as she hurried off.

Once inside the shelter, we were greeted by one of our neighbours, Grannie Davies. This old dear always seemed to be to have an unlimited supply of hard-boiled sweets, and was constantly sucking away on one of these. She loved us children, particularly me; and would gather me up in her long skinny arms, cuddling and tickling me, which seemed to give her an immense amount of pleasure. Then as a reward, she would take a warm sticky sweet from her mouth and press it into mine. She was always warm, and smelt of sweets and fruit, and another distinct smell of brandy or whisky. Her sweet sucking, everyone realised, became a habit through the need to mask the smell of the liquor.

She called to us. "Over by yer Mag, I've kept you a place".

People liked to meet in the same places in the shelter, gathering in little niches, with particular friends and neighbours. Grannie Davies was always first in of our lot, putting her bag and blankets on one of the benches that lined the walls, saving a seat for Mammy.

Maggie sat down beside her. "Where's your Mam then"? The old woman enquired.

"Gone back to the house for dad", Maggie replied.

Grannie Davies smiled wryly before saying. "Still sleeping it off is he love". She did not miss much. She knew all the gossip of the area.

Mammy soon returned, accompanied now by Joe and Audrey Lewis, but not my father. She took the baby from Maggie, and wrapping the shawl once more around her, sat down between her daughter and the old woman. They all pushed up and squeezed together on the bench: Grannie Davies, Mammy, Mrs Lewis, and Maggie who had now taken Walter from Molly, and had the little boy on her lap. Joe Lewis had wandered off to join some of the other men who were standing near the entrance. It is a great help for people to cope with difficult situations like these, when they have warm friends and neighbours for company.

Once again we settled down for another long session, most of the women seated on the benches, the men and older children standing around in groups. Harry had wandered off looking for kindred spirits, which usually meant the Smith brothers. Normally, I kept close to Mammy and her little group; but somehow tonight; I had ended up sitting in the centre of the shelter immediately beneath the single electric light. Then they came, a faint drone was heard first. Then the steady throb of the diesel engines, as the German bombers drew ever closer. It was a sound we had become accustomed to over the past eight to nine months, but the dread and fear that it brought was as strong as ever. Everyone became quiet and still, any youngsters still chattering were told to hush. Did we feel that if we could not be seen, or heard, then the bombers could not find us? It had worked in the past; so we remained silent, and daring only to breathe softly, we prayed that once more the hunters in sky would fail, or find other targets.

Suddenly, all the demons of hell were upon us. First came the eerie whistling sound of the high-explosive bombs, as they hurtled towards us. We had never heard them so close before. Then, a hush, before simultaneously, we felt the shock waves; and heard the thunderous bangs as they impacted on their random targets. The air-raid shelter was shaken violently; with flakes of concrete, and dust, raining down upon us from the ceiling; but the building, this new shelter that had replaced the older smaller one, only weeks before, stood firm. Shocked, and frightened, all those standing; turned and scattered away from the centre, pushing and pressing each other against the walls. They were all terrified, frantically clawing at the concrete, some dropping to their knees, and screaming prayers to the heavens. "Lord help us, Lord help us, forgive us Lord", they cried. They were praying to a God they had long ago forgotten.

I sat alone now in the centre of the shelter; fascinated by the sight of the single electric light bulb, which was swinging violently on the end of its flex; randomly throwing its light, then casting swirling shadows over the terror stricken people. They continued their crying, screaming and praying, long after the explosions had ceased; and the light bulb slowed its swinging and dancing on its flex, until it stopped and died. The sudden darkness; hushed the frightened people, and silence reigned momentarily. Then one small child began to whimper and cry, and then another, as the stunned people stirred themselves from their fright. Soon, there were a lot more tears and sobbing; as mothers hugged their children, and neighbours clasped and held each other close, forgetting their petty quarrels and prejudices; with loud cries of. "Thank God, thank God. Oh thank you Lord".

If my faith in a greater God, was ever put in any doubt, or questioned; in the years that followed; I stop and think back to that night; when people claiming to be atheists or agnostics, but facing almost certain death; will pray, yes beg, and even scream to God for their salvation.

We stayed there in the dark, each one alone with his thoughts; not daring to move or speak until eventually; one of the wardens who had now regained some of his composure, produced his torch and switched it on. The sharp beam of light helped to soothe and calm everyone, as he said in a stern tone of voice, more probably to give himself much-needed courage.

"Right, everyone remain calm now; stay where you are, we must take stock of the situation; I'm going outside now to see just what has happened, and if there has been any damage".

It was the younger Warden who had taken charge, and he was now going to venture outside into the night. As he left, the older Warden switched on his torch, to lift our spirits and give us a dim but much needed source of light.

The warden who had left the shelter was outside for what seemed a considerable length of time, but it was probably only minutes. Then people began to fidget and become impatient, not knowing exactly where the bombs had dropped. When he did return, we could sense that things were bad; we could not see his facial expressions because of the poor light, but could tell from his voice that he was in an agitated state. He called Joe Lewis and some of the other men to him. They were mostly middle-aged or elderly, the young men having been conscripted to the forces.

In a voice shaking with anxiety, he said. "Men I need help, the road has been damaged and the water mains gone; and some buildings hit as well". He paused for a moment, his anxious and fearful state had taken his breath away; he swallowed hard; then continued. "I'll be honest with you men, it's a hell of a mess out there".

Then came cries of. "What's been hit? Is it the railway? The bridges? The cinema?"

But no one asked about the houses; they were afraid to ask about their homes.

"I can't tell you", he said. "There's no light. Sergeant Clifton is out there now trying to organise something, and we need help. These men are coming with me now, but you are all to stay here, and remember, you must wait until the all clear signal goes before leaving the shelter".

He had been gone less than five minutes, and the all clear had still not been sounded; but the tension was building up until it all became too much to bear; too long for these people caught up in this concrete shell. They were anxious and frightened. They just had to know where the bombs had landed, and what had been hit. It was close, they knew. During the last year, they had heard many bombs drop; some near and some far, and had witnessed the terrible scenes during the three nights blitz. They remembered the damage to the town centre and the docks, and other areas laid waste. They remembered the sound; of the high explosive bombs; as they rained down on these places, which were less than two miles away; and were dreadfully aware that the bombs that had descended near them that night, was the closest thing yet to a direct hit on the shelter.

They could restrain themselves no longer; as first one, and then another emerged from the shelter. A trickle of the few became a flood of many; as almost in panic now, the shocked and trembling friends, neighbours, and families spewed out of the shelter's narrow exits. The older Warden, who had remained inside, did nothing to prevent them from leaving. He did, however, stem the flood of people at one of the exits; and provided a much-needed source of light by shining his torch on to the ceiling, casting a dim reflection throughout the building.

As the people left, Mammy, becoming anxious about me pushed her way to where I was sitting, and with her one free hand grabbed me the around the waist. With me now safely in tow, she returned to her seat and rejoined the rest of the family.

She pushed me closer to my sister Molly. "Here Molly, she said, "hold on to Handel. We'll wait here a minute", then pointing to the crowd she said, "let them go, we'll find out soon enough what has happened out there".

Finally, when everyone except our group had gone, the old warden called over, "Alright Louisa, you bring them through now," shining the light from his torch directly upon us.

Mammy stood up, her body shuddered slightly, and she sighed. Then taking a deep breath, she said, "Right, keep together and stay close to me", then added, "Watch him Molly", as she pointed to my brother Harry, who was already edging towards the door.

The all-clear siren sounded as we emerged from the air raid shelter. Its high-pitched monotone sound always brought calm, and comfort, to the people recovering from a night's bombing. Especially tonight, it was greeted with huge sighs of relief. The three-quarters moon, which was shaded by high thin cloud, was bright enough for me to see, as my eyes grew accustomed to its shallow light. Most of the people, who had left the shelter before us, were still waiting around in huddled groups; discussing the night's events and what they had discovered on the outside. I could just make out the largest of these, through the smoky haze, that had gathered around the opening in the wall.

Beyond them was the main road, where there were signs of more flashlights, and men carrying red-lighted hurricane lamps through a pall of thick blue-black smoke. The dim lights reflected eerily in the water from the burst water main, which was gushing down from the road, over the bank and on to the canal below. A chicken, bereft of most of its feathers and mortally wounded, struggled feebly against the rush of water as it swept down to the canal.

Because of the burst water main, the ground was quickly turning to mud, where a hundred pairs of the boots and shoes had churned its surface into a sticky morass. We moved slowly up the bank to the road, following Mammy, Audrey Lewis and Grannie Davies; I was with Molly and Daniel, and Maggie bringing up the rear carrying Walter.

Mammy was constantly vigilant; her sharp eyes always moving; scanning to the front and sides and over her shoulder, to see that her brood was all present and still with her.

Suddenly, she stopped and shouted. "Where is he Maggie, where is Harry? Find him a quick".

It was always Maggie that she turned to when she was upset, and received the sharp end of her tongue. "I don't know Mammy, I've got Walter", she screeched back. Maggie was angry and tired, as she put my little brother down, turned and punched Molly in the back.

"It's her fault Mammy", she said. "She was supposed to be looking after him". The force of the punch to Molly's body knocked her to the ground, into the muddy water, but she was up and on her feet quickly; wiping the mud from her faded green frock she pulled the loosely fitting black cardigan tightly around her shoulders. Her face was flushed, and she stared straight ahead, she was embarrassed but did not cry. Molly was used to the knocks of life, particularly the blows delivered from her sister's fists.

There was still no sign of Harry, who was very clever at disappearing and melting into the background, then reappearing in the most unexpected of places.

Panicking, Mammy screamed once more at both my sisters, reverting to her natural Welsh tongue. "Iesi Annwyl o' Nazareth, Dear Jesus of Nazareth", she screamed. "Find him, find him now girls".

Maggie responded, wide-eyed and desperate; breathing deeply, the burden of responsibility hammered into her by Mammy weighed heavily upon her. "There he is Mammy, up by the wall". She dug her clenched fist once more into Molly's back. "Go and get him you lazy slut", she bellowed threateningly.

I hated Maggie when she attacked Molly like this, but I was afraid to say anything for fear that she would turn her fists on me. Molly just turned and hurried off, glad of the brief respite to get away from the intense worry and anxiety of her mother and sister.

We all stood there, waiting for Molly and Harry to return. Grannie Davies and Audrey Lewis continued walking up towards the road. It was typical of Harry that as Molly approached him, he ran back down the slope to within Mammy's sight, but kept well out of her reach.

She threatened and scolded him. "Your father will find out you have been a bad boy, and you know what will happen then". He just stared back at her, then turned around and walked slowly toward the road, with his hands in his pockets and head slightly drooped. Harry exasperated Mammy, and sighing heavily now she said.

"Come on, let's go".

We moved forward slowly again as Molly rejoined us. She came and stood next to me and put her arm on my shoulder. "Did you see the chicken Handel", she said "no feathers".

"Yes I did", I replied, then laughed, but it was a hollow laugh, I was glad it was the chicken and not me that was blasted that night.

As we approached the people, who had gathered around the gap in the wall, Grannie Davies who had gone ahead of us, shouted down to Mammy. "The bastards have got our homes Louisa. Our houses have gone".

Mammy did not stop, but continued trudging her way up the muddy bank, where she joined the old woman and Audrey Lewis; and together, they pushed their way through the crowd.

The stick of high-explosive bombs, had clinically taken out the small row of six houses where we lived. They had missed their intended targets, of the railway line, that ran along the rear of the houses, and the bridges that spanned the road. These vital links remained intact, including the cinema that was only a matter of a few yards away from the houses. The air-raid shelter, from which we had just emerged, was immediately opposite across the road, and fortunately sheltered behind a stout 6 ft high, stone wall. It is extremely doubtful, whether the shelter could have withstood a direct hit, like the one, which had demolished the houses. It would have been the town's worst disaster, where probably more than one hundred souls would have perished.

Along with Grannie Davies and Audrey Lewis, we joined those of our neighbours who, like ourselves, were now homeless. The two ladies, Mammy's friends, drew closer and clasped their arms around her; knowing that it was not just her home that she had lost that night, but probably her husband as well.

## CHAPTER 4

# HITLER'S DONE US A FAVOUR

The thin, high clouds, covering the moon, were beginning to thicken now. I could see in its shadowy light, Sergeant Clifton; who was supervising a group of men that were working away at a mess of stones, timber, slates and broken furniture. This was all that remained of our homes. My father was still probably asleep, even after the high explosive bombs ripped into the house. Joe Lewis was aware of this, and it was he that had instigated the search for my father, by alerting Sergeant Clifton and the warden to begin digging away at the rubble immediately.

Now, they were frantically clawing at the rubble with their bare hands; working in the faint light of the moon, and a couple of hurricane lamps. The weak, red light, from these lamps, gave an extra sense of unreality, and a spooky atmosphere to the whole scene we were watching.

Grannie Davies was the first one to break the silence that had gripped us, as we tried to come to terms with the scene of carnage and devastation. "They'll get him out Louisa, you see, he'll be alright. He's a tough old bugger is your John".

As she finished speaking, one of the men broke away from those digging at the rubble, and quickly pushed his way through the stunned and staring crowd. It was Joe Lewis. "He's alright Louisa, he's still alive", he said, as he caught his breath.

Smoking forty cigarettes a day and working at the Copper Works; were taking its toll on the fifty year-old. "We'll get him out soon", he said, almost squeezing the words from his parched throat and mouth; which had been attacked by the acrid fumes emanating from the bomb blasted debris.

Mammy just stared straight ahead, showing no emotion, a blank stony look on her face. She was still trying to come to terms with the loss of her home and possessions, and what this meant to her children. I did not think that she could cope with the thought of losing her husband as well.

It was well past midnight, and cold, with the damp air of winter's early morning hours. But still many people remained. Some were our immediate neighbours; like Grannie Davies and the Lewis'; who were also now homeless, and others waiting to help if needed. They talked in low tones and quiet voices, almost whispering, and stealing glances at us, particularly Mammy. She had not moved or spoken since we had arrived, and still supported by the two ladies, shoulder-to-shoulder holding her closely. Some of our other neighbours, formed a loose circle around them, eager to hear the news Joe Lewis had brought. But, by the lack of reaction from Mammy, it was very doubtful, whether she had taken in what he had said. He could sense this, and said to his wife. "Stay with her now, love. I must get back and help".

He started to go back to where the men were digging, but, turning once more, he hesitated, swallowing hard trying to inject some authority into his voice. Then pointing his finger firmly at Maggie said. "You look after your Mam now". Then to Molly, "and you, both of you, see to your Mam and the boys".

Perhaps, it is one of nature's safeguards that young children are in the main, selfish little creatures. Something in the human basic instinct, that instructs children that survival is everything, and to look to their own needs first. So perhaps, it was not surprising; that throughout all of this, the destruction to our family home, and the perilous state of my father; the greatest agony I suffered that night was for the loss of my marbles, which Maggie had snatched from me and placed on the bedroom mantelpiece. I was looking at the scene of devastation, wondering just where my precious marbles were in the shattered remains of our home, and thinking would I ever have the chance to recover them. Maybe, I hoped, one of the men now frantically clawing away at the rubble would find them and keep them for me.

As the night passed, the cold and damp air began to penetrate our scanty clothing. We were getting tired and starting to fidget. I remained close to Molly and Daniel, huddling together now to keep warm. As ever, Harry stood apart from the rest of us, intently engrossed by the spectacle of the smouldering debris, and by the efforts of the men who were digging frantically to get at my father. Maggie, still carrying my smaller brother Walter, stayed close to Mammy. The little boy was in a state of half sleep, and was almost constantly, if wearily, grizzling.

This is one of the things that I remember most about Walter, he seemed to be always whimpering and grizzling. I'm sure, that in a competition for grizzling he would have been a world-beater. Having said this, I know that I am being unkind to him. He was born a sickly baby, and only just managed to cling on to life for many years as a child. He suffered many terrible illnesses, such as bronchitis and pneumonia, and had come close to death on two occasions. Our family doctor almost pronounced him dead, having withdrawn medication and given him up as a lost cause. It was another wonderful example of the great strength of character and will power; possessed by Mammy, that she persevered in nursing him, and would not let him die.

As the cold night dragged on, most of the people now began to drift away; many to their homes; and others, who like us were now homeless, to stay with relatives or friends. Then just when things were beginning to get extremely unbearable; we were so tired and very cold, news reached us that the Salvation Army had set up a refuge at one of the local churches, St Paul's. They had organized food, hot drinks, and warm blankets.

Realising that Mammy was still trying to come to terms with the night's terrible events, Grannie Davies now shook her slightly, saying. "It would be better Louisa, for you and the children to go up to the church. You can't do anything here. You must think of the baby and the rest of the children".

The gentle prodding, by the old lady, helped Mammy to shake off the state of lethargy that had overwhelmed her. "Yes you are right gran", she replied.

She realised that she had to regain her mental strength and composure. "The children need warmth and shelter, and they must go, but I'm staying here until they get John out".

Then turning to Maggie, and now with authority in her voice, said. "Mag, take Molly and the boys up to St Paul's. Keep together, and stay there until I come for you, right. I'm going to wait here until I see that your Father is alive and safe".

The baby, wrapped safe and warm in the shawl close to Mammy's body, softly whimpered, as she patted and cooed to him. "There, there, bach, quiet now".

Unhesitatingly, Maggie obeyed Mammy and moved off in the direction of the church, which was on the main road about a quarter of a mile away. Harry was still engrossed in watching the men digging at the debris. He wanted to be the first of the family to see my father being pulled out. Most of the people had left the area now, their curiosity and willingness to help defeated by the cold night air. It was much quieter, the only noise coming from the men working on the bombed site.

Mammy called to Harry. "Go with Maggie now up to St Paul's". He pretended not to hear her, and only responded when she raised her voice. "If you don't move now, Harry, you'll pay for it". Reluctantly, he shuffled off after us, hands in his pockets and dragging his feet, demonstrating his unwillingness to go.

As he walked past Mammy she said. "You stay with Maggie now" then shouted to the rest of us "Do as Maggie says". Then in acknowledgement of the responsibility she placed on her daughter's young shoulders, she added. "You are a good girl Maggie".

Bedraggled, tired, weary, and cold, we arrived at St Paul's to find most of our homeless neighbours already there. Other casualties of the bombing, people who lived in a little row of houses across the road from us, along side the canal, and had lost their homes were also there. These houses were almost under one of the railway bridges, and a single bomb had strayed from the stick that struck our houses, had made a direct hit, killing two men. Like us most of the houses in the area; these were homes to large families, and in total there must have been over forty people in the Church that night.

Looking after our needs and caring for us, were two members of the Salvation Army. One was an elderly man, with thin white hair and watery eyes; and his tight fitting, crinkled uniform, looked too small for his tall lean frame. The other was a stout middle-aged woman, with straight short black hair, and she was very much in charge.

Maggie, pushing the six of us before her, approached the woman, and without speaking, but by sheer weight of numbers, demanded her attention. "How many are you", the stout lady enquired. Maggie eyed the woman carefully. She was unsure just how to address her; was she a Miss, or a Mrs? Eventually, she said. "Six Miss," deciding that she looked like, and acted with the authority of a schoolmistress.

The woman inhaled deeply through her large flared nostrils, then sighing heavily asked. "Are you the Swain family"? "Yes Miss", Maggie replied. "I've heard about you", the woman went on. "Well I hope you are the last", she said, taking the three remaining thin woollen blankets from the table in front of her, and gave them to Maggie.

She showed little sympathy for us, no sign of emotion or pity for the plight we were in. Doubtless, the reason she appeared to be so cold hearted; was that she had seen so many people like us over the past months that pity, and sympathy, were feelings she could not afford. Practical help and providing sustenance were more important; and that's what the Salvation Army did for us that night, and on many subsequent occasions. The work that they carried out at that time is to their eternal credit, and to this day; I never pass a seller of the "War Cry", without putting my hand in my pocket.

We moved away from the Church entrance, and joined the rest of the people who were sitting or sprawled out on the oak pews. Some were talking in hushed whispers, but most were silent, alone with their thoughts, or sleeping. Death and destruction had come to them that night, and most did not know how to cope with it, but they would; the hardening process would continue, and see them through the years of war that lay ahead.

The church with its high domed roof was immense, with plenty of room for the number of people seeking shelter. It seemed strange at first; that they chose to remain huddled on one side of the building, in semi-darkness, away from the main aisle and centre seats, which were well lit; but these were facing the alter, on which was displayed the crucifix and the figure of Jesus. It was as if they felt a great despair at their plight, and they were ashamed that God should see them like this.

Walter, who had whimpered and grizzled most of the way on the trek to the church, was quiet now, as Maggie motioned for us to join the rest of the people in the pews. She led him by one hand, carrying the family bag and blankets in the other. Then herded us into one of the rows of seats, which was flanked on one side by the church wall. She positioned herself like a sentinel on the inner side near the aisle, thereby confining us in one row and keeping us all together.

The old man with the watery eyes followed behind us; with two cups of weak milky tea that were barely warm and placed them on the pew in front of Maggie. She gave one of the cups to Daniel, to be shared with Harry. The other cup was for me, and my younger brother Walter, who she once again cradled on her lap. Maggie would do without a drink, and so could Molly. She did not mind this sacrifice, even though she was parched and dying of thirst, as long as her sister was deprived as well. She knew Molly would be hurt and suffer through this, and she was glad. Maggie, as the eldest, rightly felt that life was unfair to her and resented Molly. People made a fuss of Molly and liked her. She was fair, and pretty, and smiled coyly; and got off lightly when she did wrong, even with our heavy-handed father. Whereas she, was expected to help Mammy, and look after the younger children; to be attentive; yet still took the brunt of the beatings from both Mammy in despair, and my father when he was in drink.

When we had finished drinking the tepid tea, Maggie took one of the blankets and wrapped it around her and Walter. He was by now thankfully asleep. The second blanket she handed to Molly, and told her to share this with me. The third was given to Daniel to share with Harry. As usual in these circumstances, Harry started playing up, complaining that he was cold. He did not like the church or the people, and threatened that he would run off, and Maggie would get into trouble with Mammy. I knew, and so did Daniel just exactly what Harry was after. He wanted the blanket to himself, and would create havoc until he got his own way. So once again, Daniel gave in and allowed him to keep it. Once he had succeeded in getting the blanket entirely for himself, the moaning and complaining stopped. He just sat there, with a smug, self-satisfied smirk on his face.

Out of all us children, it was probably Daniel, who suffered the most pain, from the terrible scenes of violence that frequently erupted in our family home. As the eldest son a lot was expected of him, and he could not be faulted in the example he set for the rest of us boys. He would do as he was told, help whenever he could, appease and give way to people; and sacrifice anything to preserve the peace. He was certainly not a coward, as I witnessed on several occasions his bravery in standing up for what he believed in. Like the countless occasions he defended me, when I was being picked on by Harry. I cannot remember him saying anything bad about anyone, or doing anything to hurt or harm. The one word that would describe him, or sum up his personality would be saintly. Like the colour of his hair, which was very light blonde; and his clear blue eyes, his persona oozed with trust, care, and affection. If he had a halo over his head it certainly would not, have been questioned by me. Over the years, I believe that he gradually developed a mechanism in his mind, to blank out the violence and pain that he witnessed, as a safeguard for mental protection. This enabled him to detach himself from the world and dwell in the land of dreams.

Harry on the other hand, was the complete opposite. No one word could describe or sum him up; but unruly, wicked, cunning, and unreservedly selfish spring to mind. Nothing or no one was safe when he was around. Apart from Maggie, he would bully the rest of us to get his own way, deliberately destroy things; and steal anything, even the food from your mouth. His defiance knew no bounds. But he was extremely wary of Maggie. She was up to him and gave him no quarter; and was more likely to give him a smack to the back of his head, or a clenched fist to his body, stomach or kidneys; depending on which way he was facing when she got hold of him. He received some terrible beatings from my father, and most children would have learned quickly to behave and avoid trouble, with the spirit of defiance being belted out of them. But not Harry, he only seemed to get worse as he got older.

Although it seemed like an age, Mammy rejoined us at the church about an hour later. She wearily shuffled in from the porch, across the main aisle, with the baby still wrapped in the shawl, her eyes searching the rows of seats looking for us. She had waited patiently near the remains of our house with a doggedness that was part of her incredibly strong character, until the men; urged on by

Sergeant Clifton, finally clawed their way to where my father lay and brought him out from under the rubble. The emergency services had managed to get an ambulance through, and this was waiting under the railway bridge, some fifty yards away. This was as close as it could get, as the road from there and in front of the bombed houses was impassable due to the clutter and debris, which was strewn across it.

Sergeant Clifton brought the news to her that my father was alive, but was badly injured, and he was being taken immediately to the general hospital. She could just see in the poor light of the hurricane lamps, the limp figure being carried by four men over the remains of the houses. The duty that she felt she owed to her husband had been carried out, and now it was time to fend for herself and her children.

I was in a drowsy state of half sleep, as I snuggled close to Molly under the blanket, with just my head showing. Mammy had found us, and exhausted now sat down in the pew immediately behind Maggie. Taking a little time to compose herself and sooth the baby, she leaned forward her face close to Maggie.

Then in a low voice, almost a whisper, but I heard her say. "They've taken your father to the town General, he is alive, just".

Maggie nodded her head, but it was not news that she welcomed; Mammy knew, and understood, that Maggie was full of hatred for her father.

One of our neighbours, I recognised him as the projectionist at the local cinema, called softly to Mammy. "Is everything alright Louisa"?

She turned her head in the direction of the man, and nodding, mouthed quietly back. "Yes, they've taken him to the hospital, but he's in a bad way".

The old Salvation Army man had watched Mammy as she entered the Church, and now brought her a cup of tea. He had heard the news of my father, and placing the cup on the seat alongside her said. "Your man is alright then, girl. Good news".

She gave a weak smile, thanking him for his kindness. She needed a drink badly, but there was milk in the tea and I knew that she would not drink it: Mammy drank strong, sweet tea, but with no milk. Still, it would come for the baby, but first she had to change him. She had nursed him throughout most of the night, and he badly needed cleaning. Her clothing was saturated with the baby's urine, and the stench now emanating from the little human bundle was more noticeable in the confines of the church.

She unwrapped the flannel shawl from around her, and softly uttered little soothing sounds, "sh, sh, there, there, bach", as the baby began to stir; getting angry at being removed from the comfort and warmth of his mother's body. Then moving closer to Maggie once more, she leaned forward saying, "Maggie, give me the bag".

Trying not to disturb Walter, who was still on her lap, Maggie removed the bag from her arm, then passed it over the pew to Mammy. She opened it and took out from this a piece of clean white towelling, which she was going use as a nappy.

The baby, screaming now as Mammy quickly removed the saturated but warm cloth from his body, and almost in one movement, replaced it with the clean towelling. Normally, she would wash the child before doing so, but that was impossible under the circumstances. The baby was quieter now, his screaming had ceased, but he still cried; he was sorely in need of succour and comfort.

Maggie had already anticipated Mammy's next move by taking the ever present, "titty bottle", from the family bag and gave this to her. The glass titty bottle had rubber teats at both ends, and Mammy now removed one of these, and poured in some of the cold milky tea from the cup. The baby eagerly took the teat as Mammy placed it against his lips; his grizzly sobs, ceased instantly, to be replaced by a more comforting sound as he sucked into the sweet milky fluid. She stood up and wrapped the child once more in the shawl, performing with ease the complicated ritual of nursing "Welsh Fashion".

Feeling better now that she had changed the baby, she sat down again to rest her wracked body from the aches and pains sustained during the long night. She allowed her body to sag, as her head slumped forward, and with eyes closed had a brief moment of respite. Sadly, the much-needed rest did not last long, as she became aware that the background noise and sounds of people talking and moving suddenly stopped. Sergeant Clifton had appeared in the porch of the Church, and was now walking grim faced towards us. Joe and Audrey Lewis were with him. They came straight to the pew where I was sitting alongside my brothers and sisters, and stood over us, and the policeman sat down next to Mammy. The horrifying and physically demanding events of the night had taken their toll on the old Sergeant too, and this showed as he sighed and with a resigned voice said.

"He's gone, Louisa. John is dead". Mammy stared blankly back at him, attempting to take in the dreadful finality of his words. He took her hand in his, fearing that she had not understood the news that he had brought. He patted her hand for a brief moment then asked.

"Do you understand Louisa, the loss of blood was too much. The doctor at the hospital said he was dead on arrival".

In an ironic yet cruel twist of fate, my father who had

survived the trenches and the terrible carnage of World War I, only to meet with death now in his own home in World War II.

Outwardly, it would appear that Mammy could not come to terms with what the Sergeant had told her; but the great shock to her nervous system; was sensed by the baby, who now began to cry. The need to soothe the child seemed to help. She appeared calm, and composed, as she stood up and began to rock the baby slowly and soothingly, muttering. "Well he's dead", and looking down at my baby brother quietly said, "That's alright bach, you cry now. Your father's dead".

The old Sergeant, also stood up, once more he had delivered his grim message to another victim of the war. But there were other people in the church, with their needs to be seen to, and further grim news to be delivered. For the moment he had done all that he could possibly do for us; but before he left, he said to Mammy, "Call me when you need me Louisa".

Audrey Lewis, who had been standing near to Maggie, moved now and stood close to Mammy. She put an arm around her shoulder, and sat her back down in the pew. Her husband Joe came and joined them, and sitting next to Mammy enquired, "Are you alright girl".

Mammy, replied then with words I would hear her speak so many times over the coming years; when dealing with the trials and hard times that lay ahead for our family. "Well, we will just have to get on with it".

As I looked at her face then, all the anguish of the night was gone. So too was the tired and weary sag of her body. The words she uttered seemed to transform her. She stood up once more, her back straight and head erect, her chin set firm and a hard look of steel in her eyes.

She moved round into the next pew where we were

sitting, and looking down at my eldest sister said, "Maggie, did you hear what the Sergeant said?" "Yes, Mammy," she replied.

Maggie was unflinching, firm and steady and showed no emotion. She was the mirror image of Mammy. She faced her now, reflecting the same look of determination and inner strength that is the foundation of a resolute character.

For Mammy the loss of my father was hard to bear, she would gladly endure the beatings and miserable existence, in return for the security he provided for her and her children. But I also knew what it meant to my sister Maggie. It was the removal of the constant threat of violence that she had endured for the whole of her young life. Her father was dead. Mammy understood, and could not deny Maggie's moment of truth; as she stood up, went close to Mammy, and in a slow, deliberately measured voice said. "I'm glad Mammy. Hitler's done us a favour".

## CHAPTER 5

# A ROOF OVER OUR HEADS

"If we have a roof over our heads then we have won half of the battle". This was another expression of Mammy's simple but effective philosophy, of dealing with the problems that she had to face in the days immediately following the death of my father. She had lost her husband, our home, furniture, and clothing: indeed all of our worldly possessions. We were left with just the clothes we stood up in, plus the family bag.

The family bag contained all of our family's important documents. It was multi-coloured but faded; and made of very closely woven heavy duty wool; probably from a piece of old carpet which had been folded over and stitched at the sides, with two pieces of wood slotted along the top forming the handles. This had been entrusted to Maggie the night before, but was now back where it belonged in the hands of Mammy. It would never be far away from her; taking second place only to her children, especially in the nightly dash to the air-raid shelter. It held all of the family's assets and identity; marriage and birth certificates, insurance policies, treasured photographs, ration books; and for Mammy the most treasured possession of all, my father's heavy solid gold watch chain. As precious as it had been to my father, it was not in anyway for sentimental reasons or fond memories as far as she was concerned, but very much for its intrinsic value. For gold Mammy knew, was a constant and universal means of wealth. This would be her insurance for the long-term; to be used only when all other means of survival and sustenance were exhausted. As long as it remained in her possession, then she was winning the other half of the battle.

So, to whom could Mammy turn to now for the help that she so desperately needed? Here she was; a forty three year old widow, with seven children in tow, with no house and little or no possessions. A bombed out family, living in a bombed out town, in a bombed out country; that was fighting for its very existence against the might of the German aerial and U-boat threats. The very essentials of life, food, clothing, and shelter, were getting fewer as the war progressed; and if any of these were lost, they were almost impossible to replace. The odds were stacked against her, but she was determined that the family would remain together.

Then where could Mammy start? What options were open to her now, when the family fortunes were at their very lowest? Her father, my grandfather, who never saw any of his daughter's children, had died in 1935 the year before I was born. He kept his vow, and never saw or spoke to Mammy ever again after that day she had left her family home to live with my father. Her mother, who did keep in touch with her, had died last year. The farm; was now run by her two younger brothers; and there were other members of the family; brothers and sisters, aunts, uncles, and cousins, scattered about the length and breadth of the country. But they had more or less taken the same view as her father, and had judged her to be foolish at least; or at worst brazen for what she had done and had excluded her. And in those days, there was no quick way to communicate with anyone except by telegram. Few people had telephones installed in their homes. Even so, there was no guarantee; that if she was able to contact members of her family that they would have shown any willingness to help.

On my father's side of the family there were just two, his one and only sister, and a cousin. Both of his parents had been dead for many years; well before Mammy and my father had even met. But, she needed immediate help to keep her family together; and although she would hate asking the woman, there was no alternative but to approach her late husband's sister.

Myra Ann, as she insisted on being called, was two years older than my father. She was the big sister; and according to those who knew my father's first wife, she allowed Myra-Ann to dominate her. Whereas, Mammy was strong and independent, and there was no way that she would be subservient to her husband's sister; who had made her quickly aware of how she felt. First about the illicit relationship with my father; then the child conceived out of wedlock, and even the subsequent marriage. She disapproved of the union, and had little contact with either Mammy or my father; although both families only lived a matter of five minutes walk away from each other.

Although haughty by nature; she was an attractive woman; tall and angular, with long brown hair and hazel eyes. We never referred to her as aunt, but always mimicked our mother as she with disdain called her Moirah Hahn. Her husband, Sydney Giles, he was never referred to as Sid, was a rather small quiet man, or at least this was the way he appeared in the presence of my aunt. He always seemed to be in a hurry, walking with determination whenever we saw him, either going to work or to church. Unlike my father, we never saw him walking to the pub. He was a clerk, a white-collar worker, and always wore a suit. He worked in the offices at the Copper Works.

So, the morning after the bombing, Mammy, nursing the baby; the shawl wrapped around her, walked us the short distance from the church to my aunt's house. Before we had left the church, the people from the Salvation Army had managed to get hold of some extra clothing for us. I was given a well-worn but clean navy-blue Burberry raincoat. It was much too big for me, nearly reaching the ground; but it kept me warm, and it had a belt. I felt very smart. I had never had a coat with a belt before. Harry, got a jacket that was miles too big for him too; and was walking around exaggerating this, by bending his knees and pulling down the sleeves as far as they would go, calling himself Gungah Din. Some older children at the church were taunting him, calling him names and shouting, "who died in China", referring to the Chinese mandarin dress, with very long sleeves. Like me, he did not mind the jacket not fitting him properly, or the name calling, as at least we were now warm.

Daylight was just about breaking as we left the Church. It was cold; with a heavy, grey, cloud-filled sky. My aunt's house was situated in a side street that led off from the main road, in a cul-de-sac; and always seemed much quieter compared to the hustle and bustle of the main road where we had lived. There was usually little or no traffic. However, the relative silence was shattered at times throughout the night and day, by the frequent, heavy traffic on the railway which ran alongside the back of the house. Today, the little street of terraced houses seemed almost ghostly. There was nobody about. Perhaps people were resting, still in shock from the bombing of the night before; or were they watching from behind net curtains, as we slowly trudged the length of the street to where my aunt lived at the far end. She had already received the news of my father's death, and the curtains in the front of the house were drawn.

It was my Uncle Sidney, who came to answer Mammy's knock on the door.

"Oh, Louisa, it's you", he said, in an edgy voice.

He seemed to be overwhelmed, by Mammy's presence and the knot of children tightly clustered around her. He half turned to walk back inside the house, then, paused, he seemed unsure of what to say or do. But, as he dithered he was soon relieved of making any decision, as he was now joined by the imposing figure of my aunt. He stood to one side, allowing her to come to the front; where she just stood and stared at us. Even now, Mammy would not be intimidated by her sister-in-law, and was the first to speak.

"I need help, Myra Ann" she paused briefly, "I need a place, for me and the children".

Her jaw was set firm, her eyes in a piercing stare; she was determined to break down any reluctance on my aunt's part to help us. Myra Ann clearly sensed this, you'd better come in then, Louisa" she said wearily.

Then in a more brusque and typical tone of voice she said, "Not the children mind, they must stay outside". Then she spoke directly at us, and pointing with an accusing finger said, "Mind you behave yourselves, and be quiet".

She glowered at us once more before disappearing back inside the house, and Mammy echoed those words; pointing her forefinger at Harry, half pleading and half threatening said. "Be a good boy for your Mam now".

54

Amy Bowen, my father's cousin, lived in Bethesda Street, which ran parallel to the street where my aunt Myra Ann lived. Their houses being almost back-to-back, and it was not long after Mammy had entered the house with my aunt and uncle; that she came hurrying up the street from the main road. She was a small stocky woman, with ginger hair, and a reddish, almost florid complexion, with bright blue eyes. She was a humble, yet kind soul, and although life had not been particularly generous to her, she always smiled in a soft caring way, more with her eyes than her mouth.

We were not a family, who found it easy to express feelings of warmth and affection, and so it could be said of most of the people where we lived. It was probably something to do with the times we lived in, and the harsh, drab, environment that went with it. Even so, Amy Bowen still managed to smile as she passed us, and took the time to pat me on the head, and my little brother Walter. She stood and knocked at the door and waited. No one entered Myra Ann's house until they were invited in. Once more it was Uncle Sydney who answered; and without acknowledging her or saying anything; just held the door open long enough for her to squeeze through into the house, then quickly closed it again behind him.

Having had little sleep the night before, we were all now very tired, and weary, as we sat huddled together on the wall. Except that is, for Harry; who had began to fidget, and started making a nuisance of himself; standing and doing a balancing act on my aunt's neighbour's wall, which brought a sharp rap on the window from the irate occupant.

This brought a verbal rebuke from Maggie. "Get down from the wall Harry, now, or I'll give you a hammering".

She could threaten him, but he knew there was little she

could do about it; as she was cradling Walter and would suffer anything, rather than wake the little boy up and have to endure his grizzling. Then he ran to the other side of the street, and was sitting with his feet in the gutter, daring me, and Daniel, to join him.

His taunts, "big sissy Daniel", and "little sissy Handel", were bad enough, but to make matters worse; he was gathering up the gravel from the gutter, and each handful was showered in our direction. He was annoying the rest of us, but was driving Maggie's patience to the limit.

Thankfully at last, Mammy, Amy Bowen, and Myra Ann emerged from the house. Harry immediately stopped his taunting and gravel throwing, stood up and swaggered slowly towards us. He would keep his distance, and behave himself in Mammy's presence.

She called to Molly and Daniel. "You two are to stay here with your Aunty Myra Ann". These two were the pick of the brood as far as Myra Ann was concerned. They would behave, and fit into the family household without causing too much disruption.

Mammy was not going to hang about. There was work to do. "Right, come on then" she said, "follow me, the rest of us are staying with Amy".

Then, without looking back at my aunt, she began walking down the street with Amy Bowen; who to give Maggie a rest was now carrying Walter. I followed behind them, keeping as close as I could to Mammy; with Harry, whose right arm was now twisted and locked behind his back by Maggie, struggling in the rear. Maggie was not going to forgive Harry for his antics earlier on. With vengeance in her voice now, she was asking Harry as she twisted his arm. "Do you want more of this boy, you little sod. I said I'd get you". It was only Harry's increasing yells of terror, and pain, that prompted Mammy to turn around and shout at Maggie. "That's enough now Mag, let him go".

I looked back almost in desperation, to where Daniel and Molly were standing together outside Myra Ann's house. I had a terrible feeling of being alone and at Harry's mercy, without the care and protection of my bigger brother and sister. Molly waved her arm feebly, as Mammy shouted once more. "So long now, be good. I'll come and see you later"

There was no man at Amy Bowen's house during the time we stayed there. She was married, I know, so I can only guess that her husband had probably been conscripted into the armed forces. They had a family, all girls; and I certainly remember the oldest girl who was considerably bigger than Maggie, and probably older too. But like most of the children in the neighbourhood, whether boys or girls, she was no match for Maggie in spirit; as my sister quickly gained dominance over all the children, from both families.

The Bowen's house was typical of the small terrace houses in the area, similar to our own house, but probably of an earlier type, with smaller rooms. It was still two up and two down, with an extension at the back; adding a kitchen on the ground floor, and a further bedroom on the first floor. This was going to be our home, or where we were to be billeted for the foreseeable future. But not for long if Mammy had anything to do with it: albeit that we were billeted with cousins. Our family was split between two different houses, but Mammy was determined that this situation would not prevail for long.

She knew that her first priority was to somehow get us a house, a home of our own, to enable her to reunite the family once more; but first she had to return to the scene of last night's devastation, to see if anything could be salvaged from what was left of the family's possessions. But when she returned later that morning, she was empty-handed. What had not been damaged by the bombs, had been carried off by looters. The war brought out the best in most people, but sadly, there are always those who will profit from other people's misfortunes.

All of the furniture, the bedding, and Mammy's great pride the upright piano that stood proudly in the parlour, was smashed and mangled up in the debris. And, it would be weeks or even months, before any attempt would be made to clear the bombed houses, as we had seen from previous bombings. Manpower was scarce, and needed for much more important work. By then, the looters would have taken what ever they could get there thieving hands on; and the effects of the elements, would soon quickly complete the work of destruction.

So within the space of 24 hours Mammy had lost her husband, her home, most of what possessions we owned, and the family was divided between two houses. But there was one avenue of help, an escape route open to her; which would have relieved her of her greatest problem, caring and providing for her children. The Roman Catholic Church, of which my father was a member but did not practise, was ever eager to increase the numbers of its flock; and would be only too glad to take all or some of us into care.

It was a bone of contention in my father's family, especially with Myra Ann; that Mammy did not convert to the family faith after they were married; and that we were not baptised as Roman Catholics. So it wasn't hard for Mammy to guess, who had instigated the visit of the nuns who were waiting for her when she returned that morning. They were of course, regular visitors to Myra Ann and Amy Bowen, but Mammy felt there were outside influences at work for them to arrive so quickly. No doubt the two smiling faced, patronising ladies of the church, were genuine and well-intentioned in their motives; but must have been severely shocked by Mammy's reaction to their offer of "taking the worry and strain of caring for the children", off her hands.

The meeting with the nuns took place in the front room; with Amy Bowen, Maggie, and the children from both families, either in the room or standing outside in the passageway. I was standing near the door as Mammy, her nostrils flaring, her eyes glaring, and both arms held aloft; chased the nuns from the room and the house, out into the street with her words of rage ringing in their ears. "Don't you dare come here trying to take my children away from me, they are my children, my children, do you hear, now clear off and don't come back". I can still hear the rustle of their skirts, as they flew past me to get out of Mammy's reach and escape her wrath.

As kind as Amy Bowen was, and Mammy was glad of her help; she knew that the Roman Catholic Church would not give up easily, as they believed that our souls were in danger. The nuns would be back. This made her aware, that it was more imperative than ever to secure a house of our own.

So after she had rested for a moment, and calmed down, her inner strength and resolution still intact, she said to Maggie. "There's a place for us somewhere Mag. Look after the children, I'm going to start finding us a house right now".

## CHAPTER 6

# A STRANGER
# AT MY FATHER'S FUNERAL

It was fortunate that there was no man at Amy Bowen's house, as it would have made the sleeping arrangements, even more complicated than they were. I shared a single size bed in the smallest bedroom, with Harry; Mammy, Maggie, and the two little ones, shared a large bed in another room; with Amy Bowen and her three girls in another large bed in the third bedroom. Mammy had the added complication of Harry and his problem with bed-wetting.

Meals were taken in the small back kitchen, where there was one small deal table, two chairs, and a bench. Mammy and Amy, to avoid any squabbles, agreed that only one woman and her brood would use the kitchen at any one time. They also agreed that the Bowens would eat first.

The following day Friday 14th March, Mammy left the house early while it was still dark, before 7 o'clock. She was going to the town hall, to see the housing manager. After she had seen off the nuns the day before, she had gone down to the police box and waited there for Sergeant Clifton; she knew that he visited the box at regular intervals during the day, when he would report in to the town's central police station. She remembered his words of the night before in the church. Well, she needed help; she needed a house; but the only advice that he could give her, was that the council had a duty to re-house all families that had become homeless. The extent of the duty depended on the needs of the family concerned, and that Mammy, a widow with seven children should come near to, or even top the list for the first house available.

Although it meant a walk of more than three miles to the Town Hall, she was not going to wait for some hard-pressed council official to contact her. Her mission was simple; she would find the housing manager's office in the town hall, and when he arrived, which she guessed would be just before 9 o'clock, she would be waiting for him. But, she had never encountered, or had to deal with the machinations of a local council office or its officials before; and was in for a rude awakening.

She was correct in assuming that the town hall was open for business at nine o'clock; but it was two hours later before she was ushered in to the housing department, where she was interviewed by a young man who painstakingly recorded the details concerning her request. When this formality was completed, he suggested that she returned to where she was staying, as she must obviously be concerned for her children. Mammy's reply was; that she was concerned for her children, and that's why she was there at the town hall housing department, seeking their help for accommodation. She needed a house to enable her to have all of her children with her once more, her family back together again. She stated that there must be some houses or suitable properties available for a family such as ours, and that she would wait to see what they had to offer. To his answer that this could take days or even weeks, she replied, if that was the case, she would wait for days or even weeks; but right there in the town hall's housing department. So she sat down and waited.

Saturday was a half day for the council staff, and the young man who had seen Mammy the day before, was more than a little surprised to find her waiting outside the department office when he arrived for work. She sat silently and patiently for the entire morning; ignored for most of the time by the staff, but her presence rankled and irritated the young man who had dealt with her. He spoke to her saying that there was nothing he could do, and it would be better if she returned home. His downfall was using the word "home". Her simple reply was that she did not have a home to return to; and would not have until the council provided one.

On the following Monday, she was there again; waiting outside the town hall for it to open, and once more parked herself down in the housing department's office and waited. The same thing happened again on Tuesday, and for most of Wednesday. But now, she was like a thorn in the side of the staff, and by late afternoon, was seen by a senior official.

Yes, he showed great and genuine sympathy for her plight, a widow with seven young children. This was not going to be a family easily re-housed. He started by saying that she was lucky that she had already found accommodation with relatives, and that he would probably not be in a position to provide anything better for quite some time. He promised that he would do his utmost; that she was a priority case, and would contact her personally when a suitable house became available.

But he was not going to get rid of Mammy that easily.

He had not reckoned on her sheer doggedness and tenacity. She told him she wanted a house and soon, she did not mind where, but large enough to house her entire family; and as long as it would take, she would journey the three miles to the Town Hall every working day. She never failed to turn up before 9 o'clock in the morning, and parked herself outside the Housing department's office until it closed in the evening.

Whilst Mammy was engaged in her titanic struggle with the housing department, the rest of us carried on as best we could without her. During the week, Molly, Daniel, and Harry attended school. Maggie's duty, helped by Amy Bowen, was to remain at our temporary home caring for me and my two younger brothers; and the others when they returned home.

But I was five years old now, and very eager to attend the local Infants School. Mammy agreed, and told Molly to take me to the headmistress to see if I could start; but she was adamant I could not. She was not a bit concerned about the plight of our family and the help it would be to Mammy, to know that I was safe in the school during the day; she rigidly applied the rules and regulations of the local Education Authority. I could only start at the beginning of the next term, which was after Easter. It might seem a bit strange to most people, for a boy of five to be refused to attend school, but I was bitterly disappointed.

It was during this period, one week after the death of my father; that a strange event occurred, that probably sums up the bitter and hate filled relationship I had with him. There was just one day, that Mammy missed her daily visit to the town hall and her vigil outside the housing department's office. For that day, Thursday the 20th March was the day of my father's funeral. I was blissfully unaware of this event, as I was allowed to carry on with my life, like any other day. There was nothing to indicate that this was in any way a special occasion. Mammy had left the house early, and so had Harry. As usual I was left at home with Maggie and the two little ones, and left to my own devices.

I was allowed to play in the street, or even wander down as far as the main road, where I could watch the occasional bus, car, or lorry pass by. It was still considered a big treat or thrill to see mechanised vehicles in those days; as there was still a lot of horse drawn traffic; with most of the local tradesmen such as the baker, milk man, coal man, and the local authority refuse collection, were all done by horse and cart. People would stand and stare if a motorcar went by; and air their knowledge as to whether it was a Rover, Morris, Austin, or Riley; and would be enthralled, and enraptured, if they saw a sports car or Rolls Royce. Spotting an aeroplane was another matter; then people would stop with heads craned upwards at the first sound of the approaching aircraft; and they would point skywards when it was sighted, and keep pointing until it had disappeared from view.

Sometime, during that day, I had wandered down to the main road; drawn by the crowds of people who had gathered there. It was lined with people on both sides, as far as I could see, in either direction. I had seen similar crowds before, but not as many as this, when the local Territorial Army, or Home Guard were on parade.

The houses on the main road had elevated front walls, with steps leading up to them; and nobody took any notice of me as I clambered up on one of these, and sat myself down on the wall where I had a good view. Even before I had climbed the steps, I could hear the sound of men marching. The march was steady and in unison, just like

64

soldiers. Then as they came into view, I could see them marching, three abreast; they were soldiers, old soldiers from the First World War. Over a hundred men, displaying their war medals with pride, and marching once again as soldiers. They were all dressed in black I know, but I can only remember the boots and the bowler hats they wore, as they proudly marched past me preceding the hearse and motor carriages behind. I still did not realize the significance as far as I was concerned, until the first car following the hearse was level with me; and I recognised the figures of Harry, and Daniel, also dressed in black, sitting alongside my uncle Sidney. It was at this fleeting moment, a picture etched in my memory forever, of seeing my two older brothers sitting in that big black car; that I realised that I was watching my father's funeral.

It was the custom in those days that all funerals were for Gentlemen Only. I can only suppose that Harry and Daniel qualified under this heading, and that I was considered too young. Mammy and my sisters were not allowed to attend. And as the funeral procession sombrely made its way past, I had a strange feeling of detachment; that I was looking at someone else's brothers; at someone else's father's funeral; and that it had nothing to do with me.

## CHAPTER 7

# "GO AND SEE YOUR FATHER"

Sunday 23rd March, three days after my father's funeral, and Mammy decided that we should visit the cemetery where he had been buried. It was a bright, if blustery March afternoon, when we boarded the number 71 bus; that would take us the two miles or so to the small town of Morriston. We had enjoyed Sunday dinner as a complete family again, having been joined for the occasion by Molly and Daniel. Earlier that morning, Mammy had made one of her famous rock cakes; this was just a mixture of dough with some currants and sugar mixed in, and baked in a hot oven until the cake was sugary and crusty on top, with a soft, pudding-like texture inside. This was not to be consumed at the house, but was to be taken with us on our first journey to my father's grave.

We did not realise then, that this set a precedent that became a ritual in the years that followed. Whenever Mammy needed a break from her offspring, particularly us boys on a Sunday afternoon after dinner, and if the weather was suitable; she would cut five pieces of rock cake, put these in a brown paper bag, and give them to

Daniel with the instruction, "Go and see your Father".

It was a fair distance, probably about a mile from the bus terminus at Morriston Cross to the cemetery; and as sorry as Mammy was to leave them; she had asked Amy Bowen to look after Eddie and Walter. As physically strong as she was, she knew that she would be asking too much of herself and Maggie, to cope with the added burden of having to carry the two little ones for most of the way.

The road from the bus terminus was mainly uphill, and in parts quite steep; with large semi-detached houses on the left, and farmland of open fields; which included a golf course on the right. The mood of our family as we made the journey that bright and breezy afternoon, was, even for Harry, one of quiet and sombre reflection.

We arrived at the cemetery not knowing quite what to expect, except for Daniel and Harry who had witnessed the actual burial. The graveyard was immense, and situated on a gentle sloping hillside, containing hundreds or maybe thousands of graves. The good weather had encouraged other people to visit, not many for the size of the place, and these were scattered about the cemetery tending to the graves of their loved ones.

There was a swathe of grass-covered land, about five yards wide along the lower end of the cemetery, upon which were tall, naked trees: oaks and elms. It was on this sheltered grassland, which had been allotted to those civilians killed by enemy action, that my father had been buried.

Harry led the way to the grave, which was in a small group of about twenty. There was a separate group of graves, about fifty, further along that had been allocated to local servicemen who had been killed in the war; with regimented lines of white gravestones, neat, tidy, and orderly; just like the soldiers, sailors, and airmen they represented.

I was struck by the contrast between my father's grave, which was just a mound of black earth with a couple wreaths and bunches of wilting flowers on it, and those of long standing with their gravestones of varying shapes and sizes. They ranged from great ornamental edifices of marble, with intricate lettering in gold leaf, to simple wooden crosses that were dry and cracked with the passing of time.

We watched as Mammy fussed about the grave, tidying it up, arranging the wreathes and bunches of flowers as best she could; then removing the dead heads and the worst of the dying flowers. With her bare hands, she patted the black earth, her mouth and lips moving as if in silent conversation, trying to pacify and meditate with the soul of her departed husband. She would tend to my father's needs in death, as she had when he was alive.

Maggie, who was normally very attentive to Mammy and stayed close to her, had moved quietly away from the grave, and was now sitting on a large wrought-iron bench some twenty feet away. The resentment she felt towards my father had not died with him, and never would for her. Mammy understood her daughter's anguish, and when she had finished tidying the grave; she beckoned to rest of us to follow her, as she walked over and sat down beside Maggie. The rest of us joined them, except that is for Harry. The cemetery held too many attractions for him. He had gone wandering off, and was now walking up and down the lines of military graves, no doubt seeking something that would satisfy his morbid curiosity.

Mammy called to him in what can only be described as a muffled shout. We were, after all, in a place of the dead. "Harry, come away from there this minute". Then, not to spoil the occasion with anger, she called again. "Come on Harry bach, come and have some cake".

It was a bribe, she knew, but it worked, as he came scampering back to where we were now clustered around the bench and Mammy. She had already cut the cake into six slices, and we greedily devoured it; while she just picked at the piece she had. Harry had finished his cake first, and I was not far behind; then Mammy smiled and began breaking the piece she had between her thumb and forefinger, and pushing it into Harry's and my open mouths, like a mother bird feeding her chicks.

The bright sun of the early afternoon was now being covered by an increasing layer of heavy, grey, dark clouds, and the blustery breeze had developed into a keen edged, cutting, cold wind. We were the last of the few visitors to leave the cemetery that day, as the tall bare trees began to creak and groan under the strain as the wind strengthened.

We had finished our treat and eaten the cake, as Mammy stood up saying. "Its cold. Come on, time to go". She glanced once more at the mound of earth that covered my father's lone coffin; as if she should not leave him like this, unrecognised; then defiantly added. "We must get a cross for the grave, with your father's name on it".

## CHAPTER 8

# MONEY AND MARBLES

Things started to get a little strained, which perhaps was to be expected, after we had been billeted with Amy Bowen for a couple of weeks. It was not easy for two families totalling ten people, most of them children, living in a small converted two up and two down terrace house. Naturally Amy Bowen saw to the needs of her own children before ours, which was quite understandable to Mammy and Maggie, but not to Harry. The fact that Mammy was grateful to my father's cousin for sharing her house with us, made no difference to Harry, who continued to act in his customary selfish and thoughtless manner.

Amy Bowen's three girls, who were fourteen, nine, and six years old respectively, were not exactly shrinking violets, but neither were they as robust in body and spirit as Maggie. She dominated the children from the two families, not in any way nasty, but in a bossy more motherly fashion. When Mammy was not around she took control, it was her way of keeping order in the house; and Amy Bowen and her three daughters more or less accepted this. Maggie's role was to keep order in our family, and really take on the mantle of Mammy, who was away for most of the day attending the Housing Department at the local town hall. The number one priority for her and our family, was still of course acquiring a house.

For the greater part of the day, during the week, Harry and the three Bowen girls were at school. Maggie helped by Amy Bowen, remained in the house looking after Walter and Eddie; and I as usual was left to my own devices; to play in or around the house or dream the day away as I was prone to do. The problems arose during the hours immediately after school had closed for the day. Harry had started to tease and bully the two younger Bowen girls, which led in turn to him being scolded by Amy Bowen and threatened by Maggie. Most days, the problem was solved with Harry being banned from the house until Mammy arrived back in the evening.

It was on one such occasion, that Harry, after being chased from the house yet again; unfortunately found me outside in the street, and persuaded me that we should return to the bombed out family home. When I use the word persuade, that meant that I did not argue, or disagree with him; or the persuasion would have come in the shape of his fist in my stomach. I was playing with a couple of marbles that Daniel had given me. He knew how upset I had been when mine were lost during the night of the bombing. This was typical of him, but Harry said he was glad because his marbles had gone too.

He came and stood over me, poking me in the back with his finger. "'ey, 'andel", he said, "come with me, right, lets go down to the bombed 'ouse". He could see from the frown on my face that I was not happy with the idea, but he insisted, "Come on, mun, I know where I can find some money", he hesitated briefly, then said, "and some chocolate mun". Harry would say anything to get his own way. Then as an added incentive, he said, "We'll look for uwer marbles as well, right".

This was the first occasion that I had gone back to what remained of the family home, but I knew very well that it was not the first time for Harry. He passed the bombed site at least twice a day on his way to and from school; and I expect it was only natural, that any normal boy would be drawn to the place where he had once lived. But, it held a kind of morbid attraction for Harry; of that I am sure.

Constantly, he went on about the little treasures that were there to be had from under the rubble. He could remember where the rent and insurance monies were kept, in the old teapot on the kitchen mantelpiece, above the fireplace. There were sweets and chocolates, and more money on the very top shelf of the pantry, and Nice biscuits too. Whether there were any of these things in the places he mentioned, I had my doubts. But there was a possibility; and Harry would love to get his hands on them, as he had so often attempted in the past; only to be thwarted by Mammy, or my father, and get a good hiding for his efforts into the bargain. I expect this was his way of having the last laugh, or getting his own back on my father.

Because I was not yet of school age; I was restricted to just where I could play or explore on my own, to the immediate area where we lived; and certainly for the present not further than the main road. On the other hand, Harry, who had been attending school now for more than three years, was allowed far more freedom. It was deemed by society then; that attending school was a significant step forward in a child's maturity; indeed a yardstick of achieving greater responsibility; unlike the children of today; probably because we lived in a more static and closely knit community. Once we had attained school age, children could roam and explore the locality where they lived, as freely as they liked. There was very little road traffic, but the other hazards and dangers that lay in wait for us were numerous; when you think of the environment in which we lived and grew up; we were virtually surrounded by railways, rivers and canals, workshops and factories; derelict buildings and slag heaps; and now the added problem of the war, and all of the changes that this brought.

Four weeks to the very day had passed since the bombing and the death of my father, but as I now viewed the pile of rubble that once was our home, it was as if it had never existed. So complete was the destruction and quick deterioration of the signs of where people had once lived. Looters, those evil or desperate people; of a sick and desperate world; had picked over the debris, salvaging what they could; searching for anything that could be used or sold in these times of extreme shortage.

I watched as Harry clambered over the piles of stones, slates, and timber that had been cleared from the road, and piled high on what once was the front of our house. He was sure footed, and nimble, and moved quickly over the rubble; which was sloping back up to where the rear walls of the house were still partially intact, and then stopped. This was where the back bedroom would have been; where the floor timbers had been smashed by the impact of the bomb; and rubble from the walls and ceiling had followed through, filling the void below, which was once the back kitchen.

Scared as I was to follow him, in climbing over the debris; I was even more afraid of incurring his wrath. He called to me, as I gingerly crawled over the chunks of stonework and broken timbers, "Urry up 'Andel mun, come up by yer" he yelled.

He would not bully me too much into hurrying, as long as I was making the effort to stay with him. For my part, I had to try and balance the two evils I was confronted with, of not hurting myself on the broken remains of the house, or risk a tirade of abuse from Harry. My greatest problem, was trying to avoid the bits of wood embedded in a chalky mix of mortar and plaster; studded with rusty nails, that made up the old lath and plaster ceilings. By the time I had got to where Harry was waiting, the skin on my hands and knees had suffered badly, and I was in pain from the scratches and cuts inflicted on me.

Still, I felt a great sense of achievement, as I stood there not far from Harry, who had already started on the next stage of his plan. He was swinging now on one of the roof joists, which was jammed upright and embedded into the rubble. He was trying to lever a way into the room below, but the mass of debris would not be shifted. After a while and breathless with the exertion, he gave up and rested, sitting down on the debris, his chin resting on one hand in a great posture of thought. This was not going to work he realised, and he was beginning to get angry "There is money in that teapot 'andel", he said, looking at me with menace in his eyes.

He was expecting me to come up with a solution to his problem; I didn't have a clue, but I put a pained look of concentration on my face; screwing up my eyes, nose, and mouth, hoping that this display would convince him that I was giving the matter my undivided attention.

It seemed to work, as he moved away from me, this time to the very edge of the wall which overlooked the back of the house.

"You think 'ard now 'andel", he said, as he looked down to the backyard below. For my part I continued to concentrate, closing my eyes and screwing up my face even more, as proof of my devotion to his cause. I could hear him moving about, pulling and pushing at some of the looser timbers and stones; but I was happy to remain still, with my eyes shut. Then suddenly, there was an almighty crack of splitting timber, and falling masonry; followed by yelps and screams from Harry; and I was being swept down, yelling and screaming myself now, into the back yard in a stream of debris that gravity was now claiming. It all happened and was over in less than a second, as I came to rest feet uppermost on the rubble that had spewed out from the wrecked building. My eyes were still closed, but all my efforts of pretence to please Harry were gone, they were closed now out of sheer terror. Briefly, I thought that I was dead, claimed by the debris as the house collapsed, as it had on the night of the bombing, killing my father. I only opened them again, when to my relief I could hear Harry shouting at me once more. "Stay there 'andel", he yelled, the anger and menace in his voice had now gone.

The air was thick with dust that the falling masonry had thrown up, and at first I could not see him; but as it slowly cleared, I could see that he was perched on the one piece of the back wall that had not given away. There was almost a note of triumph in his voice, as now he once again repeated his instructions to me.

"Stay there 'andel, I'm coming down", and with that he jumped from his perch on to the rubble; that had now formed a kind of bridge from the upstairs room to the ground below.

I had been more than lucky, as the part of the wall that had given way was not too big a drop to the ground. The backyard was on a split level with stone steps leading up from the rear ground floor area; where entry was gained, by the door to the back kitchen. The outside lavatory was also situated here, with its door next to that of the kitchen.

While I lay there covered in grit and dust and afraid to move, Harry had dashed past me with a determined and bright look on his face. I just managed to catch the words from his breathless and panting lips. "I can get in now".

From his vantage point, after the partial collapse of the rear wall, he saw that the door of the back kitchen was half open. He could now get the prized teapot and secure its contents. Buoyed up by the thought that at last I could come out of this with some reward, I managed to get to my feet, and followed him down the stone steps. Still partly stunned and shaken, I was limping now from the effects of the fall on my bruised body and legs; but my newly found bravado did not extend to entering the kitchen like Harry. I stood by the door and peered in, where I could just see him in the gloom crawling over the rubble.

The open fireplace and the oven, which was alongside, seemed to be still intact; but the wooden facia and mantelpiece were broken and slewed forward; covered in the debris from the ceiling and room above. Harry was now in very dangerous territory indeed. One wrong move could bring tons more of the building crashing down on him. For one so young he seemed fearless, or perhaps fatalistic; and this perhaps was one reason why even adults went in dread of, or despised him.

I meekly called to him, "Harry, come out".

He did not reply, he just crouched there engrossed in the scene before him. He reminded me of a cat waiting for its prey to move before pouncing, and oblivious to my presence. I was glad and relieved that he did not answer me; he might have ordered me to join him inside, and I did not enjoy the prospect of doing that one bit. On my toes now, I slowly backed away from the kitchen door, turned, and quickening my pace; almost ran up the stone steps to the higher ground once more.

The houses were divided at the back, by walls no more than four feet high, which enclosed a small area of ground. I expect this patch of land could be referred to as a back yard, and to some even a garden. Some people had sheds or chicken coops; and usually a clothes line, which was strung between the back of the house where it would be tied to a drainpipe; and at the other end to a pulley attached to a line-pole. All we had was the latter, and a sheet of corrugated iron; which was slanted against the wall, and used as a cover to keep a small stock of firewood dry. All that remained now was the line pole. The rest was gone.

I went and stood with my back against one of the dividing walls. The sun, had momentarily broken through the white and grey strata clouds, I could feel its heat on my face, warming my body. It soothed the aches and pains in my sore arms and legs, and I thought of Mammy. We had not seen much of her over the past couple of weeks, as she with single-minded purpose; strove to find us a house, to make into a home. My father had been killed I knew, and he could not hurt us anymore; but I was suddenly struck with a terrible sense of grief, at the horrible thought that it could have been Mammy that was now dead. I could not bear to think of it, as even just the mere thought, sent fear and panic racing through my young mind.

Although it was painful, I was happily brought back to reality from my sad day dreaming, by a malicious dig to my sore ribs from Harry. He was angry again, as he shouted at me. "Look by yer".

He pushed his hands up to my face, where he was clutching some broken pieces of the teapot; that he had been searching for. "Look mun! I've found it", he paused, "but no cowin' money".

The menace was back in his voice again. "Where is it,

who's 'ad it", he shouted, staring at me; almost accusing me that it was my fault that the money was gone.

I responded as I always did in these situations; by pursing my lips, and appearing to give deep thought to the problem. It normally bought me a bit of time, during which Harry would find his own solution, or get fed up, and move on to the next episode of mischief he had in mind.

Thankfully this did not take too long, as he now moved away from me; and clambered up on to the pile of rubble that had brought me tumbling down from the house minutes earlier. From here he had a good view of the yard next door. Surprisingly, but as unpredictable as ever, his tone of voice had mellowed again as he called to me, "Come up by yer 'andel".

He had forgotten about the teapot and the money already, as his furtive little brain, began to work out the next challenge that lay ahead.

Where he stood now, the debris was level to the height of the dividing wall, and triumphantly he cocked his leg over this and sat straddling it. Relieved, that he was once more in a better frame of mind, and this seemed like fun to me; I soon joined him and sat with legs astride on the wall.

He waited for me to settle and make myself comfortable, then with a smirk of self-satisfaction on his face, said, "Remember the paints, 'andel".

His face lit up, as he pointed to the ground in front of the remains our neighbour's garden shed, where several tins of paint were scattered. He was giggling now as he said, "We can 'ave those tins of paints now mun, an' he can't touch us".

He was not referring to our neighbour, but my father. It was sad to see the backyard; which was once meticulously clean and tidy; now in its present state. The chicken coop had gone, along with the chickens; and the small shed was smashed and damaged beyond repair; with the windows broken and the door ripped off.

\*\*\*\*\*\*\*\*\*\*\*\*\*\*\*\*\*\*\*\*\*\*\*\*\*\*\*\*\*\*\*\*\*\*\*\*

Harry's reference to the "tins of paints" brought back painful memories. Oh, yes! I had not forgotten the time of the paints. He was referring to what occurred some months previously, when he had managed to scale the wall where we were now sitting; smashed the window of the shed; and grabbed what ever he could; but the only things within his reach were some tins of paint, which were stacked on shelves on either side of the window. There were half-a-dozen tins in total, and he passed these over the wall to me, which we then hid under the corrugated iron sheet. Of course, once the initial thrill of the "smash and grab" wore off; and the probable consequences of our action began to be realised, panic set in and we bolted; for we knew, it would not be long before my father came home from work.

So as in all times like these, our refuge and the place where we always turned to was the Great Tip. To get there we had to sneak out the house; run the short distance up the main road to the Bridge Inn public house; turn right here, where there was a narrow right-of-way which led up to the railway embankment. It was here that we had to run the gauntlet of either being seen by one of our adult neighbours; or the man who operated the signal box: but, worst of all, the railway policeman, the dreaded Chinky.

Harry was so much bigger and quicker than me, and was steadily increasing the gap between us as he easily scrambled up the railway embankment, leaving me to struggle way behind. I could hear the threats and abuse, being shouted at him, by the raging railway signalman, as he started to cross the line. Alas, I did not even make it to the railway embankment; as I heard another shout, this time the unmistakable voice of my father; who unbeknown to us, had spotted us scurrying away from the house as he emerged from the Copper Works gates.

Sensing that we had been up to no good, he ran after us; and even now, I can still feel in my bones the terror that struck me as he shouted, "Handel, stop where you are". I immediately froze; and started to wail, but Harry kept on running. It came as something of a relief, that I only received one whack across the back of my head from my father; and told to "Get off home".

My father continued in pursuit of Harry, who now having heard him was inspired to a greater turn of speed; and was soon lost in the safe haven of the giant mounds of clinker and ash; that formed that part of the Great Tip. For the moment he was safe, but my father realised that Harry would have to return home sometime; and I can still hear the yells and screams that emanated from the parlour that late afternoon; as my father lashed into Harry with the strap; when he became aware of the theft of the tins of paint and the smashed window.

\*\*\*\*\*\*\*\*\*\*\*\*\*\*\*\*\*\*\*\*\*\*\*\*\*\*\*\*\*\*\*\*\*\*\*

Harry had forgotten all about the failed teapot adventure now; and the rest of the treasures he had come to find, including my marbles. Getting his hands on the tins of paint would be a just reward. He quickly got down from the wall and into the next-door backyard, calling me to follow him as he hurried to where the paints were. "Urry up mun", he said excitedly, "Come an' 'elp me".

The tins were old and rusty, with the lids on two of them stuck firmly; but the third tin had no lid, and was half full of green paint, the surface of which was covered by a thick layer of hard skin.

He picked up the two tins, which had the lids, saying, "I'll carry these two right, and you can carry only one". He nodded his head in the direction of the remaining tin of paint, which was without a lid; and like the obedient younger brother that I was; I immediately, without question picked it up.

The next thing he had to work out was how to get away with the booty. To go back the way we had come; via the bombed house, would be too risky; and the back wall leading up to the railway embankment was too high and steep. There was however, another way. We lived at number three, and we were now in number two, so there were only two walls to climb to get clear of the bombed houses and drop to the side street, which was Railway Terrace. Getting over the smaller wall into number one was easy; the problem was the final boundary wall. Inside that backyard, the height was the same as the others, about four feet; but the problem facing us was the drop to Railway Terrace on the outside, which was almost double.

When we reached the final obstacle, we both sat on the wall; and Harry could see that I was not at all happy with the thought of dropping the eight feet or so to the ground. With a mixture of encouragement and threats, the latter being that he would leave me there, I agreed to make the drop.

He decided that he would go first; and dropping the two tins of paint he was carrying to the ground, followed on by lowering his body against the wall, then hanging on by his fingertips easily made the drop. The plan that he had figured out; was that I was to copy him, to do exactly as he did; only he would stand so I could put my feet on his shoulders, when he would gently lower me to the ground. We had almost completed this manoeuvre, when he suddenly realised that the third tin of paint, the one that I was responsible for, was still on the wall.

At this stage of the plan, I was just about hanging on with my finger tips; my legs stretched, and toes barely on Harry's shoulders; when he yelled, "Grab the paint 'andel". I refused to move, as he repeated his words, "Grab the paint". He raised his feet now, and standing on his toes; he screamed, "Get the cowin' paint 'andel"; pushing me up the few inches necessary to grab the tin, which I foolishly did, then, losing balance, came crashing to the ground, with the tin of paint following.

Prostrate as I was now; I was in direct line, as the paint filled missile hit me with enough force to dislodge the layer of hard skin; releasing and spraying me with its bright green liquid contents. Harry, of course was unharmed and free of any paint splashes, as he quickly got out of the way; when he realised just what was happening. As for me, I was severely winded by the fall, and now covered in bright emerald green paint; and Harry burst out laughing, which perhaps was a natural reaction; being relieved that it had not happened to him.

Shocked and winded from the fall, I was soon to discover that there was little time for me to dwell on my predicament, or to feel sorry for myself. For then, as if from nowhere, appeared the great looming figure of Sergeant Clifton. Harry's burst of merriment came abruptly to a halt; as the policeman grabbed the back of his neck in a vice-like grip, causing his face to screw up in excruciating pain. The sergeant knew Harry of old, and tightened the pressure, squeezing any thoughts that maybe going through the boy's mind of trying to make a run for it. As for me, he was sure that I was not going to cause any problems, as long as he kept Harry under tight control. Not daring to put a hand on me, or come too close, because of the blobs of green paint that now adorned my body and clothing. He gruffly looked at me and said, "Get up Handel, and stand against the wall".

At the same time he was applying downward pressure on Harry, whose eyes were watering, and bulging, and was now down on his knees.

We; were just a dammed nuisance as far as Sergeant Clifton was concerned. He was a tired old man, who was sick of the war; he should be retired now and enjoying his pension; instead of which he was hard pressed by the general shortage of manpower, and all the added problems with the advent of war. He could certainly do without the responsibility of curtailing the mischievous antics of two wayward and belligerent small boys.

As ordered by the Sergeant, I stood now with my back against the wall. He still maintained his stranglehold on Harry, whose face now was almost purple, with weird gurgling sounds emanating from his mouth. I was just about to celebrate his demise, when the sergeant slightly released his grip, allowing him to gasp some air. The policeman had no qualms with doling out the punishment, for he was only too aware; that where Harry was trouble would not be far away. I did not have any feelings of guilt, seeing Harry and his plight, and the pain he was suffering: I was glad that he was having some of the torture and treatment, that he usually meted out to me; but not so glad at the thought of whether it would be my turn next, despite the paint.

Then mercifully, a very familiar figure suddenly appeared, hurrying along the main road. My relief was so great, that a spontaneous long and painful cry of "Mammee-yah", came wallowing up from my throat; and at the same time spouting great flowing tears which were now running down my cheeks. For one heart-stopping moment, I thought that she had not heard me, as she hurried along walking with her usual purpose and determination. But then she stopped, and turned her head, looking directly at us. My cry had startled her, which was more meaningful, as she had just passed the remains of our bombed out home.

She muttered quietly at first, "Handel", then in a louder voice. "Sergeant, Harry, what's going on here". The sergeant was almost as relieved as I was, as he said, "Just in time Louisa". Look at them. Been up to no good again".

We must have looked a pitiful sight to Mammy; with Harry firmly pinned down on his knees; and me almost unrecognisable; covered in dirt, and dust; and blood from the cuts and grazes on my arms and legs, all topped up with a coating of green paint.

I could feel the anger in Mammy's voice, as she reverted to her native tongue once more. "Iesi Annwyl. Dear Jesus". But the anger was short lived, and she quickly recovered her composure. For today was a special day, a very special day, as a broad smile now spread across her face.

Holding up her right hand she said, "Look boys! See what I've got", and there dangling on a rough piece of cord was a single key.

She swung the key tantalisingly; once, twice, three times; and almost laughing with relief and delight said, "Look boys, the key for our new house. I've got us a roof over our heads".

## CHAPTER 9

# MOVING ON

After many weeks of trudging daily to the town hall housing department; at last, Mammy had the key to our new house. It was almost a month to the day since the loss of our home, and the death of my father. She was determined that our family would be reunited, and would remain in billeted accommodation not a day longer than was necessary. The use of the words "being billeted" with the reference to our family was dreadful and abhorrent to Mammy, especially as we were divided between two households. She was grateful to Amy Bowen, and to a lesser extent even Aunty Myra Ann for taking us in; but she was a proud woman, who valued her independence and self-reliance. This was yet another demonstration of her strength of character, that she was to bestow on us children; to enable us to get through the many trials and tribulations of the years that lay ahead.

We could take possession of our new house right away. It was vacant and ready for occupation. Mammy had received the key late on Thursday afternoon, and she decided there, and then, that we would be moving in the following day, Friday 4th April 1941. This date conveniently fell on the day that the schools were breaking up for the Easter holidays; the two weeks' break would give her a little breathing space to get us established in our new home; and to prepare for that wonderful day when I would be allowed to attend the Infants School. So she immediately put into effect, the arrangements to remove us, and our scant belongings, the half a mile or so to our new home.

The Salvation Army promised us help with bedding, blankets and sheets, as they had already helped in providing us with essential clothing. Everything else came at a price, the most vital element being the means of transportation for the few sticks of furniture Mammy had acquired. This came in the very rough and frightening form of Jackie Smith, the local odd job man, with his pony and cart. I am sure though, that Mammy would have found some alternative means if at all possible.

Although small in stature, he was a brutish foul-mouthed man, a braggart who liked to curse and flog whichever unfortunate beast happened to be pulling the cart at the time. He always seemed to wear the same crumpled suit; with a collar and tie; he was a businessman after all; and a flat cap with the peak pulled down on one side; with the remains of a cigarette, or meg-end, stuck in his mouth. It was a terrifying sight, an almost demonic spectre; to see him in full flight racing down the road; standing on his cart with legs astride, whip in hand, cursing and damning the pony as he wilfully laid into it.

He had two teenage sons who were almost as evil as their father. Like him, the eldest boy was a weasel-faced creature; small and wiry with lank thin hair; but the youngest lad was like his mother, a large lump of a boy with short black crinkly hair. Whether it was to do with their diet or the foul conditions under which they lived; their hands, faces, and legs, always seemed to be covered in purple blotches, and red, running sores. Again like their father; they used the whip on the pony almost non-stop; and should the poor creature show any reluctance to move; then it would be reminded just who was the master, with one of the Smith brothers delivering a hefty kick to its stomach.

The family lived in two bare rooms above the stables where they kept their ponies, at the back of the Mile End pub. Access to their dwelling; if indeed it could be called that, was by way of a rickety wooden staircase, which led up from the stable yard below. This structure, which seemed and most probably was an afterthought, was built of wood and covered entirely in black felt. It jutted out from the main building and was supported from the ground by stout wooden pillars. The rooms inside had no ceiling; being openly exposed to the timber roof, with the wall of the pub at the back; the sides made of timber, and the front almost entirely made of small panes of glass. To a stranger looking at the building from a distance, he or she could hardly be blamed with mistaking it for a gigantic pigeon loft.

One of the rooms served as a bedroom for Mr and Mrs Smith, with a large double bed; and what could be seen of the floorboards, were bare, and unpainted. The room was crammed with junk Mr Smith had hoarded over the years. There were pieces of old wood, old tins of paint, cardboard boxes, and stacks of old newspapers. There were also a lot of wooden shelves of different shapes and sizes; which adorned the walls, and were lined with old paperback books.

The other room was much larger and contained a table, two wooden chairs, and a huge leather couch, with bits of lino of varying sizes and colours covering the floor. But there was no fireplace or oven. They did not use coal or gas. For heating and lighting they used paraffin oil only, with the stench of the stuff constantly permeating the air. Again, this room was also littered with more items of junk; and in one corner there was a small oil drum, which contained the paraffin oil. It was widely believed by the local community; that the two teenage boys slept in the stables with the ponies.

There was something very odd regarding these two boys; which was entirely out of character with their social standing in life, and the area in which they lived. They both had very posh, even aristocratic, Christian names. The older boy was named Algernon, and the younger one Percival. Why on earth the Smiths decided to saddle the boys with names such as these, when they lived in an area that was predominantly made up of very poor working-class people; was a mystery. Perhaps old man Smith's motive for doing so, was that he knew that it would be open season on them regarding taunts from other children, and this would help toughen them up.

Mrs. Smith was a tall, well-proportioned woman, with short, tightly curled, dark grey hair; her face was round, with strong features; but with a sallow complexion. She came from the London area; and had met Mr Smith, when he returned from serving with the army in France during the First World War. Whatever life she had before; it must have been a miserable existence for her to change it for her present one with Mr Smith. But there was another member of this dreadful family; a small waif-like child who like her brothers, was always covered in blotches and sores; a little girl called Rosie.

\*\*\*\*\*\*\*\*\*\*\*\*\*\*\*\*\*\*\*\*\*\*\*\*\*\*\*\*\*\*\*\*\*\*\*

Rosie had been involved in a road accident some months earlier, just before Christmas; and unfortunately I had been a witness to this terrifying scene. I had watched, as the poor emaciated child ran into the road, where she collided with a bicycle; which was travelling at quite a high speed. She seemed to get all entangled up in the machine's wheels, chains and cables, and was dragged some ten to fifteen feet on the rough surface of the road. I remember becoming extremely distressed, as I heard Rosie's screams of pain, and bitter sobbing; and listening to the cyclist, a young man, cursing her for the damage she had done to his smart new touring cycle.

The accident occurred just outside Mary's sweetshop; and the clatter of the bike scraping along the road, accompanying the cyclist's curses and Rosie's painful screams, brought Mary racing out.

She screamed at the cyclist. "Be quiet, you stupid man, never mind about your bike, look what you've done to this little girl!"

Then, she gently extricated the limp figure of Rosie from the mangled wreckage of the bike, and carried her into the shop; but not before shouting at the cyclist once more, "You'd better pick up your bike and go boy, before this girl's father finds out what you've done".

The thought of old man Smith, with whip in hand, meting out some raging punishment on the cyclist as he did with his pony; filled me with terror. I did not wait for the reaction of the cyclist, as sick with fright; I turned and ran the short distance home, desperately seeking the comfort of Mammy.

As hard pressed as she was with her own problems of a drunken husband, and trying to cope with the needs of seven children, she still understood the pain and concern I felt for poor Rosie. So later on that evening, when it was cold and dark, she took my hand and we walked the short distance to the Smiths' house. Mammy had raided the store of chocolates and sweets she was keeping for Christmas; and had given me three chocolate pennies, which were covered in gold foil. They were for Rosie, to make her feel better.

This was the first time that I had ever been to the Smiths household, and was very glad that old man Smith and his two sons were not there when we arrived. We could just about see the wooden stairway, aided by the dim light from the single paraffin lamp that faintly glowed in the room at the top. As we climbed the stairs Mammy called out, "Yoo-hoo, Mrs Smith, I've brought Handel to see little Rosie".

I kept as close as I could to Mammy, squeezing her hand tightly as we eventually got to the small landing at the top of the wooden stairs. There had not been any response to her call that we were visiting, so she knocked on the door and called out again "Hello Mrs Smith".

It was difficult to see inside the premises, because of the grey dirty net curtains, and the grime that covered the windows; but eventually, after Mammy had knocked for the second-time, the door was slowly half opened to reveal the looming presence of Mrs Smith. Because of the poor light, I did not see her at first; but peeping out from behind the great bulk of her mother, with her head almost entirely covered in bandages; was Rosie.

Not a word was said, and an awkward silence prevailed until Mammy spotted the little girl. "Oh! There you are Rosie. Look, Handel has come to see you".

I held out my hand with the little white paper bag containing the chocolates, offering them to Rosie, but the little girl did nothing. She just stood there clinging to her mother's dress. Her head was cocked to one side like a baby sparrow, as she looked to her mother for some direction, but there was no response; Mrs Smith just stood there, a blank expression on her face. It was quite evident that we were not going to be invited inside the Smiths' home.

Later, I discovered that no one was allowed to enter the property under any circumstances, when old man Smith was not at home. But this did not apply to me when visiting on my own. Mammy sensed this, and not to embarrass Mrs Smith any further said, "Well, it's getting dark. There you are, Rosie, you take the sweets from Handel now, there's a good girl, and get better soon".

There was still no response from either of them; so Mammy took the bag of chocolates from me, and put them in Mrs Smith's hand. I took hold of Mammy's hand once more and held it tightly, as she turned to descend the stairs saying, "Well, so long now Mrs Smith, and Rosie. Handel will call and see you again tomorrow."

Being extremely careful because of the failing light and the unsure state of the creaking wooden stairs, we made our way back down to the stable yard below. I looked up to wave goodbye to Rosie, but the door had been silently closed and the little girl and her mother had gone. This was my first visit to the Smiths household; but I returned again the following day, and many more times in the weeks that followed, as Rosie became an integral part of my young life. But I always checked first; that the pony and cart were not in the yard, to ensure that Mr Smith and his two sons were not at home.

*************************************

So the day arrived when we would leave Amy Bowen's house, to start our new life without a father, but reunited as a family once more. At first light, Mammy, and Maggie, and the two little ones had gone to the new house to meet the Salvation Army; who were going to deliver some bedding, and whatever else they could manage to help us settle into our new home. Molly, Daniel, and Harry were at school, and as usual at times like these I was left on my own.

Old man Smith and his sons were going to collect an old kitchen table from Aunty Myra Ann's house, some time during the day. Mammy had agreed to pay her the sum of £1 for this, when she received the money from the government for her war damages claim. I spent most of the time in the back bedroom of the house, looking directly into my aunt's backyard; as I was hoping to catch a sight of them at work. And although I despised the Smiths and felt very frightened and insecure in their presence, they still provided a curious fascination for me. I was happy with this, as long as they remained at a safe distance, or I was in the comforting presence of Mammy.

The day was sunny and warm. Then, in the early afternoon, I heard the sound of the pony and cart going at a trot along the main road. I was sitting on the stone step outside the front door, and looking down the street, waited for them to come into sight. When they did appear, I had a funny feeling of being frightened, yet excited at the same time. Old man Smith was as usual, standing at the front of the cart, and the two boys sitting one on either side. Then, as they disappeared from sight, I dashed into the house and up the stairs to the back bedroom. The net curtains protected me from being seen by anyone outside, but I had an excellent view of my aunt's backyard. It seemed like an age, but soon the Smiths emerged from the rear of the house, preceded by my aunt. She, no doubt, harboured great thoughts of supervising the removal of the table from the workshop; through the house and outside to the front, without any damage being done.

I watched, as a stern-faced Myra Ann strode towards the lean-to shed, open the door, and pointing her hand inside said, "There's the table, now take your time, and be careful bringing it out".

She ushered the Smiths inside the shed, while she remained outside still holding the door. A couple of minutes later, old man Smith reappeared walking backwards now, with arms waving from side to side and up and down. He was shouting what proved to be unnecessary instructions to his sons, but in reality, mocking my aunt. "Right now, be careful, come-on watch the door".

The table had to be placed on end to get it through the door, which the Smith boys had now done; and with commendable care, still under the watchful eye of Myra Ann and the arm-waving Mr Smith; half of the table, with one pair of legs first, slowly emerged from the shed. The Smith boys knew exactly what they were doing, having carried out similar manoeuvres in the past; and now showed their expertise; by quickly turning the table around the door jamb and the open door, and triumphantly extricated the other half.

The second part of the operation was carried out at such high speed, that it caught my unfortunate aunt off guard; as she rapidly disappeared behind the now fully open door, which was being pressed by the weight of the table, pushing her into the side of the shed. I could just about hear the mocking voice of old man Smith crying out, "Hold on boys, where's Mrs Giles".

He paused, and waited for the answer to his question, which he knew would be coming soon enough, "Get me out of here", she screamed, "move the table now, and get me out of here". Shaken, by the extreme tone of her voice, the Smith brothers quickly moved the table away from the shed. They were not as brave as their father in taking on the biting tongue of Myra Ann. But the old man, as malicious as ever, was still mocking my aunt saying, "Dew, Dew, boys, there she is behind the door. She was there all the time".

Scowling now, but still trying to retain her dignity, she emerged from behind the door, straightened her dress and shouted at Old man Smith. "Be careful Smith, I know you and your tricks; now bring that thing through the house, and if you do any damage I'll report you to Sergeant Clifton".

The odd job man had a bit of a reputation of sailing close to the wind, in his various and nefarious dealings, and the mere mention of the old policeman's name rapidly removed the smirk from his face. He quickly changed his attitude and tone of voice, immediately protesting his innocence, "No harm meant Mrs Giles". Then, almost pleading, said to his sons. "It was just an accident boys, isn't it".

Although I had no great love for my aunt, at that moment I did feel some sympathy for her, being at the cruel mercy of old man Smith. I was still watching from behind the net curtains; but crouched even lower now as Myra Ann disappeared back inside the house; and I could hear the old man cursing and venting his anger on his sons. He would not use foul language in front of my aunt, but did not mind if she heard it. "Come on you cowing idiots", he shouted. "Get that cowing thing on the cowing cart".

The word cowing; was the favourite expletive used by almost every adult male in the area, and by a great deal of the boys as well. The Smith brothers then lifted the table once more and following their father, eased it through the back door and into the house.

Five minutes later, I was once more in the street outside

the house; when I heard the crack of old man Smith's whip, the clatter of the pony's hooves, and the grinding of the metal trimmed wheels as it moved off at a trot, pulling the cart with the table now safely on board. I did not have to wait long, before I saw them on the main road; with the old man now sitting at the front with his legs dangling over one side, his meg-end in his mouth, and his offspring one on either flank running alongside.

Their next stop would be to the Mile End pub, where they were to pick up three kitchen chairs, which Mammy had bought at a bargain price from the landlord. He had agreed a reasonable sum for these with Mammy, perhaps through a feeling of guilt; or as a tribute to one of his best customers. For he knew that John Swain my father; had more than paid the price of three kitchen chairs; over the bar room counter, during the past thirty or more years.

When I felt it was safe to do so, I quickly ran down the street, keeping well out of sight of the Smiths. I watched as they loaded the chairs on to the cart, then they quickly moved off, up the road passing the bombed family home, until they disappeared from sight under the railway bridge.

Heeding Mammy's warning to stay close to Amy Bowen's house, I dare not follow them any further. Anyway, I was unsure of the territory beyond the bridges, and I could get lost. Besides, Mammy had told me, I must wait for Molly and my two older brothers to come home from school, when she would come to collect us. My excitement increased as the afternoon progressed, with the thought that finally today all of our family would be together again. I was particularly happy; that I would be with Daniel and Molly once more.

## CHAPTER 10

# TOGETHER AGAIN

That evening after tea, we said our goodbyes to Amy Bowen and her girls, and left Bethesda Street to walk the half a mile or so to our new home. We probably looked a sorry sight, to those friends and neighbours that we passed in the street, and on the main road. Mammy led the way, setting a firm walking pace, carrying Walter in her arms and Maggie beside her with the baby. Walter was nearly two-and-half years old now, but was still a delicate and woeful little boy, and was getting heavier to carry; which was why Mammy had him, and Maggie carried the baby. Molly and Daniel were immediately behind; taking it in turns to carry the small cardboard box, which held the remnants of our meagre food rations and other essentials, such as matches and candles.

I walked between them, happy and comfortable in their company; holding the hand of whichever of them was not carrying the cardboard box. Even Harry, seemed to sense the great importance and significance of this day, and was surprisingly calm, and placid; trudging along at the rear with his hands in his trouser pockets.

Why, Mammy had decided to return to Amy Bowen's that afternoon, I do not know. It would have been far easier for her and Maggie and the two little ones, to stay at the new house, to be joined there after school hours by Molly, Daniel, and Harry. Either Molly, or Daniel, could have then come and picked me up from Bethesda Street. There was really no sound reason why she did this, other than symbolic, demonstrating to those people who would try to break us as a family; that they would have a fight on their hands. She was showing her defiance by leaving the neighbourhood, our friends, neighbours, and relatives, as a united family; and we would remain so.

Mrs Joe Lewis was waiting for us outside Mary's sweetshop, and greeted us as we passed. "All the very best of luck, in your new home Louisa. We'll call and see you once you've settled in".

"Thank you Audrey", Mammy replied, "don't forget now love, we'll have a nice cup of tea".

She did not stop to chat; there was no time for that today. The house she had fought long and hard to get was waiting for us.

We passed the cinema, then crossed the entrance to Railway Terrace; and in a deliberate silence we shuffled past the bombed out family home, each with our own thoughts; with Mammy not giving a second glance at the pile of rubble. It was only when we had walked past the place; that Maggie, who was never slow to vent her feelings said. "I hated living there, Mammy", she paused, "and him". "We will be happy in our new home won't we"?

Briefly, for a split second then, Mammy rested her hand on Maggie's shoulder, just a light touch. There was rarely any expression of affection between Mammy and my older sister. "Hush now girl", she said, "don't dwell on the past".

We continued under the first railway arch, passing the

Bridge Inn pub and the footpath that led up to the railway line. The pavement narrowed once more as we approached the second bridge, and Mammy halted our little procession; as a South Wales Transport red double-decker bus, laden with people many of them standing, sped through the gap on its way to the towns and villages up the Swansea Valley.

She shouted now, "Keep in, keep in, let the bus through", and we all pressed against the bridge wall as the bus hurtled by, almost sucking us into the roadway in its draught as it pulled against the air beneath the bridge.

We were witnessing what I expect could be called the rush-hour in those days; as the bus was followed under the bridge by two cars and a flotilla of about a dozen cyclists.

Mammy repeated her warning, but this time with emphasis; she cried out "Gan bwyll, Gan bwyll, take care take care".

We all knew that she meant business, and took heed, when she started to express herself in Welsh. We waited, struck like statues by the tone of her voice. I gripped Daniel's hand tightly, as the road under the bridge was finally cleared of all traffic. Then quickly she hurried us through calling us as she went, "Right now follow me, quickly now".

As we all scurried after her, Harry now decided to abandon his loitering at the rear, and scampered to be with Mammy at the front of our little column.

Once we were clear of the railway bridges, there was a high, stone, wall, which separated the roadway from the wastelands of the Tip. Here, there were some buildings set back from the road behind the wall, with steep stone steps leading up to them. One of these was the Mexico Fountain Pub, which was on the corner where we turned from the main road into Pentremawr Road, and our new home.

Pentremawr Road is quite wide and on a slightly curved incline, that sweeps up to the open area of Hafod Square. There were terrace houses on one side, and the tip, which was much closer to the road here, on the other side. To the west of the road was the district of the Hafod proper, which was built in a block or grid system; of narrow little streets, with rows of back-to-back terraced houses. The streets were all named after members of the family that owned and founded the old Copper Works, the Vivians.

As we approached the open area of Hafod Square, I saw for the first time the neat row of half a dozen semi-detached houses where we were now to live; the third one of which was to be or new home. Directly opposite to these, and on land which was predominantly made up of the tip, was an old run-down white cottage, which we discovered was still lived in. There were also the remains of some stone outbuildings, indicating that this place was probably once a farmhouse. The occupant was like the cottage itself, a frail white head old lady, who no doubt remembered the land on which the new properties were built, as flat open grassland known as the Summer Dwelling; which is the English equivalent for the term Hafod. Sadly we never got to know the old lady. She died shortly after we moved there, and the cottage quickly fell into decay and ruin.

The centrepiece of the square was a large slightly raised tar macadam island, which was almost heart shaped without the top indent, and ringed with concrete kerbstones. It was about 20 metres long and 10 metres at its widest point; and there was an old green painted metal lamp post on one side of the island; but because of the black out which was in force at the time, we would not see in use for many years. The square, and particularly this raised island, was a favoured and alternative play area for the children living in the vicinity. We played games such as football, with anything from a tennis ball, a bag of rags, or a tin can; and other games such as rounders, cricket, and hopscotch.

Our excitement was getting intense now as we crossed the square to our new home; with Harry becoming more and more worked up, running ahead then returning to Mammy shouting, "Where is our house Mammy, where is it, show me where it is". These houses were much bigger and better than the majority of the houses in the area, and occupied by better-off people. They were mostly shop-keepers, self-employed tradesman, and white-collar workers; and already, word had got around that their semi seclusion-away from the riff-raff was now to be invaded by this large bombed-out family.

As we passed our immediate neighbour, the front door of the house was open and we were greeted with these words emanating from the lady within. "She's got seven bloody kids, and no man".

As young as I was, I felt humiliated and stunned by this remark; and it must have felt like a dagger to Mammy's heart. But, she showed no outward sign, that she had heard this deliberate and offensive slight to her and our family. But that was not the case with Maggie, who responded immediately, "Did you hear her Mammy, the old cow".

Mammy was stern but quiet, and replied, "Hush now Mag, I'll see to her, all in good time", and in keeping with her simple philosophy in life added, "Remember Mag, people who throw stones must not be surprised if great boulders are hurled back at them".

We gathered in a tight cluster around her, as she stopped briefly outside the gateway of our house; and pulled the key, still hanging from the rough piece of cord, from her handbag. It was scruffier than the other houses, with only one brown battered gate left of a pair; as the place had not been lived in for a while, the other had probably been taken for firewood. The front walls were built of red brick and about 3 ft high, and looked sound enough; and there was a small lawn at the front of the house, with a spindly privet hedge close to the wall. At the side of the house there was a rough cinder path that ran down to the back; and parallel to this was an uneven bumpy lawn raised at a slightly higher level. Still, to our family, and me in particular, this was a grand house. Indeed it was a palace, compared to the one that once was our home.

Harry, impatient as ever was first in through the gateway, and was now banging away at the front door with his fists, and shouting, "I'm going to be first in. Open the door Mammy".

She strode past him, smiling now, with the rest of us crowding tightly behind her "Then you had better get round the back quick son", she said, "this key is for the back door".

Like a flash he rushed past us and disappeared round the back of the house, where there were two solid pine doors.

As we followed him, he was now pushing on the first of these doors, and it flew open. "It's open Mammy, he shouted, we don't need a key". Mammy laughed; and so did the rest of us when she said, "Dew, Dew, silly boy, can't you see that's the lavatory".

The ground at the back had been concreted over between the house, and a slightly raised patch of land, which was overgrown and covered with thick couch grass and weeds. In better times, this was probably a kitchen garden or vegetable patch. Like the front of the house, there were similar red brick boundary walls to the side and the back; and once again, there were planted along these the inevitable privet trees. Apart from the two pine doors, there was a large window, and standing in the corner was an old iron clothes mangle.

Mammy put the key into the lock now, as we all gathered there in eager anticipation of what we would discover once we were inside. She turned the key but hesitated before shouting for Harry, who had run off to the front of the house in a sulk, after he had mistaken the lavatory door for that of the house.

She called to him, "Come on Harry bach, you can be the first in". He did not need calling a second time, as he sprinted back and squeezed in front of her. She pushed at the door, but it opened slowly and with some difficulty; it had dropped slightly on its hinges; scraping against the floor covering of lino, the pattern of which had been stripped away and revealing the black felt underneath.

Finally, after one last push, the door was open sufficiently for Harry to bound through, with Mammy and the rest of us, shuffling in to what was to be the main living-room-cum kitchen. Harry had already disappeared through into the front room, and I could hear his boots thumping against the bare wooden stair boards as he clambered up to the first floor. He was calling me to follow him, "Come up by yer 'andel, come-on mun, it's great up yer".

He seemed compelled, that wherever he went, to reach the highest or furthest point before stopping. But before I could make a move, Mammy had got hold of me saying, "No, wait now bach, let's take our time, see there are the table and chairs".

There were some old newspapers neatly laid covering the top of the table, as a substitute tablecloth; and the three chairs that Mammy had purchased from the Mile End pub had been placed around it; one at the top and one at either side.

There were no curtains at the windows, not even nets; but at least they were whitewashed on the inside, which would give us some privacy. Then, with a grand gesture, her arms open wide Mammy approached the fireplace and with pride said. "Look here, a double oven, the bottom one for cooking, and the top one for keeping things hot".

It was much grander than the one we had in the old house. We all stood gazing and admiring the black leaded fireplace, with its modern oven, as she added. "I'll get some sticks and coal tomorrow, and cook us a nice dinner. Some Cawl is it".

She knew that this would please us; for the very thought of having a hot bowl of Cawl, the traditional Welsh soup or stew, made with mutton or lamb, with potatoes and all the vegetables that were in season; or during these times, whatever she could lay her hands on.

She turned and walked back across the room to the two doors at the opposite side. The first one she opened revealed the pantry, with its rows of bare shelves and cold slab. She closed it quickly, as it was a reminder that we did not have a great deal of food, apart from the little box of provisions we had brought with us. Then with another grand gesture she pushed open the next door, and proudly said, "Look here, see all of you, a proper bath with hot water, and a proper wash hand basin to wash your hands and face".

We all pushed and shuffled after her; crowding into the bathroom; the like of which we had never seen before. There was the large white enamelled cast-iron bath, with two chromium-plated taps, one for hot water and one for cold water. Alongside it, directly under the window was the wash hand basin. Once again with two chrome taps. We were almost overwhelmed by the sight of these modern appliances, and quickly got caught up in Mammy's enthusiasm for this splendid addition to our lives. It was a far cry from the old zinc bath that we used in the old house, in front of the fire on a Saturday night, with the saucepans and kettles of hot water being boiled on the open fire. "Oh Mammy, Molly piped up, can I have a bath now".

But Maggie was quick to dash her hopes, "Don't be so stupid girl, you've got to have a fire first for the hot water". "Oh never mind girls", Mammy said, as she fondly tousled Molly's hair. "Tomorrow night Moll, before bed, you and Maggie can be the first, you can have a bath then. We'll get a good fire going to cook the dinner, and then we will have plenty of hot water for baths too".

The thought of getting hot water just by turning on a tap, and bathing in this gleaming white bath stunned us into silence momentarily; until Mammy broke the spell. "Well that's enough of the bathroom for now", she said, as she shooed us back into the main living room. "Come-on, you haven't seen it all yet".

She now ushered us into the front room, and walking to the centre, danced a little twirl with her arms outstretched, she said, "and this is the parlour".

It had a large bay window at the front giving plenty of light, and again like the back room window was without curtains and similarly whitewashed. The room wasn't strictly rectangular, with the innermost corner angled to take a small open fireplace and mantelpiece. The solid concrete floor had been covered with red cardinal polish, and a large square of linoleum, which was predominantly green in colour, with specks of red and black. What the Red Cardinal polish actually consisted of I do not know, but it was all the rage at that time.

We all seemed to gravitate towards the centre of the empty room, with its grimy cream painted featureless walls, and the single electric light socket dangling from the off-white ceiling. This room was not at all inspiring after the excitement of the bathroom, and Mammy sensing this said, "Well, there's no furniture yet, but we will make it nice in time, you see. We'll have a nice settee and comfortable chairs", then she paused and almost as an afterthought said, "and definitely a piano one-day"

She knew that having a piano was very much a long-term aim, and this was another way of showing us that we had to think in the long term, and build up our hopes accordingly. Yes a piano was very much a luxury; an important status symbol for her, but there were many other things; other essential household items to acquire first. She was under no illusion; and was fully aware of the hard and difficult struggle in the years that lay ahead for us, to survive and keep the family together.

Harry was still walking about upstairs, occasionally stamping his feet on the bare wooden floor boards, shouting and calling me, "'Andel, come up by yer quick".

He was getting impatient as he was now out of things, and he liked to be the centre of attention. The next time he shouted, "Come up by yer and see, everybody come-on up".

But, before anyone could respond, Mammy had moved out of the parlour to the foot of the stairs and shouted back at him, "No boy, you come down here, it will be dark soon and time for bed". Then turning to Maggie she said, "We'll have a hot drink now Mag, some tea is it, and get the candles and matches ready".

This puzzled Molly, as she chipped in, "But there's electricity in this house Mammy, like in our school, we don't need candles we can have electric light".

I am sure that we all felt the same way. Here we were in this modern house that had a bathroom, with hot and cold running water, so why couldn't we have electric lights. With puzzled faces we all look towards Mammy, searching for the answer. "Ah, true Molly", she said, as she ruffled her younger daughter's hair, "but first we need a shilling piece for the meter, to get the electricity switched on, and then we have to buy light bulbs. So we shall have electric lights when we can afford them and not before, and until then, we will have to make do with the candles".

Harry, reluctantly at last yielding to Mammy's insistence that he should return downstairs; as no one, particularly me, was going to be allowed to join him; quickly descended creating as much din as he possibly could as he clumped into the bare wooden stair boards. Mammy scolded him as he came into the room; he went and stood by the window, and immediately started to pick away at the covering of whitewash with his fingernail. Mammy threatened him once more. "Harry if you don't stop doing that and start behaving yourself, new home on not, you shall have a good hiding". Luckily for him he was saved from this, as Maggie now shouted from the back-room. "I've got the matches and candles Mammy, how many shall I light".

Like chicks following the mother hen, we all trooped back to where Maggie was standing near the table; she was holding our entire stock of three candles in her hand. She repeated her question, "how many shall I light Mammy". Just the one, girl", she replied, "but not yet, it is still light enough to do without".

Then pointing to the single gas ring, which was precariously balanced on a plank of wood that spanned the large porcelain sink in the corner, she said. "Light that gas ring Mag, we need to boil water for some tea".

Maggie, always prepared to exercise her authority over her sister, now dug her knuckles into Molly's back, saying, "Come on you, give us a hand, fill that saucepan with water while I light the gas".

So in a cold twilight, we settled into our new home on that first day, with half a cup of lukewarm tea, with a little sugar but no milk; drinking from an assortment of teacups of various shapes and sizes; sitting in front of an empty, cold, fireplace. Our entire seating capacity; the three kitchen chairs were occupied by Mammy nursing the baby on one, Maggie, with Walter on her lap on another, and Harry, with legs spread wide; had commandeered the sole remaining chair. Molly and Daniel sat on the floor with their backs to the wall, with me on Molly's lap. We sat there in silence for a while, happy but tired; each one of us reflecting on the day's events and thinking of what lay ahead. Content to be together again, albeit a cold, tired, and weary family.

Even Harry seemed to sense the reverence of the occasion, and managed to remain still as the night drew in quickly. At last, the silence was broken, as Mammy said, "Right the beds are made, so light that candle now Mag, and let's put the boys to bed first".

The sleeping arrangements were simple. In the front and largest bedroom was the one complete bed unit that our family possessed; and in here would sleep Mammy and the baby, Maggie, and Molly. In the back bedroom was a large mattress that had been placed on the floor; neatly made up with sheets and blankets, and this was for Daniel, Harry, Walter and myself. Mammy had decided, out of necessity, that Walter was big enough now to sleep with us boys.

Evening rapidly turned to night; as Mammy, with Maggie leading the way, and guided by the light of the solitary candle, led the four of us up the stairs to bed. As she tucked us in; with Daniel and Harry at the top of the bed, and Walter, who was fast asleep, and myself at the bottom, she gave a final warning to Harry, "be a good boy tonight Harry, and try not to have any accidents".

She was of course praying that he would not wet the bed that night; and those thoughts were echoed by Daniel and myself; also praying that we would not wake up in the morning, sticking to the bed clothes and reeking of urine.

So with that earnest prayer; that we would wake up warm and dry in the morning, and no visit from the Luftwaffe, we settled down for the first night in our new home. I slept that night on my side facing the window, with Harry's feet firmly planted close to the back of my head; and the last sounds I could remember was him giggling and tormenting me by saying. "When you turn over 'andel, I'm going to stick my big toe up u'er nose".

# CHAPTER 11

# STARTING SCHOOL

The Easter holiday was over, and at long last the day that I had yearned for finally arrived. It was the start of the Spring school term; I was five years old, and could now take my rightful place in the Infants School; unlike the previous attempt a couple of months earlier, when I was denied entry. This time I could not be refused.

Hafod school was an imposing structure, three stories high, built on sloping ground, with a split level between the main boys and girls schools. The Infants school was on the ground floor of the lower part, with the first and second floors providing the Girls' School. Both the girls and the Infants shared the same playground; as it was considered safe, for the small boys and girls who made up the Infants, to share their playtime with the older girls. The older boys were strictly segregated, being confined to the upper part of the school.

So, on that Monday morning after the Easter holiday; and escorted by Maggie and Molly, I made my second appearance before Miss Thomas the Headmistress. I was dressed in a soft silk-like white shirt, with large mother of pearl buttons on the front, and a similar button on each sleeve. This splendid garment came with other items of clothing, in a parcel donated by the people of America, and given to us by the Salvation Army. The rest of my attire was made up of a pair of navy blue short trousers, handed down from Harry, a pair of black woollen socks, and black boots. Boots, with hobnails on the soles, and iron plates on the heels. This was the normal footwear then, for the majority of boys from working class families. We could certainly be heard coming.

Mammy was fully aware of just how important this occasion was for me, and shared in my delight. She was very proud of me. The white shirt with the mother of pearl buttons had been selected, and kept, for this very important day. Normally, we were left alone to our own devices to dress ourselves in the morning; when Mammy would be fully engrossed, in preparing what ever food was available for breakfast. This was usually a piece of stale bread kept from the day before, and if we were lucky, there would be some jam or syrup to spread on it.

She had risen much earlier that morning. She was always an early riser; before six o' clock on most days, a legacy from her life on the farm. Breakfast had been prepared, and the washing of hands and faces supervised. She was keenly aware of tidemarks on the upper neck of any child; when the soap and water was applied to the face only; and after a couple of days, evidence of this would be manifested in a thick line of dirt running from under the chin to the ears. This meant that these appendages as well as the neck had also been missed. The remedy, or punishment as we would liken it to; was that the offending child would have his head; it was always the boys in our house, placed in the vice like grip of Mammy's powerful hands; and a flannel liberally soaked in warm soapy water feverishly applied to the neglected neck and ears. The painful result of this; would be a sore head and neck, tears in your eyes, and worst of all; the spine-chilling sensation of the warm soapy water, rapidly cooling as it ran down your back. The discomfort this produced as it soaked into your vest, or shirt, would prevail until the garment dried out. It was never a pleasant feeling at the best of times; but was particularly horrible, as you walked to school on sharp and frosty winter mornings. But there was no scrubbing of necks and ears this morning, just as when she was extremely angry, or happy, as she was on this occasion; she reverted partly to her native Welsh tongue. "Du du cariad, she said, as she walked me to the gate of the house with Maggie and Molly, "you are my handsome boy today".

So off to school I went, feeling very smart and grown-up; and to give credence to this feeling; I now had strung over my shoulder a loop of stout twine, to which was attached a light brown cardboard box. This contained the hated gas mask, the device which all children of school age had to carry with them whenever they attended school. Any child found without a gas mask would be promptly sent home, and not allowed to return without it; and drills, were regularly carried out by the teachers; to ensure that the device was functioning properly; and that we were capable of putting the things on. Like most children; I found it extremely difficult to stretch the thick rubber straps, which enabled you to place your head inside the mask; without them viciously snapping back and biting into the sides and back of your head. My ears especially, seemed particularly vulnerable to these fiendish attacks from the gas mask; a device allegedly designed to protect us.

In those days, the school year began in January, and ended in December; and your school career began at the start of the term, which immediately followed your 5th birthday. I was five in January, and along with about a dozen other children I was about to join Miss Parsons' class. She was a small, quiet, and demure creature, a rather sad little woman who almost appeared to be detached from the world. Whether it was unwitting or not, she seemed to transmit her state of lethargy to the children under her control. My recollection of the short time I stayed in her class, was not one I would normally associate with a bunch of newly arrived five-year-old children; some of whom bitterly resented being snatched from the loving arms of their mothers, and had to be dragged kicking and screaming into the school on the very first day.

We all assembled in the school hall, where we were met by the headmistress and our teacher Miss Parsons. Each child waited in turn to be introduced, or rather come under the scrutiny of the stern and strict; but fair headmistress. We were then escorted one at a time to the classroom, where there were neat rows of two-seater desks; occupied wherever possible by a one boy and one girl. The door of the classroom had been wedged open, and the children already seated were in the temporary charge, or care, of one of the older girl pupils.

It was then as I entered the classroom; that my eyes fell on and became transfixed on what I thought was an angel, the most beautiful girl that I, or the world had ever seen; Daisy Davies. The Hollywood child star Shirley Temple was all the rage at that time, and parents who could afford it; tried to copy or emulate the dress style and looks of the actress, for their own little princesses. She was the sweetest thing in the whole of the universe I was convinced; dressed in a soft pink dress, with long rolled plats of golden hair, peaches and cream complexion, with sparkling blue eyes. They say that the eyes reflect the soul, and through them she oozed confidence. I was completely entranced and captivated by her, and would swear even now; that the whole picture of Daisy Davies was bathed in a glowing halo of warmth. She was sitting at a desk all alone, and I desperately wanted to be the boy who would sit next to her. But the aspirations to my first great romance were quickly dashed, as from the furthest corner of the classroom came the soft but distinct call. "Come and sit by me 'andel".

Without stopping, Miss Parsons who still had one hand clasped firmly on my shoulder; turned direction away from the centre of the room, and headed straight towards the source of these words. My eyes however, were still locked and fixed upon the sweet smiling face of Daisy Davies; but a little jolt from the teacher, with the added words of, "look Handel you have a friend you can sit next to", persuaded me to look ahead. The teacher's hand was now firmly gripping the top of my head, which was being twisted, forcing me to look in the direction in which we were now moving. The radiant features, the glowing warmth of Daisy Davies vanished; and was now replaced by the pitiful sight of the blotchy and sore covered face of Rosie Smith. She was dressed in a faded navy-blue frock, with a loose black cardigan that was much too big for her, draped over her shoulders. Her short, cropped black hair, had been parted to one side, and held in place by a small white rag. It was a pathetic and pitiful attempt to adorn her hair with a ribbon. I could not hide my feelings, and she could see the look of disappointment on my face, as Miss Parsons sat me down next to her. Sadly, she dropped her head and unsmiling face, staring blankly down at the desk. We sat in silence, and at that time I felt no pity or compassion for this girl, who had denied me my chance of sitting next to the girl who had claimed my heart. Little girls like Rosie

Smith rarely smile, they do not know how. They can laugh at things that are funny, and ironic or mocking laughs come easily, but there are no smiles where there is no love or genuine affection. I was fully aware that this was so in sad little Rosie Smith's life.

As for Daisy Davies I could only watch in jealous rage, as minutes later Miss Parsons brought in and sat beside her one Norman Lloyd. He was much taller than me, but then, although I was well proportioned, it was true that most of the children in my class were taller than me anyway. It was a fact of life that I had to endure. Throughout my entire school years, my height was well below the average of that for boys in the same class or age group. I was never the smallest child, as there was nearly always one boy in each class who was really tiny. One lad who comes to mind, who was in this minute or tiny category was Dinky Miles; who although a year younger than me, was to become one of my best friends during my early school years.

Norman Lloyd I realised was going to be formidable competition for the favours of Daisy Davies; and he had many advantages over me, not least by the fact that he was now firmly ensconced sitting alongside her. I have already mentioned that he was much taller than me, but then he was much taller and well built than the rest of the boys in the class. His hair was well groomed, with a parting in the middle, which was unusual; and quite different to my hair-cut, which was little better than a basin cut. We had our hair cut by an amateur barber who worked at the Copper Works, and cut hair in his spare time. But Norman Lloyd was smartly dressed as well, in a red blazer with grey trousers and a gleaming white shirt; but the part of his splendid attire, that the majority of the rest of us envied; was his shiny new shoes, instead of hobnail boots like the rest of us. He had everything going for him; with his good looks and physique, and the way he was dressed meant that he came from a home entirely different to mine.

My first day at school had not got off to a good start; I was sharing a desk with Rosie Smith, which meant that we would remain together until we were assessed; sometime in the future, regarding the progress of our schoolwork. It was the custom in those days to segregate children; with the brightest pupils occupying the desks at the front of the class, and receding in order to the back of the class where the less bright children were placed.

So the long process of acquiring the art of mastering the three R's was put into place. We were duly issued with pencils and sheets of lined paper, both sides to be used; and began to learn our numbers 1 to 10, and the alphabet, ah,bu,cu,du. Soon the anguish of losing out to Norman Lloyd and his favoured position of sitting besides Daisy Davies was forgotten. The issue of the pencils and paper meant; that at long last that we were getting down to serious learning, and just how important, school was to me. I had already mastered through my own efforts, and the guidance of Mammy, the numbers up to 100 and most of the alphabet, including being able to recognise and read some simple words. I did not mind having to start from the very beginning; as I realised that the majority of the children in the class had no idea of what the three R's meant, and had no wish to understand them or have anything to do with school anyway. For me it was different. I was thirsty for knowledge; curious of so many things in life, and it meant that I could shine in the presence of my peers. I was lucky in as much as I had an ability to pick up knowledge quickly, to understand it, and had a great capacity to retain information.

Over the coming days and weeks, I was able to demonstrate to the teacher; that I was very well prepared for school, and made swift progress to one of the front seats of the class. By the end of the spring term I had parted company from Rosie Smith, and was now sitting beside a different girl. No it was not Daisy Davies, for she was languishing somewhere in the middle of the class; but this did not disturb her or lower her confidence; she had been taught that a pretty girl can achieve most things in life, without having to prove how clever she is. Norman Lloyd however, was a different proposition. He applied himself to his work with great vigour; and although not spectacular, he too made good progress, and ended the term sitting at the desk immediately behind me.

As school broke up and we started our long summer holiday, I realised that I had learned a valuable lesson; that life has many surprises, and one should not be deterred or discouraged when the odds against you seem over-whelming. Circumstances can change quickly; and alter the course of your life, sometimes for better and sometimes for worse, as I had discovered during my first few months at school. Happiness and success in life comes with a lot of hard work and a little luck, or an abundance of luck and a little hard work. However you approach it, these two ingredients are essential as you steer down that uncertain path through life.

## CHAPTER 12

# FRIENDS AND NEIGHBOURS

During the following weeks and months, we gradually settled in to our new home, and we began as a family to establish ourselves with our new neighbours. Mammy, forever on the lookout to increase the family possessions, acquired more household items, pots and pans, and some incredible tin mugs. As the war progressed and things got increasingly scarce, then the ingenuity and resourcefulness that characterise the British nature got going.

Molly had discovered from one of her friends at school, of this old chap, a Mr Brooks, living not too far from us, who would make the mugs at no cost. All he required was the raw material; i.e. a clean tin such as those used for tinned fruit, milk, or vegetables; though these items were also becoming less plentiful, they could still be acquired occasionally. Mr Brooks' method was simple but effective. The tin was turned into a mug by simply cutting off the top inch or so, straighten this bit out, then forming a small handle out of it, which he then soldered onto the side of the remaining piece of tin. The finished product had to be used with care; as the rim of the mug could still be a little on the sharp side; but still it was better than some of the old cracked and chipped cups that were the only alternative.

We even got some net curtains for the back room, the main living room and kitchen, where we spent most of our time. But our most desperate need was more seating capacity to supplement the three chairs we already had; and for this Mammy scrounged an old orange box from one of the greengrocers. Even though this was intended to serve as a bench for the smaller and lighter members of the family, there were many doubts expressed by neighbours and others as to the wisdom of this. The flimsy structure, everyone advised, would never support the weight of three kittens, let alone the three intended members of the family, Daniel, Harry, and myself. But Mammy was to prove them all wrong; by stuffing the inside of the box with cardboard and balls of paper; which gave it sufficient strength, and thus sturdy enough to get several months use out of it.

Most of our new neighbours were reluctant to mix with or even speak to us at first, preferring to keep us at a distance; and one or two, particularly our immediate neighbour Mrs Morris; were downright hostile in their attitude, and would say and do things which caused us severe embarrassment and be deliberately hurtful. We were from a much poorer part of the town and normally would not be living in such an area as this, and certainly not in a modern semi-detached house. But gradually, Mammy, as resolute as ever, bided her time, and knew that it was up to us as a family to show these people that they had nothing to fear from us. She might have had precious little possessions, but was not lacking in dignity; she had received a good education and was well read, and could hold her own in most company.

So in time we settled in, and as in most communities we

made friends to a greater or lesser degree, and were generally accepted by most of our new neighbours. We also made some enemies. There are always those people who when seeing someone or a family such as ours, having suffered a severe setback in life, are prepared to add to that hardship if they can. Unable to impress their peers as they would wish, and left wanting in self-esteem; they will attack those that they feel are vulnerable, to bolster their own inadequate lives.

Such a person was Mrs Morris, our immediate neighbour in the adjacent semi. It was she who had made the arrogant remarks about Mammy having, "seven kids and no man", which we as a family had overheard the day we arrived at our new home. She was either a widow, or a rare animal for those days; a divorcee, for there was no Mr Morris around. This lady had a biting tongue and waspish nature, but for all of her faults, and she had many, she did have one overriding virtue. She could cook. She had the knack of turning simple fare into items of gastronomic delight, by the subtle addition of seasoning and spices, and I can vouch for this from personal experience. It was probably on the strength of this, her expertise in the kitchen; that enabled her to secure a second husband. The honeymoon however did not last long, as we were soon subjected to many lengthy slanging matches emanating from their back room. There was one particular occasion I recall, when even her culinary delights proved insufficient to keep him at home; and as he stormed out of the house, his dinner still on the plate, followed him, flying through the air and smashing into the back of his head. I watched this from our back garden; as the man just kept on marching in the direction of the works, or perhaps the pub, the way he had come from minutes earlier; with bits of potatoes, carrots, cabbage, and gravy running down his back.

Over the following years she was to become a nagging thorn in Mammy's side; with her constant harping that we children were too noisy, or were playing ball where we should not be. Strange as it might seem, in as much as she was always on our backs, we rarely saw the woman. She made her presence felt with her voice; with venomous screeches emanating from the back room of her house, which always had the door fully open. But even she mellowed with time, and many years were to pass before she and Mammy were on speaking terms. And it was only then that I was to discover just what a wonderful cook she was; when she would send over the occasional plate of roast dinner, or casserole, which Mammy would share with any lucky individual of our family who happened to be present.

On the other side of us in the adjoining semi, lived the Evans family. They were a quiet, polite and courteous family, keeping very much to themselves. Without being over friendly they made us feel welcome, and were kind in as much that they would give us the occasional bag of apples or pears; when they were in season, with some runner beans and peas as well. They probably got the fresh fruit and vegetables from friends or family living outside of the town, for they certainly did not grow anything themselves.

They had one daughter who was a couple of years older than Maggie, but we saw little of her. She did not attend the local school like the rest of us, as Mr and Mrs Evans had grand aspirations for their Sylvia, who was taking a course on shorthand and typing at the Greggs College in the town; and Mammy alert to the possibilities and opportunities to better her own children's future, made a mental note of this, that one of her girls could do the same. These were the two families then; that I remembered being in contact with at first, simply because I was now confined to the area within the perimeter of our new house, unless I was in the company of one of my older siblings.

We had been fortunate, since taking up residence in our new home; that we were spared any of the dreaded air-raid warnings, whether real or false, during the first couple of weeks. Then on one bright moonlit night, the familiar siren started wailing its distressing sound; that brought us running from our beds, to the air-raid shelter of our new neighbourhood. It was one of the older types of shelter, which was small and divided inside into compartments; and surprisingly, although we were now in a more densely populated area, it was not as full as I expected. This, was probably because a lot of the people living in the posh semis had their own Anderson shelters, or had become complacent once more, as the raids were becoming fewer and less severe. Those people that did use the shelter were also now better prepared, and most had warm blankets and torches. We however did not have any such luxuries as blankets and torches, but made sure that we brought our warmest garments, which was usually an overcoat or jacket.

It was on this night that I first met Dinky Miles, a boy who was to become a firm pal of mine over the coming years; during which we had many adventures together; and as his nickname suggests he was rather a small person. We had squeezed into one of the shelter's inner compartments, which, was already occupied by Dinky, his mother, and grandmother. They had with them an old bicycle rear lamp that provided light; a red eerie glow, that made the inside of the shelter look like a fairy grotto; with little Dinky standing there dressed in striped pyjama trousers, a woollen jumper that was much too big for him, and a woolly hat perched on his head; greeting us like a little elf.

"What's uwer name", he enquired of me, as Mammy pushed me in first; but before I could reply, his mother had grabbed hold of him and sat him on her knee. Sit there, boy" she said, "and let the good people come in".

The eight of us crammed in and settled down; Mammy nursing Eddie, with Maggie holding Walter on her lap; and quite soon she and the other two ladies had begun to exchange their views on the war, the weather, the food shortages, and life's hardships in general. I was standing close to Mammy and watching Dinky, intrigued by the little boy who had now begun to pull faces at me. They were funny faces rather than nasty or malicious; as Dinky I was to discover, didn't have a malicious thought in his head. He was an only child whose father was away in the army, and was desperately in need of company. His grandmother was very much aware of this, and without interrupting her conversation with Mammy, got hold of my arm and pulled me on to her knee so that I was now sitting close to and facing Dinky. He leaned towards me and repeated quietly now, almost in a whisper, "What's ewer name mun". 'Andel", I said, and he started to giggle, putting his hand to his mouth to stifle the laugh.

I wasn't quite sure what to say or do, so I thought I had just better ask him, "well what's ewer name then". This at least stopped him from giggling, then, startling me he shouted out, "Dinky". At this his mother briefly interrupted her conversation, saying, "Your name is David, not Dinky".

But she did not pursue the matter; obviously she was resigned to the fact that everyone called him Dinky, and that is what he would be known as anyway, and resumed her conversation. Then to avoid drawing his mother's attention he reverted once more to whispering, as he cupped his hand over his mouth he said, "You call me Dinky right".

He quietly giggled once more; he had an infectious laugh and I soon got caught up in the mood as I said, "Right, and you call me 'andel". My name was too much for him, but I expect it would have happened sooner or later as he replied, "right Andy". So it was that I had been renamed by this mischievous little urchin, and would be known forever by him and most of the other children, by the nickname of Handy, or more often Andy.

I enjoyed my first experience in the air-raid shelter that night, because of my first encounter with Dinky and his family, and was sorry when it ended with the sound of the all-clear signal. There had been a raid that night, and enemy planes were overhead; but somehow because of the warm and pleasant atmosphere in the shelter, their presence did not affect us.

The raid was over and we made our way back outside the air raid shelter, and as often happened on nights like these, although the air was crisp but not too cold, the bright moonlit night encouraged people to hang around, mingling and talking with their friends and neighbours. Mammy stopped only briefly to say good night to Mrs Miles and her mother, before getting hold of my hand and ushering the rest of the family back across the square to home and bed.

It was not until Mammy was lighting the candle in the kitchen, and instructing Maggie, "Right Mag, let's get the boys to bed first", that we noticed that there was one boy present who should not have been with us. Somehow Dinky had broken free from his mother, and got caught up in the throng that was our family, and had willingly come home with us. Realising that his mother must have been distraught with anguish when she found that he was missing, Mammy told Maggie and Daniel. "Get hold of him quickly and take him back to his mother", despite

Dinky's loud protestations of, "No mun, no mun, I want to stay with Andy".

Now Maggie was quite used to dealing with wriggling children, and few would escape her clutches when she set her mind to catch them; having to deal with Harry, and to a lesser extent me, had sharpened her expertise in catching children to an extremely high level. So it was with great amusement and laughter all round; that when she tried to get hold of Dinky, the little lad wriggled and squirmed out of her grasp; sidestepped Daniel and Molly who were also trying to get him, and dived under the table. We were all in fits of laughter including Mammy, as Maggie, confident that she had him now, squatted down and got under the table after him. There were howls of delight from the rest of us, and Harry encouraging Dinky now pointed to the cupboard under the kitchen sink shouting, "Go in there quick, get under the shelf".

In the poor light of the single candle, Maggie had difficulty in locating Dinky under the table, as he hid behind one leg and then another. She was thrashing about trying to get her hands on him, while Harry was still encouraging him to make a dash for the cupboard. He was holding the door open calling the little boy, "over by yer Dinky boy, get in the cupboard".

Mammy moved quickly and got hold of Harry, giving him a clout across the back of his head and dragged him away. In the confusion that followed, as we all scattered out of Mammy's way, this was just the opportunity that Dinky was waiting for. By the time things had settled down again, and Mammy had Harry firmly in her grasp, Dinky was safely ensconced under the shelf in the cupboard. He was an incredibly small boy for his age, but extremely agile and nifty, just like a little mouse. We could just about make him out, crouching under the shelf, hanging on for grim death to the lead water pipes, which were secured to the wall.

Given the confined space under the sink, Mammy thought it wise not to try to yank him out of there as he could be harmed. Besides, she was worrying about the little boy's mother, who must by now be distraught with the worry of where her son could be. We were all over excited and wound up by what was happening, with a lot of giggling and shouting going on, as Mammy now tried to restore some kind of order, in a stern voice said. "All right, be quiet now the lot of you. Maggie take Daniel with you and try and find his mother".

It was then that Maggie retorted, sullen now that she had failed to catch the little boy, "But Mammy, we don't know when he lives".

The sudden realisation of this threw Mammy into a minor panic as she cried, "Iesi Annwyl" but for once did not repeat it in English. Just asking the same question, saying, "Oh! Dear, dear, where does he live"?

Then Daniel intervened with what seemed to be the only solution to the problem, "We must go back to the shelter Mammy they will be looking for him there".

But before anyone moved, we had a stroke of luck. To this day I do not know why I did it, but to quote out of the mouths of babes and sucklings, I simply said, "Where do you live Dinky". We were all more than a little shocked, and Mammy gave a huge sigh of relief as a little voice piped up, "Dinky lives in Odo Street, Hafod", and with that he extricated himself from underneath the kitchen sink, took hold of my hand and said, "Come on Andy, you come to my 'ouse with me, is it"?

The whole episode had taken less than 10 minutes; as Maggie, Daniel, and myself with Dinky still holding my hand, found his mother and grandmother, and most of the people who had been in the air-raid shelter that night, searching its immediate surrounds and calling his name.

The last thing I heard that night as we once more made our way home, were the great sobs and yells, emanating from Dinky as his mother rendered a few sharp slaps to his bare bottom. It was probably more out of relief than anger, that his mother had smacked him that night, but it would not be the last time that I would witness such an act over the years that followed.

## CHAPTER 13

# COLLECTING FIREWOOD

Every single day life was a constant battle for Mammy; just to provide the very basics of living such as food, clothing, and fuel, that most people took for granted; even during the dark days of 1941, when Britain stood alone against the might of Hitler and the Nazis. She received a war widow's pension of £4.3 shillings (£4.15p) a week, to keep her-self and seven children. There were no other benefits; this was her entire income, and everything had to be paid at the going rate. Although there was never any money left at the end of the week, I never heard her complain that this was not enough. She was grateful for the money that she received from the state, even though she had lost her husband and breadwinner through the country being at war with Germany. She always believed that no one owed her a living.

From conversations I had with her later on in life, when I was better able to understand these matters; she told me that she added to her income by taking money from her meagre savings, and the small amount of insurance money she obtained on the death of my father. She only ever did this when it was absolutely essential, to maintain the vital necessities of life. If, she ran out of funds by Friday, and we could manage on what provisions we had until she received her pension on the following Monday, then, that is what we did.

When we could afford a decent joint of meat for the weekend, of beef, lamb, or pork, which was mainly for Sunday dinner; then Mammy went to the butcher's herself. She knew the best cuts, and what would be good value for money. The joint of meat would be cooked on Saturday night, and this provided some dripping, which was spread on a piece of bread as a treat for us after our weekly bath. Any meat that was left over from Sunday dinner would be served cold, but with fresh hot vegetables, on the Monday.

However, when money was tight, she would send one of us in her place. I often waited in the corner of the local butcher's shop on a Saturday morning, as customers were served, waiting for a decent bag of bones to be made up. A good joint of meat could be had for two shillings; but a big bag of bones, which would make a huge cauldron of Cawl, would only cost 6 pence. Then, as now, weekends were to be celebrated as best we could, and she always tried to ensure that we had good hot food, especially on Sunday. One of the high spots of the week would be Sunday tea; when she made one of her special rock cakes, or a rice pudding, or some jelly.

During the week it was a different story, after Monday when we had used up the leftovers from Sunday, we would make do with what ever Mammy could scrape together. Dried egg powder, which came in large round tins; made an excellent meal when mixed into a paste and fried with some onions. When this was running low; Mammy would eke it out by adding flour, and some lard, or margarine, if she had any to spare. Fresh eggs were even better if they were on the ration that week, even if sometimes we had to share one hard-boiled egg between two. Other meals we enjoyed would be tinned corned beef, sardines, or my particular favourite pilchards in tomato sauce. On the whole our diet was pretty good, particularly in summer and autumn when fruit and vegetables were in season. Potatoes and bread were generally in good supply, and most days the bulk of our food intake was made up of these. There were times however; more perhaps than I care to remember; when the main meal of the day would be some bread and jam, or cheese if we were lucky.

Bread and milk were delivered daily to the house, except Sundays; and the standing order for these essential foodstuffs was four large loaves of bread, and a pint and a quarter of milk. The milk was delivered by pony and cart, carried in huge churns, and sold by one pint, half pint, and quarter pint measures. Mammy had worked out that a pint and a quarter would be sufficient for our daily needs; or more probably, this was the amount that filled our one and only milk jug up to the brim. If however funds were required elsewhere, then a quarter or a half pint measure would have to suffice; but the daily order of four large loaves of bread, was never compromised, as this was a vital part of our diet, and we simply could not manage without it.

It may seem strange for someone brought up on a dairy farm, but Mammy thoroughly hated the sight, and smell of milk; she liked strong sweet tea but without milk, and would eat with relish a rice pudding that was made with water and sugar only. But she did of course realize that milk was a very important part of our diet, particularly for the younger children. The rest of us, myself now included, were getting free milk in school. Sometimes I would get an extra bottle, as there were always spares. Not all the children liked milk, and as much as they were encouraged to drink it by the teachers; they gave up with certain children, when the bottles were opened but the milk wasted.

Coal was also delivered to the house weekly by horse and cart; two one hundredweight bags a week was the minimum requirement needed, and the maximum amount we could afford. It was delivered summer and winter, and supplemented by sieving the ashes of yesterday's spent coal every day. The stock was conserved in the summer, to enable us to build up a reserve for the harsh winter months when more was required. Should things become desperate during this time of the year, then, we would once more turn to the Great Tip and raid her great store of cinders.

Although there were fireplaces in every room of the house, for the first few years we only ever lit the fire in the main living room. This single fire, provided us with warmth, heat for the oven for cooking, and the back boiler for hot water. A huge cast-iron kettle, which I believe came with the fire and cooking range, was in constant use on the hob, and its water, could quickly be brought to the boil for hot drinks. This would almost certainly be tea, but occasionally Mammy would buy as a treat, a bottle of Camp coffee; it was not real coffee, but made from chicory, which had been processed and treated, and came in liquid form not unlike gravy browning. In fact on one occasion, I remember my older brother Daniel mistakenly using the wrong bottle; and he swore that the gravy browning, if anything; tasted better than the coffee. I tried this myself, and with the addition of milk and sugar I certainly could not tell the difference between the two.

The kitchen fire was in constant use both summer and winter, but was always allowed to die out overnight, and then lit again the following morning. Once the cooking of the main meal had finished, the fire would be banked up. This involved topping it up with sieved ashes, cinders, and small coal, which slowed down the burning rate and give a greater length of life to the fire; but because it was re-lit every morning, there was a great need for a steady supply of firewood. It was an essential commodity in any household in those days, and many shops, ironmongers, and general stores, sold bundles of firewood. There were even full-time firewood merchants, who delivered by the basket or cartload. Of course this was a luxury that we could not afford, it would have been a sheer waste of money; besides there were other sources where it could be obtained, such as old fruit and vegetable boxes from the grocers and greengrocers.

But if all this failed, we could again always turn to the sprawling mass of waste that lay on our doorstep, the Great Tip. It stood out in all its majesty, a giant slagheap that was to us children of the Iron and Copper Works, railways and docks, as was mother earth to the heroes of legend. She was the provider of warmth; wood and cinders for the household fires when the coal and money ran out; a land of adventure; with high plateaux, hidden valleys and caves; and treacherous marshes and precipices. All this provided a battleground; where rival gangs of boys would fight for the riches she had to offer; and a place of refuge where they could run and hide when the world turned hostile against them, which was often the case. For me, and a multitude of other children for generations, the Great Tip was the centre of the universe. It was an all embracing, vibrant living entity; which had a soul and personality of its own. This was no ancient mountain that might contain the lairs and workshops of elves and gnomes; but was the product of mineral ores that had been brought from many parts of the world, and stripped of their valuable metals. It was a grand tip of long standing; built by the muscles, sweat, and blood of men, when little or no mechanical aids were available. But for us children it held the same primitive magic; as did the sun for Neolithic Man; such was the reverence and wonder it presented.

It never failed to amaze me; that despite going over the same piece of ground time and time again; we always managed to find the odd bit of wood; and in five or ten minutes we usually had enough to start a fire. The member of our family; normally assigned to carry out this essential task of foraging for firewood was Daniel; accompanied when, and if he was in the right mood by Harry. I remember very well, my first expedition to the tip to collect firewood with Daniel and Harry, which turned out to be an extremely frightening experience.

It was late August; the long summer holiday was coming to an end, and I was eager to return to school; and now that I was attending school I was allowed a little more freedom; but still confined to the immediate surrounds of the house. I could cross the road as far as the White Cottage; or play on the square with the other children; but I was not permitted to venture on to the tip itself.

On this particular day, Daniel had a large Hessian sack, with instructions from Mammy to collect as much firewood as he could. She intended to build up a stock, or reserve of wood, for the coming winter. Harry had told her; that he had discovered a place on the other side of the tip, where there was an abundance of firewood; enough to last us the whole winter.

Unlike previous occasions, when he had been told to help Daniel on these wood collecting trips, he seemed eager to go. Normally, he would put up some resistance; and skulk about defying Mammy; and it would take a couple of hefty blows to his shoulders, or the back of his head, from her clenched fist; to persuade him to do as he was told. But not on that day, he was full of pride; he would lead Daniel to where he could fill ten sacks of wood in an hour. But, the biggest surprise of all was that he suggested that I should go along as well; more hands to lighten the load and to help. I should have immediately smelt a rat; as from past experience, he only wanted my company when he thought I would prove useful on one of his nefarious deeds of mischief. But foolishly, I was too excited at the prospect of exploring deeper into the tip, than I had been before; and finding the great wealth of firewood that Harry had already discovered.

So on that bright sunlit day after dinner; with Harry leading the way, and me following, and Daniel keeping a watchful eye on both of us from the rear; off we trooped like indefatigable explorers of old going into uncharted territory. At least that is what it felt like for me, but Harry I knew had already covered most of the tip and its surrounding area. There was a final warning from Mammy; "Be good boys now; Daniel, take care of Handel", and more of a threat to Harry, "Behave yourself Harry, I want a good report on you".

The initial part of our journey; was on the road, that led back in the direction of where we once lived. We were making for an area where part of the tip had been cleared, reducing the height on one side, and making inroads into it, forming a long narrow valley. We had to pass through this valley, to get to the spot, where Harry had discovered the stack of firewood.

The site was being worked on by a local firm of hauliers by the name of Jones Brothers, Dai and Ianto; two cantankerous old men, who always seemed to be at odds with the world and each other. They had won the contract of working the tip; to supply hard-core materials for building and road works; but after the war had started the demand for their services began to improve. Their entire fleet of lorries consisted of two small, old, ramshackle tippers, with the faded logo of Jones Brothers just about discernible on the doors of the cabs. They also had an old tracked mechanical shovel, which they used to load the ash on to the tippers.

Each brother insisted on loading his own lorry; and Dai the older of the two brothers, could just about handle the array of levers that were necessary to work the machine; which appeared to be rather complicated. Ianto, on the other hand, was completely useless, but still insisted on having his turn in operating this mechanical monster. The long handled levers, controlled the various movements of the machine, for opening and closing the mouth of the shovel; and moving it up and down the jib, as it dug into the tip. When the first part of the manoeuvre of filling the shovel was completed, the entire machine was swung around until it was directly over the lorry. This manoeuvre I believe required a steady hand and nerve; as each load had to be placed in a slightly different position before releasing it; thereby distributing it evenly across the back of the tipper.

Ianto was operating the machine as we approached, and was being watched from a safe distance by his brother Dai. It was not a smooth operation in any shape or form; the engine was grunting and groaning, the gears screeching and grinding, and Dai Jones cursing and screaming at his brother.

"Take your cowing time mun", he screamed at his brother, who was feverishly pushing the pedals to the floor, and with both hands trying to control the erratic behaviour of the shovel and jib.

The whole machine was rocking on its axles, as it

jerked around the lorry; then Ianto released the load too early. Still moving, its contents of ash, cinders, and clinker, showered down first on the cab of the lorry; before depositing the remainder of the load half in and half outside of the tipper; doing further damage to its already battered timber body.

As all of this commotion was going on, we were slowly approaching the place where they were working. Our intention was to pass them by, and walk through to the other side where Harry had found the new supply of fire-wood. But this was not going to happen. Dai Jones was not going to allow three scruffy kids, anywhere near the site where they were digging. He was a short, fat little man probably in his early fifties; and always dressed in the same dirty blue dungarees, with an oily flat cap stuck on his head. The fact that he wore glasses was the only real distinguishing feature between him and his brother Ianto, who was of identical build and dressed in similar garb.

He moved towards us raising his fist and shouting, "Bugger off you bloody kids, go on bugger off. If I ever see you around here again I'll break your cowing legs".

He emphasised this threatening posture by kicking into the ground, and spraying us with bits if ash and cinders. I took fright and hid behind Daniel, I was so glad that he was there to look after me.

We backed away from the menacing figure of Dai Jones, who was still walking towards us. "Alright mister we're going, we're only looking for some bits of wood for the fire", Daniel said, as he took my hand and turned around and quickly walked back towards the main road.

This seemed to appease the man momentarily, until it dawned on him that originally there had been three of us. "Where's the other cowing one", he screamed. "Where's he gone"?

Harry was nowhere to be seen. Ianto was still totally engrossed in operating the mechanical shovel, and we had reached the comparative safety of the road. There we turned and waited, and soon we could see, and so could Dai Jones; the furtive figure of Harry who had somehow got behind the lorries and mechanical shovel, and was now scampering through the narrow valley to the other side. Dai Jones was now running after him, cursing as he went, "You little bastard, I'll wring your cowing neck", he screamed.

But there was no way; that he could catch Harry with the head start that he had, and the man would be no match for him on the loose and broken surface of the ash and cinders. I was in no way fearful for the safety of Harry, and neither was Daniel; we both knew and realised that our brother was a law unto himself. He could match any evil or malevolence that came his way, and we were sure that all too soon we would find him unscathed, safe and well.

Daniel had a fair idea of the layout of the tip, and the place most likely where Harry was now heading, via the short cut. We hurried along the road, still in the direction of our old home, with Daniel still holding my hand tightly; and it was not long before we reached the main road, where I could see the two railway bridges that spanned it. This was now familiar territory to us, and I immediately thought; that we were going to approach the tip from the path that ran along the back of our old home.

We had passed the Mexico Fountain pub, which was set back and elevated from the main road, where access was by a steep line of steps. There was another building next to the pub, an imposing structure of red bricks. This was the Copper Works laboratory. It was completely surrounded by a high wall, and like the pub could only be approached by a steep line of steps. Daniel paused here outside the entrance, and looked up at the building. The gate at the bottom of the steps was open, and he was watching the windows of the laboratory; studying the offices inside, where there appeared to be a lot of activity. He was weighing up our chances, of sneaking around the back of the building without being seen. But before we could make a move, his mind was made up for him; as suddenly the front door opened and two men dressed in white overalls emerged, and quickly hurried down the steps towards us. This prompted Daniel to move away from where we were standing, grabbing my hand and dragging me with him. We hurried further along the road, "Come on Handel", he said, "we'll have to get to the tip from somewhere else".

We were getting close to the first of the railway bridges now, and Daniel stopped once more, outside another gap in the wall. There was no building here; but there was a path, where there were once probably steps, leading up to waste ground. I could see the tip in the background, and I obviously thought that this was the way that Daniel had in mind. I broke free of his grip, and started to scramble up the path; only to be brought back sharply as Daniel dashed after me, and lifted me bodily back down to the road.

Then dropping the sack to the ground, he began shaking me by the shoulders with both hands. "Don't ever go up there again Handel", he said, pointing to the path from where he had just dragged me. "We can't go that way to the tip ever, we'd have to go near the Devil's Inn. Come-on we'll go along the path by the Bridge Inn, and cross by the signal box".

I knew that Daniel would always take care of me, and I grasped his hand even tighter, now that he had mentioned the Devil's Inn; I had heard of it, but no one ever went near there. Not even Harry.

As we walked under the first railway bridge, I welcomed its dark shade from the harsh early afternoon sun. With all the excitement, I had not realised how hot the day had become. When we emerged into the gap between the two bridges, I could see the entrance to the Copper Works, which immediately brought back memories of my father. I expected to see him any minute trudging along the works road with the other men, his old haversack slung over his shoulder. It was the first time that I had thought about him since the night of his death, and I felt sad; I wanted him out of my mind and thoughts, and happily responded to Daniel's words. "It's all right Handel, he's gone now". It was as if he had read my mind, then swinging my arm he said, "Come on let's go up to the railway, perhaps Harry's waiting for us".

The next obstacle was getting across the railway line, without being seen by the man in the signal box. This section of the railway was not as busy as the main Swansea to London track, but it did take the Swansea to West-Wales traffic. Not far from where we intended to cross the line, it curved in almost a hairpin bend which was known as the Swansea loop; where the Swansea and West-Wales traffic met before going directly east to Cardiff and London.

Getting on to the railway embankment, which was quite steep, got easier the further along the footpath you went. The only drawback to this; was that you came closer to, and within the sight of, the man in the signal box. There was no way that the signalman could get to us; but there was always the chance that the local railway policeman, the dreaded Chinky would get you. I had never seen the man myself; but I had heard many frightening tales of youths and boys, and even grown men falling foul of this custodian of railway property. No one ever challenged Chinky. Even the bravest of men or youths caught unlawfully on his patch; would cut and run at the first sight of this long-legged giant of a man. He had narrow slit like eyes that gave him his nickname, and Harry who boasted that he had several encounters with him; likened him to the comic strip character of the time; Dr Fu Manchu. As it happened, Harry's description of him turned out to be quite accurate, when I finally saw the man. Unlike the ordinary policemen of the time, who always wore helmets to give their appearance added height, Chinky wore a flat cap with a peak. He certainly did not need any extras such as helmets, to make him appear taller. His pallid features and drab black railway uniform; meant that he could blend into the background of railway lines; signal boxes, sidings yards, and engine houses, where he operated; and spring upon unsuspecting youths and boys who had strayed illegally into his domain. Whenever we were anywhere near railway property, we had to be constantly vigilant of this man, who seem to operate in and appear from the shadows.

Daniel put his forefinger to his mouth, indicating that he wanted silence as we proceeded cautiously along the path, ever mindful of the dangers that lay ahead. There was a rusty old chain-link fence dividing the path from the railway property, and not very secure. It had many gaps at the bottom, where people had pulled at it to get on to the railway; and Daniel finally stopped at one of these, where he decided; that this would be the place to get up on to the embankment and cross the railway line. He crouched down by the gap; pulling me down with him, and whispered, "Right Handel, now you be quiet and stay by yer, while I go up and take a look by the line. If it's OK to cross I'll wave my arms, then you come up to me, right".

He was concerned that I might panic, or lose concentration, as he warned me. "Don't you move a step now mind, until I signal for you to come, right".

I took his words of warning to heart; there was no way that I was going to move. My eyes were fixed on him as he got under the fence, and began to claw his way gingerly up the grass covered gravel embankment. As he got closer to the top, he stopped for a few seconds; then popping his head clear and scanning the line in both directions, before giving closer scrutiny to the signal box. He crouched there for what seemed an incredibly long time, probably all of two minutes. Daniel was ultra careful, always; he did whatever was necessary to minimise the risk of any danger. If it were not for the fact that Harry had run off when we had encountered the Jones Brothers, Daniel would not be in this part of the area at all. But of course, Harry was somewhere on the tip, the other side of the railway line; and Daniel as the eldest brother was responsible for us both. I can honestly say; that both Daniel and I were not terribly concerned for Harry's safety. For myself, I would have been very happy if he had disappeared and was never seen again; and I am sure that Daniel felt the same way. What he was afraid of was Mammy's anger, and the wrath that would be unleashed on him should anything untoward happen to Harry.

Daniel was vigorously waving his hand now for me to follow him up the embankment, then putting a finger to his mouth, again indicating that I was to be as quiet as I could. I got under the fence easily; but found the embankment at this part to be much steeper than where I had attempted to cross the line before; when I was on the run with Harry trying to escape from my father. Slowly but surely, by digging into the ground with the front of my boots, with the hobnails gripping into the gravel embankment, I made my way up as quietly as I could and crouched down beside Daniel.

Boots with the soles protected by hobnails, and the heels by steel plates, were essential footwear for children who lived and played in the wastelands of an area of great industrial age. The type of footwear worn by today's children of plastic, and synthetic cloth; would not have lasted for weeks; certainly not the years of use we got from our boots, which would be passed down from brother to brother.

"Right now boy", Daniel uttered the words quietly but firmly. "When I say go, we run like 'ell and don't stop until we reach the tip".

We crouched there by the side of the railway line; where there were double tracks with a wide gap between them. The sun was still bright, and harsh; its light glinting on the shining steel railway track; having a dazzling effect on my eyes, which made me feel slightly giddy. The excitement of the day's events so far, were beginning to take their effect on me. I was slowing down; and I did not respond as quickly as I should have to Daniel's sudden movement, so he grabbed my hand and in a muffled voice yelled. "Right, go".

He was pulling me up to the top of the embankment, and in a voice still stifled by fear, was encouraging me to move, "come-on mun Handel, wake up, and run".

My legs were beginning to turn to jelly, as Daniel frantic now that we were out in the open, began to cross the railway line; dragging me along as my brain tried to regain control of my reluctant legs and wobbly knees. Daniel I knew would not let go of my hand, and somehow he managed to get us both to the other side of the tracks. My legs responding better now; as we raced to the relative security of the tip.

To the right of where we crossed the railway line, and in the direction of the signal box, the tip's perimeter was formed of massive misshapen slabs of clinker. The various shapes and sizes of these gigantic chunks of congealed residue from the copper smelting; ranged from three feet to eight feet across, and heaped one upon the other to a height of between fifteen and twenty feet. They formed a kind of massive honeycomb structure, a maze-like composition of nooks and crannies and tunnels. This part of the tip was known as the caves. There were many of these great lumps of clinker loosely strewn about where we had crossed, and we quickly got in amongst them out of sight of the signal box.

Hiding behind the largest one we could find; we were thankful to sit down in its protective cover, and welcome shade from the heat of the sun. Daniel was concerned over the way it had been necessary for him to hurry and drag me across the track, and said. "Be quiet and rest now Handel, we'll wait by yer for a minute".

I certainly did not have to be encouraged in this. My head had now regained control of my legs, and the giddy sensation had gone; but I was completely out of breath. We sat there in silence for at least ten minutes, until Daniel was satisfied that we had not been spotted, and I had rested long enough to regain my strength and was breathing a lot easier.

"Are you all right now son", he said, "come on then we had better try and find Harry".

We hurried away from the railway lines, and our temporary refuge amongst the lumps of clinker. Daniel knew that the ground ahead of us; in the direction we intended going, was impassable. This was the part of the wastelands known as the bog, a broad expanse of flat marshy land; wedged between the tip, the road, and the railway line. It was the area where the rainwater running off the tip, drained and got trapped by the railway embankment and the high wall, which lined the main road. Anybody, particularly children who ventured on to this part of the tip, quickly came to realise that it was a place to be avoided. The slimy ground, which was made up of a mixture of peat, ash, and cinder, was covered now in late summer; by clumps of grassy weeds, which produced flowering stems tipped with what resembled balls of cotton wool. This seemed to be the only plant that could grow and survive on this putrid land, not even the dreaded Japanese knotweed could take a hold here. For the greater part of the year; large pools, of oily, black, scum covered water formed, some of them three to four feet deep. These, combined with the sponge-like soil could suck you in like quicksand, which it had been said; happened to many a foolhardy child. I had heard of children being stuck in the gluey treacherous ground, and having to be rescued by grown-ups. But there were no fatalities as far as I know, not anyway during my time.

To avoid this area we had to climb up the side of the tip to a height of about fifteen feet, where it levelled out and became a ledge of about ten feet wide. Walking as quickly as we could; but careful because the ash and cinder here was not compacted, but loose, we made our way in the direction of where Harry should be waiting for us. The ledge, precariously narrow in places, sometimes disappeared altogether; then it was necessary to pick our way carefully over the slope of the tip, until we reached the ledge or level path once more.

Throughout all the trials and setbacks we had encountered that afternoon, Daniel was still not deterred from achieving what he had set out to do, and carry out our mother's wishes of filling the sack that he carried with firewood.

After we had safely skirted around the bog, the flat

ground beneath us broadened out; and I could see in the distance the high red brick wall at the back of the works laboratory. Closer to us, and set much further back from the road, was another much older building built of stone. It was a tall, lofty building with part of the roof missing; but apart from this the remaining structure looked sound enough. It was too big for a private dwelling, and it had three storeys. The windows on the ground floor had been roughly boarded-up, with a mixture of wood, plywood, and sheet metal; but most of the windows on the first and second floors had been smashed, exposing this part of the structure to the elements.

This part of the tip curved back much further here to an almost U-shaped indent, and set within this concave; were the remains of a massive wooden structure of pillars and beams, which once supported the viaduct carrying the drums of waste from the works to the tip. I understood now what Harry had meant; when he said there was an unlimited supply of firewood, and sure enough there he was sitting underneath the structure; alongside him he had gathered a great mound of the stuff.

We scrambled down from the tip and ran towards him. Daniel knew; that it would be useless and a complete waste of time, to remonstrate with our wayward brother. His words would fall on deaf ears. The relationship between my two older brothers was surely not close, but built really on a degree of tolerance of each other, born out of necessity. They never went anywhere together on a voluntary basis. Harry could usually be found hanging around with any group of boys waiting for mischief to happen, whereas Daniel never seemed to go anywhere or do anything. The contrast between their personalities was even greater than that of their physical make-up. Harry was thick set, and swarthy, with jet-black hair and dark brown eyes. Daniel was the complete opposite, with a fair complexion and blonde almost white hair and blue eyes.

Harry yelled at us as we ran up to him, "Come on 'u two mun, where've 'u been. I've been by yer for ages. Look at all the wood I've collected".

He sat there with a smug look on his face. Daniel laughed wryly, saying, "huh! u've been busy son, that's a good pile of wood u've got there". His tone of laughter and speech was one of irony; as he was frankly amazed that Harry had spent his time while waiting for us to join him, in gathering all this firewood. It was quite evident where the wood came from, as several large pieces of the timber that had once supported the viaduct, were strewn across the ground. Someone had recently been attacking one of these with an axe, splitting and splintering the timber into manageable lengths ready for the fire.

Daniel was anxious now, to put the firewood Harry had collected into the sack and get home. The bright and sunny afternoon changed quickly, as the sun began to set behind the higher peaks of the tip; taking on an entirely different atmosphere. As the lengthening shadows rapidly faded, the increasing gloom revealed the place as it truly was. The breeze, which had been gentle and warm earlier, became sharper and colder, and rustled the cottontails on the marsh grass. The railway lines, on which there was a lone shunter engine; were still bathed in bright sunshine, and reflected the strong harsh light which erased the distant skyline; making the image of the solitary engine appear to be floating in the sky.

Whilst Daniel was engrossed in filling the sack with firewood, Harry had wandered off in the direction of the old stone building; and I was sitting on one of the fallen beams, still resting from the afternoon's exertions. Then Harry called me, and I pretended that I had not heard his first shout of, "Come over by yer 'andel", and got up intending to help Daniel. His next shout was more of an order, "Get over by yer 'andel quick, I know where there's another sack for more firewood. Come and 'elp me".

I looked pleadingly at Daniel, hoping that he would tell me to stay where I was. But he was ever mindful of our family's needs, and agreed that another sack of wood would be very welcome. He yelled back at Harry, "Why'd you need 'andel, can't you get it on your own". Harry was quick to respond, "It's there in the old buildings and I need 'andel to help me get in".

************************************

What I did not know then and neither did Daniel, was that this old building was in fact that, which he had referred to earlier as the Devil's Inn. The story went that the inn was a meeting place for thieves and vagabonds in olden days, and on one fateful day three of these villains had conspired together, to relieve what seemed to be a well-heeled traveller of his money and valuables. They enticed him to join them at their table, inviting him to join them in a game of cards. The stranger was polite and courteous, even generous, happy and eager to ply the three men with copious amounts of beer and liquor. But their evil intention of cheating the stranger with their faked deck of cards went horribly wrong. No matter what ploys they used, or tricks they employed; the stranger's luck was always better, and they in their frustration became angry and bitter. The night's revelry of card-playing and drinking, culminated when one of the vagabonds pulled a knife and threatened to kill the traveller unless he handed over his money. With this the stranger dropped the card he had in his hand on to the floor, whereupon the villains discovered that this was the Ace of Spades, the Devil's card. Then, to their horror, and astonishment; as they looked down saw that the stranger was without shoes or boots. Instead of feet, the man had cloven hooves. They then realised who the stranger was, the devil himself.

The skies darkened and a great storm erupted. Thunder and lightning rained down on the Devil's Inn that night, wreaking terrible havoc on the building; and death and injury to the three unfortunate thieves. When the storm had abated the stranger had disappeared, and of the three vagabonds; the one who had drawn his knife was dead, and of the two survivors one was struck deaf, and the other struck blind.

*************************************

So that was the tale that kept children and indeed many adults away from this part of the tip; why Daniel had told me not to venture up that path from the main road. Whether he believed the tale was another thing, but I am sure that he did believe that the place meant trouble, and kept well away from it. But Harry was a different matter. With his curiosity and natural disposition in seeking out trouble, this place would be like a magnet to him, and he would be dying to know just what mischief the Devil's Inn had to offer.

As I had already observed, the windows on the ground floor of the building had been boarded up, and the main entrance door seemed secure. But Harry was making straight for the back of the property, where there was another door, but this one was slightly ajar. The windows, like the front, were all boarded up; but Harry knew exactly where he was going and what he intended to do. He had probably done a quick reconnaissance of the place while he was waiting for Daniel and me to join him. Reluctantly, I followed him to where he had stopped, about five yards away from the door, then pointing at it, he said, "Right 'andel, you can squeeze through there and get the sack".

Then he got hold of my arm and pushed me towards the door. The impetus of the shove took me to within a couple of feet of it, I stopped and hesitated, and turned round to see inevitably, Harry with a look of menace on his face, and holding up his right hand fist threatening me. "Get through that door 'andel", he glowered, "and look for a sack".

I had no choice; it was either walking into the unknown, or the certainty of being thumped by Harry. So I decided to take my courage in my hands, and face up to what ever was lurking behind that door. Harry, I knew, was using me as a guinea pig. Uncertain of what was inside the building yet wanting to find out, he was sending me in first to see if it was safe for him to follow. Looking for a sack for the firewood was just a pretext; he had already schemed and conjured up this plan to enter the building; but he was going to put my head on the block first, as always.

My legs shaking and heart thumping, I gingerly squeezed through the gap between the door and the wall. The place had an unmistakable smell of cooking, or food, or to be more precise gravy. I waited whilst my eyes grew accustomed to the dim light, provided by the gap in the doorway; then when I could see, discovered that I was in a kind of passageway, which had two doors leading off it. One door was straight ahead, about 10 feet away, and another on my left about two feet away. They were both slightly open, so I decided to take the easy option and look inside the door that was nearest to me, the one close to the outside door should I need to make a quick exit. Although

I was desperate to get out of the place, I realised that I needed to take my time. Harry would expect a report on just what the old building was like inside. I was going to wait as long as my nerve would hold; then push open the door and beat a hasty retreat; I would tell Harry precisely what he wanted hear, that it was all right to enter the building and hope that he would believe it. Having done my part, then it would be up to him to decide if he would enter, or if he was still frightened make some excuse not to.

After a couple of minutes had elapsed and holding my breath, I pushed at the door which swung back smoothly hardly making a sound. Then came the shock, when the hooter heralding the end of the day's work at the Copper Works was sounded; the sudden noise breaking the eerie silence of the dark passageway as I stared into the room, and the rustling movement inside, churned my stomach as panic set in. There in one corner of the room, which had a table and chairs, I could just make out the rough outline of a figure emerging from the floor. The thing stood up to its full height, but I did not wait around to find out who or what it was. For a brief moment I froze; but then the natural instinct of survival took control as I turned and fled. The narrow opening to the outside door which I had gingerly squeezed through minutes before, seemed much wider now as I flew through this screaming as I ran, "'arry, 'arry, there's something after me,"

As I emerged from the building, I spotted Harry who was already in full flight; he was prepared for something like this, heading in the direction of the main road down the path that Daniel had forbidden me from using earlier in the day. This was the wrong direction, it would take us away from where Daniel was collecting the firewood. But I had no choice other than to chase after Harry, my incredible turn of speed inspired by the noises coming out

149

from the property I had just rapidly departed. I heard the door being wrenched open, and a cry of, "Cowing kids, I'll cowing kill you if get my hands on you", and the sounds of heavy footsteps pounding after me.

The Copper Works hooter had ceased its blaring, as Harry disappeared down the path that led to the gap in the high wall at the main road. The path here was lined with scrub and patches of Japanese knotweed; and with Harry now out of sight I felt desperately alone, quite sure that whoever was pursuing me would have me in his clutches before I reached the safety of the road.

I kept on running, almost tripping, then stumbling down the path until I finally broke out through the gap, and I was on the pavement of the road, just missing the legs of two men who had just passed by. The road was full of men; they were pouring out of the gates of the Copper Works, and with relief I realised that in their company I was safe. But I did not look back I kept on running, passing the Works Laboratory, the Mexico Fountain pub, and turned the corner into Pentremawr Road where I finally stopped. There was no sign of Harry, but I did not care, I just wanted to go home. I was weak and exhausted and almost in tears; as I stood there my hands on my knees, head bowed and gasping for breath.

Momentarily my heart stopped as I once more heard the sound of hobnail boots running, they were noisy but much lighter steps, in desperation I looked up and almost passed out in relief as I saw Daniel running towards me. He had heard the commotion coming from the Devils Inn, and seen the man running after Harry and me. The man chasing us, for Daniel assured me that it was a man and not the devil, had stopped well short of the road. Daniel thought that he had no intention of catching me, he was just going through the motions of frightening me away, hoping that I would stay away in future; which I most certainly did.

My first day venturing deep into the tip was over, and what an exciting if sometimes frightening day it had been. I learned later, that the man that I had disturbed in the Devils Inn was not at all frightened by its reputation and was living rough there. It was fortunate that Harry and I had run in the direction of the road, taking him away from Daniel who was collecting the firewood, for it was his, and he had put in a considerable effort in chopping it up. Daniel was only too happy and thankful, that it turned out all right in the end. He had been able to drag the sack, which he had filled with firewood, through the narrow valley in the tip, passing the mechanical shovel, which the Jones Brothers had finally stopped abusing for the day.

## CHAPTER 14

# THE SWEET SMELL OF SUCCESS

The long summer holiday was over, and it was time to go back to school. There was always a fresh feeling about this time of the year, when jerseys, shirts, trousers and boots; that had been battered and damaged, needed to be repaired; or even worse, worn-out and beyond repair; they had to be replaced. It was a question of salvaging what could be repaired, and hand-me-downs. Daniel was the lucky one; as the oldest boy he invariably had new clothes and boots, then as he grew out of these they were handed down to Harry. Anything passed down from Daniel to Harry was generally in good condition, as Daniel took care of his clothes. But the same thing could not be said of Harry, as a great deal of running repairs were required by the time the items got to me. He was particularly heavy on boots, not only wearing out the soles and heels, but the uppers as well, with much of the stitching coming adrift. It certainly required a good cobbler to patch up and make serviceable again, any pair of boots in which Harry had kicked his way through the summer. If by chance, I was unfortunate enough to receive his boots, one thing would be sure; the laces would have long gone, and replaced by cord or string. Laces were a luxury that we could not afford. We never discarded even the shortest length of cord or string; which would be rolled up and stored in the cardboard box, where we kept the boot blacking and brush.

Footwear was probably the most difficult of all items to hand down, as it is almost impossible to wear ill-fitting boots or shoes. We could get away with it sometimes; improvising with larger boots, by stuffing newspaper into the toe-end thereby ensuring a tighter fit. Trousers, jerseys, and shirts, brought their own problems, with missing buttons, tears and holes, which Mammy would hand stitch and patch. As with cord and string, we never discarded any buttons, of any shape, size, or colour. These would be cut off old garments and stored in the button box. But it was not a great problem if a jumper, pair of trousers, or socks were one or two sizes too large; the main object was having sufficient clothing to keep out the elements. We might look a bit odd wearing an oversize jumper with a pair of trousers that might be a little on the tight side, but that did not worry or embarrass us, as there were many other children similarly dressed or even worse.

Mammy would try her hand at fixing or repairing anything, and her skills with a needle and cotton were just about adequate. But she never learned to knit, and had a real problem when it came to repairing any woollen garments such as jumpers, jerseys, and socks. For all her efforts, she was unable to come to terms, and never mastered, the skill of darning. Her attempts were rather pathetic; she was either too mean, which meant the hole being covered in a loose lattice of wool, or by being over-eager; the end result would be a large hard tangle of wool which would just about hang on to the garment she was attempting to repair.

There was not much going free; but there were times when Mammy would be given clothing that other children had grown out of, with no younger siblings of their own to hand down to. In fact the nearest I ever got to Daisy Davies, the girl of my dreams, was wearing hand-me-downs from her older brother Clive. Nothing was ever wasted; and I remember once having knee length trousers, that were in fact a youth's full-length trousers, which had been cut down. They were a little baggy, and draughty in the nether regions, especially when we did not have the comfort of wearing underpants. We always wore vests but never underpants. I suppose it was thought that these were luxuries we could do without. I remember during the occasional P T lessons in school; the master taking the class would order the boys to remove shirts and trousers for this lesson, but only if they had the necessary under-garments. Very few of the boys in my class could totally comply with this request. A lot more shirts would be removed, but not many trousers. It was not until I was 15 years old, when I had left school and started to work, that I had my first pair of underpants.

I cannot remember exactly what I wore that first day at school after the summer holidays, but it would be in the order of jersey, trousers, socks and boots. If it rained, especially as winter approached, for the first couple of years, I still wore the Burberry given to me by the Salvation Army. After that I remember a succession of old raincoats, which I would throw over my head if it rained, and wrap it around me if I was cold.

We still had to carry our gas masks with us when attending school, but the numbers of actual air raids had dramatically been reduced. Although life was still interrupted by the frequent false alarms; resulting in an orderly withdrawal from the classroom to the basement during school hours, or a mad dash to the air-raid shelter if at home. The threat of damage, death, and injury, were never far from people's minds, as almost everyone in the town had been directly affected by the bombings. They had either experienced loss of, or injury to a loved one, or knew of a bombed out family like ours, and quickly came to realise that no one was safe. People go to extremes in times such as these, becoming religious zealots practising caution and safety first, whereas others throw caution to the winds and live every day as if it were their last.

The week we started back to school for the autumn term coincided with the third anniversary of the outbreak of the war, and for the greater majority of the townspeople it was still very real, with virtually every family having some member serving with the armed forces. But for us, our family was entering into what I can only describe as another period of the phoney war. Being bombed out, and the death of my father had altered our lives dramatically; but for Mammy her main aim in life was still to keep the family together and survive. Although she was aware of the dangers that the war brought to us as a nation, and despite the reduction in the numbers of air raids; there was still the greater threat to the country's supplies being cut off by the German U-boats. But for the time being and indeed for the rest of war, we were still able to obtain more than adequately the basic necessities of life such as bread, meat, potatoes and vegetables. Our problem was the lack of funds to buy the produce that was available; which would have been exactly the same in peacetime. But there were also two essential supplements added to every child's diet, issued by the government free of charge, providing vital minerals and vitamins. One was the dreaded foul tasting cod liver oil, which was taken neat, one tea-spoonful at a time; and the second was very sweet orange juice, which was added to water and drank eagerly by the child to remove the taste of the cod liver oil.

Now that the family's income had been considerably reduced by the death of my father, I do not think that our way of life would have been any different had the war ceased the day he had died. The only foodstuffs we really missed were imported fruit such as bananas and oranges, and probably most of all for the children, sweets and chocolates. The last time we had had some in any quantity was last Christmas, and apart from very rare occasions, we would not enjoy them again until 1943. One of these rare occasions; would be on Friday afternoons when our week's work was assessed by the teacher; and if she was sufficiently impressed, you were sent to the head-mistress's room for a reward. This entailed being warmly congratulated by the great lady; who then continued the ritual by attaching a gold star to your exercise book, and with a great show of pride, opening the bottom drawer of her desk and taking out her famous round red sweetie tin. The lid would be removed with a great flourish, revealing its contents of small multi-coloured hard-boiled sweets. To this day, I can still smell the sharp sugary aroma of lemons and strawberries that filled the room, and my mouth still waters at the thought of that special visit to the head-mistress's room. Where on earth she got the sweets from, heaven only knows, but she probably had to forfeit her sugar ration in exchange for them.

The gold stars and sweets were a bonus as far as I was concerned, as I did not really need any encouragement to work hard and hone my learning skills. I was thirsty for knowledge; with a competitive spirit, and I easily maintained my position at the front of the class. I did not see much now of poor little Rosie Smith she was stuck at the back. Like a lot of children from similar backgrounds she did not make friends easily; and I feel ashamed now of my attitude, that perhaps I could have been more kindly towards her. She was an ailing child, and constantly missed long periods of school, although nobody seemed to miss her.

Success breeds confidence; but can often lead to disaster through over confidence. My confidence grew as I acquired knowledge of reading, writing, and arithmetic; especially my success in gaining one of the top places in the class. It was definitely not my bearing and manner, or having good and stylish clothes, as was the case with my rival Norman Lloyd. I had felt a little intimidated by him in my early days at school; but this diminished as time went by, and I must confess my increased confidence and success went a little to my head.

Norman Lloyd was an only child and wanted for nothing, and his parents had probably instilled in him from an early age that he was better than the rest of us. His father was a bus driver; but it was only many years later that I learned where the family's wealth came from, his mother. She indulged in the illegal, and squalid occupation of money lending. She was a big bustling bully of a woman; who would lend money to others, usually women, and charge exorbitant rates of interest; sometimes doubling the original amount of money lent. Whereas I came from a poor family and needed all the help I could get; and a great deal of this help, and strength; came from having brothers and sisters. The knowledge that you have older siblings to turn to when needed, earns a certain amount of respect among your peers. It is a great comfort to know that you are not alone in the world.

As I have already stated the infants shared the school

playground with the older girls, which was fortunate for me, as had both Maggie, and Molly, in close attendance should I need them. Although I was only in my a second term, I had built up quite a considerable following amongst the five year-olds in my class, and enjoyed being the centre of attention. My cause was in no little way helped, now that I had one trusty henchman. A certain Dinky Miles had joined the school in the most recent intake, after the summer holidays. He had attached himself not only to me but to my family as well; as an only child he enjoyed his visits to our home, and being involved in the hustle and bustle that it entailed. Dinky was a funny and clever little boy full of pranks, and mischief, he made the other children laugh. This was in contrast to my style, which was now becoming a little bossy. Still, I was the leader of my own little gang and I enjoyed it, and the feeling of importance that it gave me.

Norman Lloyd too had his own little gang, and like me, had his own trusty lieutenants who remained close and acted in concert with his wishes. The less assertive children would hang on to be part of one gang or the other, sometimes even switching loyalties.

At that age when left to their own devices young children's play is not very organised, and most of the time it consisted of us rushing aimlessly about; creating as much noise and pandemonium as possible. Then of course the inevitable happened; with two rival gangs of boys hell-bent on creating panic amongst the other children, especially the girls; one day I clashed seriously with my rival. It was more of a brush really; but with Norman being a much larger boy than me, I ended up sprawled on the tarmac playground in an indignant state of shock.

My pride was seriously dented, and although I knew that our clash of bodies was not intentional, I shouted accusingly at him as I stood up, "'u did that on purpose".

To which he replied, "No I didn't do anything on purpose".

I could feel the first pangs of fear beginning to affect my knees, but I could not back down now, not in front of my gang. "Yes 'u did", I screamed at him, and mimicking the older boys I had seen fighting, I raised my right fist in a threatening gesture.

It was obvious that Norman Lloyd was better prepared for a confrontation that I was; when no sooner had I squared up to him, that he planted his clenched right hand smack on the front of my nose. The force of the blow knocked me backwards, and once more I was back on the floor; but this time on my backside.

The other children from both gangs were now screaming, chanting, "fight, fight, fight," as I sat there with no fight left in me at all. Then a curious thing happened; the children became suddenly quiet, and silence reigned as the first great blob of blood spurted from my nose; then becoming a torrent, streaming onto my jersey, and trousers, and finally splashing against the hard surface of the playground.

Throughout all this I was still in eyeball contact with my adversary, whose look of triumph after delivering the blow, quickly changed to one of horror at the sight of so much blood. He was frightened now, probably more so than me; and so were most of the other children, as they scattered to the four corners of the playground. I could to hear the unmistakable voice of Dinky, bellowing in the distance, "Maggie, Maggie, come quick, 'andel's having a fight".

Norman Lloyd heard it too, and with that his legs finally buckled as he collapsed to the floor sobbing, "I didn't mean it, I didn't mean it".

The bell was ringing now, which signalled the end of playtime, as Maggie and Molly helped me to my feet. Molly produced a piece of rag, which she used as a handkerchief, and held this against my nose to stem the flow of blood; whilst Maggie was remonstrating with Norman Lloyd, "Don't be a cry baby, you're not hurt, get up".

He did as he was told and slowly got to his feet. No one argued with Maggie. The rest of the children were lining up to return to their classes; as we two combatants were lead slowly to the washroom by my sisters, to have our wounds treated and more importantly our pride salvaged.

Dinky said that it was a lucky punch that floored me, and it was fortunate for Norman Lloyd that my nose began to bleed. The rest of my gang seemed to concur with this, and anyway they were not too impressed with Norman Lloyd and his performance either. So another painful lesson of life had been learned by us both; but the rivalry would continue albeit with a lot more caution and subtlety as we grew older.

As the year declined and autumn turned to winter, there were no more monumental events in my life either at school or at home. Apple and candle, night came; we never heard of, or referred to it as, Halloween. We had the candles, but no apples; so we used potatoes instead, and our new enamelled bath replaced the old zinc tub we used in our old home. A candle was lit in the bathroom, and with our hands clasped behind our backs, we knelt over and fished for the potatoes with our teeth. We got soaking wet as usual; but we had a lot of fun, laughing at ourselves for being so silly, and mocking the situation we were in.

Then at the beginning of December, just over two weeks before Christmas, two new words, "Yanks", and "Japs" were added to our vocabulary; which we would forever associate with the war. One we understood to be good, and cheered when it was heard; but the other was bad and would be booed. Japan had attacked Pearl Harbour on 8th December; and the word "Yanks" was now to be added to the good side, along with the British Tommies and the Red Army. The "Japs" were included with the baddies, the Jerrys and the Itis. These words apart, it did help me realise that the war was not confined to air raids over Swansea. This stunning and infamous attack on America, by the Japanese, had no real immediate effect on my life. The fact that Christmas was only a matter of weeks away, was of far greater significance, and much more important to a five-year-old going on six.

In material terms, the fare for Christmas 1941 was meagre indeed. We were warned that Father Christmas was on rations as well, and not to expect too much when we hung up our stockings on Christmas Eve. In previous years, they would be filled with apples, oranges, walnuts, Brazil nuts, chocolates and sweets. But this year Father Christmas's sack was light indeed; he could only manage one apple and some home grown hazel nuts; but he did add some potatoes, carrots, and turnips for fun, and to make up a little bit of weight. There were no presents this year, but we did have a chicken for dinner. This was very special for us, and for the majority of families at that time. Having a chicken dinner was like Christmas itself, an annual event; we never had chicken at any other time of the year. Later on Mammy produced a quarter pound bar of chocolate, which she had saved for this occasion; and I remember having four squares of this delicacy being pressed into the palm of my hand. Then at teatime, we fed sumptuously on pudding and Christmas cake. So we celebrated our first Christmas Day in our new home, without my father, and I can honestly say that we enjoyed it as much as any Christmas prior to this or since.

CHAPTER 15

# WHAT'S IN A NAME

"Puss, puss, puss", Mammy was quietly calling the long lean scrawny cat, that had been hanging around our back garden for days now. Dere m'laen puss". "Come on puss".

Why on earth she was trying to encourage this aloof, and even hostile looking feline vagabond to enter the house was a mystery. She, it was a she-cat we found out later to our cost, was not a pretty cat, we all agreed; not a nice black and white tabby cat, or a strong haughty ginger Tom cat; but a mouldy brindled specimen with a mixture of brown, black and grey streaks. I did not know then, but now believe it to be true; that you do not choose a cat as a pet, or houseguest; but rather the cat chooses you. It will take its time in making its choice, but once its mind is made up it usually remains with you.

Mammy also took her time; she knew that trying to rush or hurry things, would only make the cat more wary of the situation; risking the chance that she would choose someone else to live with. Being a farmer's daughter, and brought up in an environment of working with and tending to animals; she was aware of just how stubborn they can be; especially cats. But after a few more days of gentle encouragement, Puss the cat, took up residence in the Swain household. She stayed with us for many years; but she was never given a pet name such as Tiddles or Fluff, we just called her Puss.

Where she came from we never found out; but she was probably the victim of a one of Hitler's air raids, a bombed-out casualty just like us. Perhaps Mammy sensed this. The cat was a kindred spirit, and that was the prime motive in offering to give her a home. Maggie, who was very much involved in running the family household, showed her concern and even went as far to remonstrate with Mammy. "Why are you encouraging that scraggy old cat Mammy, we can't feed it, we haven't got enough food for ourselves". To which Mammy replied, "Oh, cats are no problem Mag, they look after themselves, cats will never starve".

Remarkably these words proved to be true, there was very little food wasted in our house. Perhaps the occasional piece of bacon rind, or bones to be gnawed on, after the marrow had been removed. Occasionally there would be scraps of vegetables and potatoes; that would be mashed up with any gravy left over, and she would tuck into this. She always looked lean and hungry; but I believe she was a very fit cat; and she could certainly shift when speed was required; like when she got under Mammy's feet, and had to scoot to avoid the toe-end of her shoe, which would be lashed out at her.

It was about this time, in the early spring of 1942; that I the first became aware of the wide white streak that suddenly appeared in Mammy's jet-black hair; it seemed to come overnight, and was a great shock to me and my older brothers and sisters. Some people believed that this was her body's way of reacting, to the great shock it had received from the events that happened almost a year ago. She was probably aware of its development for sometime, and was feeling a little sorry for herself, but she would never show this to us. Love and tenderness, passion and even anger; these are feelings and emotions she would willingly reveal. But self pity, never.

It would only have been natural if she had felt sorry for herself at times; for though she had the great joy and love of her children, there was no other person in the world who really cared for her. She had lost her husband, her mother and father were dead, and her brothers and sisters had little or no time for her. Her only friends, her neighbours from Landore, Audrey Lewis and Grannie Davies, were still homeless themselves, and she had not seen them since the day we had moved to our new house. So it might have been a yearning, for companionship, that led to her interest in the cat.

Anyway she had very little time for socialising or keeping company, and the only other people to call at the house apart from the tradesmen were the dreaded Nuns. They would still call on us from time to time; at various hours of the day, testing Mammy's resolve to keep the family together; asking how she was and how she was coping. But they were met with the same reception every time. They were not allowed to put their feet over the door, as Mammy would firmly but politely send them packing. She made it quite plain that for all their good intentions, their company she could do without. They gradually got the message that Mammy was keeping her children; and; she already had a plan in mind that would end their visits for good.

Daniel, Harry, and I, had already started going to the local Sunday school, after dinner on Sunday afternoons. Mammy's plan; was to get all seven of us children baptised into the Protestant or Anglican Church. She had already sounded out the vicar about having us all christened, and he could see no objection to doing this. Of course, part of the deal was that we should as a family become members of the local Protestant Church, St John's; starting with the older children attending the Sunday school; but Maggie and Molly who had been included in the original deal rarely attended. They would both accompany us to the Sunday school, which was held in the old parish hall in Odo Street, and was only a hundred yards from where we lived. This was mainly to ensure, that Harry would not run off and spoil things, putting Mammy's plan in jeopardy.

Although she rarely attended church herself, Mammy was a staunch Christian, brought up in the ways of fire and brimstone of the old Welsh Congregational Church. She was well aware of Harry's reluctance to go to Sunday school, and threatened him with the wrath of God if he misbehaved or failed to attend. "Remember now son and listen to your Mam, you are going to the Lords house, and he is watching you".

She eyed him menacingly, and in a stern voice went on, "I will be told if you don't go".

She drew the line at suggesting that God talked to her directly; then as an afterthought, to make Harry think seriously about her words, she added, "and if you lie to me you will be struck down by lightning".

I am sure that Harry would have given a great deal of thought to what she had said, and would take his chances on incurring the wrath of the Lord, or being struck down by lightning. But he was well aware that he would not escape the wrath of Mammy, who would surely find out if he missed Sunday school, from Maggie or Molly.

Daniel and I were quite happy with the thought of Sunday school, and looked forward to Sunday afternoons particularly in the winter, when it was dark, damp, and dreary. It was a place to go where you could meet some of your school friends, especially my pal Dinky. We quite enjoyed the stories of the Bible being read by Miss Whitehorn the Sunday school teacher, and receiving the little pictures or texts of the day's lessons she handed out. Daniel became quite engrossed with the teachings of the Bible, and Miss Whitehorn encouraged this, even lending him a Bible so that he could continue reading it at home. The news of his devotion to God, and his eager study of the Bible; soon reached the ears of the vicar himself, which culminated in Daniel being invited to join the choir. Mammy was very proud of this, and even made one of her rare visits to the church on that Sunday-morning, when Daniel took his place as one of the boy choristers. He looked splendid in his royal blue cassock and sparkling white surplice, which seemed to add to his angelic air, with his fresh complexion and light blonde hair. Everyone was so impressed that there was even talk that Daniel would enter the ministry, and one day become a vicar himself.

If there were any doubts remaining in the vicar's mind about Mammy's wish that we should be baptised into the Anglican Church, then these would have surely been removed by Daniel's strength of belief and devotion to the Bible. The auspicious event took place one Sunday morning after the 11 o'clock Service, in the early summer of 1942. We all gathered round the font with the vicar, in a half circle facing the altar. The morning service had not been very well attended, but about half-a-dozen people of the congregation had remained behind to witness this event. The vicar said it was an historic occasion, as he had never before heard of so many children from one family being baptised at the same time.

For me it was a particularly revealing occasion.

Although I knew that I had just one Christian name, and my four brothers all had second Christian names, it never seemed to bother me before this day. Suddenly, standing there before the vicar in front of the font, I became puzzled and felt out of place as to why my parents had not bothered to think of a second name for me. Today it mattered greatly; as this act of christening within the Church had a certain feeling of finality about it. This was it; it was being made official. The vicar went through the motions of dipping his hand into the cold water of the font, then making the sign of the cross on the foreheads of each one of us, saying. "In the name of the father, the son, and the Holy Ghost I baptise thee", and starting with Maggie she said in a voice that was almost a whisper, "Margaret Ann", and the vicar repeated "Margaret Ann".

Molly was next, and taking her cue from Maggie she also whispered, "Molly Elizabeth" and the vicar repeated this, then on to, "Daniel James", and "Harry John".

Now it was my turn, and I desperately wanted to have a second name; I was waiting for a miracle to happen, but it never came. So in contrast to the others who had quietly given their names to the vicar, I almost shouted "'andel", which took the vicar by surprise. He stepped one pace backwards, and looked down at me; then to Mammy, who was standing alongside me holding Eddie in her arms, with Walter in front of her. The puzzled look on his face said it all, as Mammy almost apologetically said, "its Handel, just Handel".

So I was baptised with the single appendage of Handel, and the christening continued with Walter Peter, and concluded with Eddie Idris. It is surprising now to think, that Eddie was the only one to have a Welsh name; but then, Welsh names were not in fashion in those days as they are now.

167

The historic event of the christening of the Swain family children was successfully concluded as far as Mammy was concerned, but not for me. The designs of the Roman Catholic Church and their agents, the dreaded Nuns, had finally been thwarted. We were now beyond their reach, and they would surely lose interest in trying to convert us to their faith.

But, for me a big question mark had been raised in my mind, as to why I had just the one Christian name; the thought that I had been treated differently by my parents, worried me; and I could not let it go. So as we headed home to a late Sunday dinner, I was looking for an opportunity to tackle Mammy on the subject. She was hurrying ahead of us, the Sunday joint had been left to roast slowly in the oven; she had broken with her normal practice of cooking it the night before, and her mind was now firmly fixed on preparing the day's main meal. She shouted back at Maggie, who was carrying Eddie. "Keep them altogether Mag, I'm going to get on with making the dinner".

I knew that Maggie would be more concerned with looking after my two younger brothers, and as usual keeping a watchful eye on Harry. So she was not at all concerned when I skipped away, and ran after and caught up with Mammy.

"Mammy", I said as I ran alongside her, "why have I only got one name"?

She knew from the tone of my voice that I was not a happy boy, feeling that I had been wronged, and that she was to blame. "Well son", she answered, "I don't really know why you were given only one name".

Then she took the easy way out, not knowing what else she could to do or say. "Your father always chose the names for you children, and perhaps he could not think of another suitable name for you at the time".

She was aware that it was rather a feeble reply, and that I was not going to be satisfied or easily placated by what she said.

We had reached the house now, and she tried to change the subject by saying. "Come on, let's have a look at that meat, I hope it's not burnt".

She got hold of the rag from the table that she was using as a tea cloth, and lifted the latch of the oven door and opened it. The Sunday joint was a large shoulder of Welsh lamb; it was the family's favourite dinner, which she got for this very special occasion. For a brief moment, I forgot the heartache I was having regarding the lack of a second Christian name, as my nose and taste buds grappled with the tantalising aroma, which was now emanating from the oven. She removed the pan holding the meat, and placing this on the hob began to baste it. I watched as she scooped up the fat and ladled this over the sizzling surface of the roast lamb. She was pleased how the joint of meat was cooking, and with the successful christening of her children at the church. It seemed to inspire her, as her thoughts were still with the question I had raised regarding my name.

She finished basting the meat and put it back in the oven, then turning to me and putting her hand on my shoulder, she said," Son, I remember now what happened when you were born, what your father said to me. "We'll call this boy Handel", he said, "and no other name, because he'll make a name for himself".

At the time I did not realize or know exactly what she meant, neither did I believe that they were my father's words, but her's. However, what she said seemed to imply that they were something special, and I felt good and reassured once more as she reiterated. "You will Handel, you see; one day, you'll make a name for yourself".

CHAPTER 16

# WORK FOR YOUR KEEP

July 1942, and the long summer holidays would soon be
with us once more. These were worrying times for Mammy.
It was much easier to manage the family, particularly the
younger ones, when most of them were at school all day.
Maggie and Molly were developing their own circles of
friends, and they were both taking a natural interest in some
of the local youths, becoming more reluctant to help her in
looking after Walter and Eddie. Being as realistic and
practical as ever, she had a certain amount of sympathy with
them. She had to give the girls some respite from the
family duties, Maggie more so than Molly. Her eldest
daughter never shirked her responsibilities, and had endured
great pain and worry for one so young.

So it was agreed that Daniel, who ran the family errands
would take over some of Maggie's tasks, and that I would
take over the role of errand boy. It was a role that I was to
excel in, even earning the odd penny or two by running
messages for some of our neighbours. Monday was the
most important day for running messages; with two
essential journeys to be carried out during the school

midday break between 12 o'clock and 1.30.

It took me less than five minutes to cover the ground from the school to our house, where Mammy would fold her pension book, put it in my trouser pocket, and secure it with a large safety pin over the pocket opening. Then off again I would run across the square down the hill to the main road, past the Works Laboratory and the Devil's Inn, under the two bridges, past the remains of our old house and the Bug cinema finally arriving at the Post Office. The postmistress would undo the safety pin, take out the pension book, stamp it, then, fold four large £1 notes back inside and replace it in my pocket. The balance of three shillings, always made up of one Florin and one Shilling piece, she also stuffed into the pocket before securing it once again with the large safety pin. Running all the time, I would be back home before 12.30 to carry out the second part of the operation; which was to pay the bill for the week's rations that Mammy had collected that morning at the Star Supply Stores in town.

This was a bit trickier than the first bit, since it involved catching a bus for part of the journey. My timing had to be spot on, for I had very little leeway, and could not afford to miss the bus back again. With the bill and the money to pay it; once more secured in my pocket by the safety pin, I tore off in the opposite direction to catch the twenty-five to one, number 73 bus for the 10 minute journey to High Street station. I could reach the Star Supply Stores in under a minute from there, but I had an anxious five-minutes wait then: in the queue of people also waiting to pay their bills.

It was a worrying time, as I only had 10 minutes to get the bus back home again. But paying the bill at this shop never lost its fascination for me. The bill and the money would be taken from my pocket by one of the counter staff, who would place it in a little metal cup, which was then screwed into a receiver that was suspended overhead on a line of wire. There was a spring mechanism attached to the wire with a handle, which was then sharply pulled down, releasing the spring and with a whoosh! shot the contraption to the other end of the shop; where seated in superior splendour in her well lit glass fronted office was the cashier. She would unscrew the cup, tip out its contents; stamp the bill in big black letters PAID, put it back into the cup with any change; screw it back into its receiver, and with an air off great authority pull on the handle of the spring loaded contraption sending it whizzing back to the counter once more.

If things went according to plan, then I would return home about ten past one for my dinner. It was always the same on Mondays, cold meat from the Sunday joint, and any potatoes and vegetables left over would be mashed and warmed up in the frying pan. I bolted this down with the aid of a cup of tea, which generally left me with the margin of about five minutes to get back to school. The services were frequent, but should I miss the bus in either direction then I would have a problem. A lot of the people who worked in the town would travel home for their midday meal, and the buses would quite often be full. This would cost ten or fifteen minutes of my precious time; which meant that I would miss most of my dinner, and still be late for school with the inevitable penalty that this incurred; a scolding from the headmistress in the infants, and in the boys' school at least one stroke of the cane. No feeble excuses like running messages would be accepted.

With the coming of August and the school holidays, Mammy received an unexpected letter from one her brothers who now had the family farm. He suggested, that she might find it helpful if some of the older children were to visit to help with the coming harvest. "The fresh air and farm food would do them good, and honest work on the land would keep them out of mischief". It was an opportunity too good to miss. Maggie and Molly would look after Walter and Eddie, while Mammy took Daniel, Harry, and myself, to the farm. She would return alone the following day. The general idea was for the three of us to stay at the farm for a period of two or even three weeks; but a great deal depended on how well we got along with her bachelor brothers, and I expect what help we gave them.

Within a week of us breaking up from school, on a dull and cloudy Monday morning Mammy, Daniel, Harry, and myself, were boarding the early number 18 bus for Ammanford. We did not carry any luggage, we had no change of clothing; it was a case of having to make do with what we stood up in. Mammy was however, carrying her large shopping bag, made from the material of an old barrage balloon. Inside this she had some provisions for the journey, and a couple of old brown paper carrier bags. She did not intend returning empty handed from the farm, but would bring back as much produce as she was able to carry.

It was a journey that seemed to last forever, the bus stopping frequently once we were out in the country, at every lamp-post it seemed. Sometimes the bus would wait at the bus stop for several minutes, waiting for some regular passenger to turn up who happened to be late that morning. Whether it was official or not, the bus crew seemed to be running a profitable sideline in a parcel delivery service, dropping off and collecting various packages and parcels along the route. Mammy explained that this was part of country life, with the buses providing a much-needed service to the scattered country and farming community. She made us laugh when she quipped, that she would not be surprised if they collected the odd goat or sheep.

We finally arrived in the small town of Ammanford at midday, and the heavy clouds of the early morning had now turned to rain; it was my first visit to the town, and on this rain-soaked day it looked bleak and gloomy. The initial excitement of visiting the farm was beginning to rapidly wear off. So I was feeling a little sorry for myself, as we got off the bus and hurried to the nearest shelter from the rain, which was the local bus station. "Do we have to get on another bus by yer Mammy", I asked in a forlorn voice. "Yes son", she replied, and added firmly, "now, don't be a baby Handel and cheer up".

Then turning to Daniel she handed him a brown paper bag which she took from her shopping bag. "Take this Dan", she said, "its some bread and cheese, share it out amongst the three of you", and looking sternly at Harry she said in a slow determined voice; "make sure Handel gets his share, and don't move from this spot until I get back. I'm going to the office to find out when our bus is due". She paused briefly and looked around the bus station, it was full of people waiting for their buses to take them home after a morning's shopping in the town, and others seeking shelter from the rain. Then she hurried off, as we tucked hungrily into the thick slices of bread and cheese. We waited for nearly two hours, so Mammy said, for that bus to turn up; but it seemed twice as long as that. I was really sick of the whole idea of going to the farm now, even though as the bus left the station the rain had stopped and the clouds were beginning to lighten. The bus was a very old charabanc type of vehicle, and as it pulled into the station it was already half full. People seemed to appear from nowhere, carrying bags and parcels, all pushing and jostling to get on. Fortunately, Mammy was ready for them, and she had placed herself and us in a strong position; ready to board the bus as soon as it entered the station. With her arms out-stretched and loudly calling, "Gan bwyll, Gan bwyll, careful, careful", she shepherded us through the pushing throng until we got inside. She managed to get herself a seat and pulled me on to her lap, with Daniel and Harry having to stand. The old bus groaned, as it pulled out of the station, to start another bumpy bone juddering journey into the hinterland of the hills north of Ammanford. Now crammed full of people, packets, and parcels; but amazingly, everyone who wanted to board the bus, got on.

It took us another half-an-hour to travel just over four miles down the narrow winding country road, stopping once more at the entrances to most of the farms, and the little hamlets along the way. Finally we arrived at our destination, having more of a struggle to get off the bus than on, Mammy having to push and shove, to clear a path through the aisle of reluctant bodies and their belongings. When at last we were back on firm ground, and I had recovered my composure; I found that I was standing outside a five-bar gate, with a wooden platform beside it; this was where the farm milk churns were left to be collected by the lorry and taken to the dairy. All of this, of course, was familiar territory to Mammy. She then opened the gate and led us through on to a rough stony path that seemed to lead to nowhere.

The view from the gate, to the right of the path, was of a large open field, or meadow; which sloped gently down to a small river in the valley below. This was now in full flow after the morning rain. The land on the other side of the valley; was mainly covered by trees, which were tightly packed at the river's edge but gradually thinning out as the land sloped quite steeply back. On the ridge at the top of the hill, stood a small building surrounded by a dry-stone wall.

To the left of us was a drainage ditch, then a grassy bank on which there was a hedge, which was showing signs of severe overgrowth. The path followed the bank and hedge around to the left, and as we trudged along Mammy pointed up at the small house on the ridge opposite. "Mind now", she said, her voice filled with caution. "You remember what I told you about the rustlers".

Her words stopped me dead in my tracks I certainly did remember, and by my brothers reaction they remembered her gruesome tale as well. "Is that where they live Mammy", Daniel asked, while Harry just stopped and gazed up at the ridge; his eyes narrowing at the thought of the word rustlers and the images this conjured up in his mind. "No Daniel", she replied, "I don't know who lives there now", still pointing across the valley at the building, "but that's where they lived, all seven of them in that little shack up there".

She hurried us along the path now, which gradually straightened out, where we came to another five-bar gate. Beyond this, the path rose slightly following the general lay of the terrain, and finally led to the imposing stone farmhouse where Mammy was born and raised. As she opened the second gate she gave a final warning. "You take heed now, and stay on this side of the river"

My thoughts were racing, and I was frightened yet excited at the same time. I had now actually seen where the rustlers had lived, where the crime took place, and could recall by mother's tale.

\*\*\*\*\*\*\*\*\*\*\*\*\*\*\*\*\*\*\*\*\*\*\*\*\*\*\*\*\*\*\*\*\*\*

It happened over 30 years before when she was a young girl of 12 or 13, at lambing time in the early spring. Several of her father's lambs, had gone missing. At first, they believed they had been taken by rogue dogs or foxes, but there had been no evidence that this was the case. Normally when a dog or fox attacks, some remains of the lamb like blood, or skin, would be left on the ground. This went on for a period of about two weeks, with one or two lambs disappearing most nights. So my grandfather decided to keep watch on the flock at nights, taking it in turns throughout the night with his two older sons. Nothing happened, no one approached the flock, and there were no dogs or foxes, but still more lambs went missing.

My grandfather had his suspicions of the family that had moved to the small hill farm across the other side of the valley. They were not farmers, keeping just a few chickens and a couple of pigs. The family consisted of the husband and his wife and five boys, the two younger ones being of school age, but they did not attend the local village school. It was believed that that they were itinerant workers, or tinkers who were trying to settle down. The man would often be seen with his horse and cart and the three older boys, at the local markets mixing with the more dubious traders. Still, my grandfather realised; that suspicions on their own were not good enough. He needed hard evidence to put before the village constable. The lambs were certainly not being taken at night, and he was at a loss to establish exactly where and when they went missing.

It was obvious really, as there were only two times during the day when Mammy's entire family were fully occupied and could not keep watch. That was during milking when all hands would be needed. There were no machines then, and indeed even now on my first visit to the farm, the milking was still carried out by hand. In the end it was a stroke of luck, and a small lapse in discipline on Mammy's behalf, that led to the thieves downfall.

The village school that she attended was over two miles away, and she walked that distance every day. Summer or winter, she never failed to attend when she could, the only exceptions being if her presence was vitally needed on the farm. She was in the final year at the local school, and was now studying and developing her use of the English language. A young lad from London, the same age as Mammy, was visiting Wales and staying with relatives in the village. His own parents who were Welsh; but now living in London, had sent him down to Wales to familiarise himself with their native tongue. It was a good opportunity for both these young people; to help each other in acquiring greater knowledge of the language they were each studying. On this particular day, after school had finished, instead of hurrying home, as she should have to help with the milking, Mammy became engrossed in conversation with this young lad. Then well over an hour later, and as time does not stand still even for young lovers; with night drawing in she was to be found feverishly running home, desperately worried of the scolding she would get from her Mam and Dada.

Part of her duties was to bring the cows into the sheds for the evening milking, but she knew that it was already too late for this. The milking would have started without her, which meant that her Mam would be needed to help, instead of preparing the evening meal. If she hurried she thought there was still time for her to help out, then things would not be so bad for her.

It was almost dark now as she hastened along the road and approached the gate leading up to the farm; when from out of the gloom she saw two figures walking quickly down the path towards her, their shoulders bent under the weight of the sack each one was carrying. Her first thoughts were that one of the figures would have been her father, who had come looking for her. But where was Meg her father's dog. He could not go anywhere on the farm without her, and she would have sensed by now that Mammy was close by. Also her father was quite tall almost six ft, and so were her older brothers; but not these two even allowing for the heavy sacks they were carrying, were much shorter. Her instinct told her immediately to be wary, be on guard, obeying the safety mechanism inbred in the genes of generations of farmers; through necessity forced on them by their lives of isolation. She had already stopped walking, and was now crouched down in the ditch that ran alongside the road, only a few feet away from the gate. One of the men was already opening it, just enough to allow him and his companion through, then quickly closing it again. Mammy pressed herself down, almost lying in the ditch, and prayed that the men would not see her. Fortunately luck was with her; they turned and hurried away up the road in the direction of the cottage up on the hill.

Nightfall had closed in on the farm and the milking almost finished, when Mammy breathless now and with mixed feelings of fear and elation burst in to the milking shed crying out. "Mam, Dada, the rustlers, I've seen the rustlers, with heavy sacks, now, down by the road they were". "Carrying sacks you say girl," my grandfather said, "so that's how they do it, and when we're busy with the milk".

Before he could add any more, Mammy was already advising him what his next move should be. "Get the policeman Dada, I saw them almost running they were, up the road towards the cottage on the hill". "Yes I will get the policeman Louisa," he answered, "but whilst I'm doing that", he turned to his two elder sons, "you Sam and you Tom, go up to the cottage and watch. Don't do anything mind you, just watch until I come with the constable".

It was gone midnight when my grandfather returned with the local policeman, when both men joined my two uncles who were keeping watch on the rustlers. There they waited and their patience was rewarded, when in the early hours of the morning three figures emerged from the cottage, the man and two of his sons. All three of them once more carrying sacks. Inside two of the sacks were the dismembered bodies of two lambs, and in the third two fleeces. They were caught red handed; literally; for they still had the blood on their hands of the two lambs they had slaughtered that night.

That was where Mammy's story finished, but I can only assume that the rustlers must have received a lengthy prison sentence, as rustling or sheep stealing was and still is a very serious offence. The family too, quickly disappeared from the cottage up on the hill, as they never featured again in Mammy's tales from her childhood.

*************************************

The rain had stopped, and the clouds that contrived to make a miserable morning; had now been burnt off by the early afternoon summer sun. We continued walking along the rough farm track, and as we got closer to Mammy's family home, I was amazed by the size of the place. The earth bank and tall hedgerow ended at the front of the house, which was surrounded by a dry-stone wall, about five feet high. It was set back from the rough farm road on a rising slope, and access was gained through two stout black hardwood gates, then steps of large flat stone slabs.

Built of brown stone, with five windows at the front, three on the first floor, and two on the ground floor, with an imposing tall, wide front door in the middle. Just like the gates this was also painted in a stern black, as were the window frames, with blue-black slates on the roof that seemed to give the building an air of impregnability; like a fortress. This effect was enhanced by some large trees, larches I think, which were on either side of the steps; their lofty, but sparsely covered branches giving a thin shade from the bright afternoon sun.

Harry as always had forged his way ahead, and was now standing outside the gates looking up at the house. Then as impatient as ever he began jumping up at the gates, attempting to raise the latch, which was just beyond his reach. Mammy quickened her pace and in a muffled voice shouted. "Stop that Harry", as she grabbed hold of him by the shoulders and shaking him saying, "we don't go in that way".

She paused briefly to compose herself, and releasing Harry from her iron grip to his shoulders; she took his hand in hers then called, "Come here Handel, and you Daniel".

With her free hand she took hold of my arm. "Now listen", she said, it was a plea more than a threat or warning, "you all must behave, for if you don't, then your Uncle Idris won't let you stay". Then in a calmer voice said, "Come on we don't go in through the front door, we must go round through the back of the house and in through the dairy".

This must have been a strange and trying time for Mammy; as she had not seen her brothers, my Uncle Idris and Uncle Jack for many years; and of course neither of them had laid eyes on any of her children. It was only natural that she would be apprehensive of meeting them again.

There was yet another five-bar gate where the farm track ended and the farmyard began. The garden at the side of the house was triangular in shape, and narrowed to a point near the gate where there was a small hut, which Mammy pointed out was the cooling shed; where the warm milk was brought here, and poured over chilled metal rods to reduce its temperature before going into the milk churns. We passed through the gate and into the farmyard, where the ground was much stickier, due to the slurry coming away from the large dung heap, which dominated the centre. To the right of us was a large covered barn where hay and straw was kept, and was also used to stable the two massive shire horses. Further along there was another five-bar gate where the farm track reappeared, and continued to the upper fields. We picked our way to the back of the house, over the farmyard ground that was now a gluey morass after the morning rain. On the far side of the dung heap, stood a long white washed building; which was the cowshed or milking parlour, and at the far end of this building was a small pigsty.

There was a strange silence about the place. Apart from a few plump chickens quietly clucking and scratching at the ground, nothing moved. This was a working farm; and you could almost feel the need, for people and animals to be fully engaged in the work that was the husbandry of the land. Weird and sinister thoughts were beginning to fill my head, that the place was deserted, and that no one had lived here since Mammy had left all those years ago. Then I was startled back to reality, by a long low threatening growl; which was emanating from the throat of a wiry fearsome looking welsh sheepdog, that had suddenly appeared at the open door of the house. Mammy still had hold of my arm, and she could feel the shocked tension arising within me, as the dog growled and then snarled its defiance at us.

"Gan bwyll, gan bwyll", Mammy whispered, "steady boys, don't be afraid of the dog".

Then soothingly she called the dog to her, "dere dere, ci bach, dere m'laen, ci bach". Then for our benefit, "come on little dog".

She waited a second, then enthusiastically she patted her leg and called the dog once more, but with more authority in her voice this time, "dere m'laen, ci bach, dere m'laen".

The voice was new to the dog, but the words and tone of command it understood, as it ceased its guttural threats and started slowly walking towards us with a distinct if only slight wagging of its tail.

The dog had no sooner reached us, and Mammy began patting its head, when another figure appeared at the doorway. A tall lean, early middle-aged man, with black hair showing heavy signs of greying and dark brown eyes. Even with a few days' growth of stubble on his face, I could tell without doubt that this man was Mammy's brother. She recognised him immediately uttering the familiar, "duw duw, Idris, shumau bachgen, shumau. Hello boy, Hello".

He responded by nodding his head and saying, "Louisa merched". He had not seen his sister for over 13 years, and he now welcomed her back to the family home by just saying "Louisa girl". The dog's barking had woken him from his nap. It was customary Mammy had told us, for my uncles to have their afternoon nap after dinner, they needed it; as they had to rise early every morning to see to the first milking of the day. She had already warned us that we were to keep quiet at this time of the day after the midday meal, or keep well away from house.

Uncle Idris was a man of few words, and he always had a worried look on his face, an almost permanent frown. He rarely smiled, just sighing with relief when anything pleased him, a sure sign of a man who was always expecting the worst to happen. An awkward silence prevailed for a second, then, as if he had become suddenly aware of our presence he said, "So these are your boys then".

Before Mammy could reply, a second figure now appeared at the door. Like my uncle Idris, this man was tall with black hair, but tinted with much less grey, and yet again with dark brown eyes. His head was slightly bent, and he held his cupped hand close to his face partially obscuring his broad grin; but his eyes twinkled brightly giving away his delight at seeing his older sister once more. This shy, childlike man was my Uncle Jack. Mammy's face lit up when she saw him, she walked over and embraced him. I could sense that there was a much warmer, loving relationship with Jack, than with her other brother Idris, as she said, "duw duw, cariad". The Welsh word cariad is used only when expressing a special term of endearment, as when greeting a loved one or a child.

The dog that had greeted us was now lying at the feet of my Uncle Idris. It had remained quiet and placid, during my uncles' brief welcome, but now suddenly it stood bolt upright, its lips curled and back arched as it emitted a long low and menacing growl. It was not clear at first just what had made the dog react like this; then breaking through the background noise of the few hens scratching and clucking, came the strong if somewhat distant tones of a man singing. My uncle patted the dog to calm it; then beckoning the rest of us to follow him, he walked back inside the house. He raised his arms and shrugged his shoulders as he went, muttering something in Welsh to Mammy, but the only word that I could pick up and understand was "Italian". The singing was coming from the upper fields at the back of the cowshed; but whoever was the perpetrator and the owner of the voice, we could sense that my uncle Idris was not in a favourable state of mind to discuss it. We would have to wait until later in the day to find out just who the singer was.

The first room we entered inside the house was the dairy. It had large stone slabs on the floor and whitewashed walls and ceiling. It was here that the butter sold at the market would have been made in the old days, but not anymore. Nowadays my uncles made sufficient for themselves only. There was a huge butcher's table in the centre of the room, and two large white porcelain sinks. They slaughtered any sheep or pigs for their own consumption themselves, and the carcasses would be cut and cleaned here. There was evidence of this hanging from large hooks attached to the oak beams above, of two freshly cut haunches of pork that were soon to be cured. Mammy, her arm still around her brother Jack's shoulders, called to us to follow her as she went through to the next room, "Come on boys, come and sit down, and we'll have something to eat".

We now entered the main living room of the house, which served as the kitchen, sitting room, and dining room. It had a large open fireplace with a range of ovens on either side, and with the inevitable big black cast-iron kettle simmering away on the hob. There was an assortment of cured hams of different sizes hanging from the blackened oak beams on the ceiling, and two large rocking chairs, one either side of the fire. Dominating the centre of the room was a massive round oak table, with stout six-inch square legs, the top of which was at least two inches thick; and at the centre of this was the only source of lighting, an imposing brass oil lamp. There were eight equally stout kitchen chairs placed around it. Beyond this and covering most of the inner wall, was a magnificent oak Welsh dresser. This was adorned with plates, cups, and saucers, all with gilt edges, and painted with pictures of summer and autumn fruits, raspberries, strawberries, apples, and pears. Next there was a door that led to the passageway at the front of the house, then on to the front wall with one of the ground floor front windows.

There was dust everywhere, the thickness of which depended on the frequency of use. The table and the big oil lamp at its centre, and the rocking chairs were relatively clean, whereas the Welsh dresser, mantelpiece and their ornaments were thickly covered. The rays of the mid-afternoon sun penetrated the room sharply, slanting down from the front window; cutting a swathe of light across the room accentuating the dust particles that danced and sparkled in its beam. The great amount of dust, I later discovered, was generated by the type of fuel that was used for the fire. This was called Pala, a mixture of clay, which was taken from the banks of the river, then blended with small grains of coal or even coal-dust. It was a convenient and extremely cheap form of fuel, which had many advantages over the conventional burning of logs. Unfortunately it generated a very fine ash, which in turn produced an abundance of dust.

Mammy had quickly reverted to her native tongue, and was now busily chattering away to my uncle Idris, as if she had never been away from the place. It seemed that she had forgotten that we were present, as she sat down beside the fire on one of the rocking chairs, and uncle Idris on the other. But we were soon to enjoy a meal; of such succulence and mouth tingling delight, that will live in my memory forever. Uncle Jack had already brought the water in the kettle to boil, and was making a pot of tea. Then from under a cloth on the table he produced a large breadboard, on which was half of what must have been an enormous oval-shaped loaf of bread. He attacked this with what looked like a razor sharp butcher's filleting knife, slicing huge chunks of bread, over an inch thick. I watched Daniel and Harry's facial expressions, which must have reflected my own; they were full of anticipation of just what he was going to do next. With the bread sliced and piled high on the breadboard, he shot back into the dairy and got involved in a lot of plate clattering and banging of cupboard doors. Soon he returned, his eyes still twinkling and face smiling, loaded up now with plates, cups and saucers, knives and spoons, and a large white jug of milk, which he set out on the table in front of us. He dashed back into the dairy, returning this time with a dish in one hand on which sat a huge lump of yellow butter, and in the other a great big two-pound pot of red jam. This was topped with some kind of cloth, which looked like muslin, and tied in place with string instead of a metal lid, which we were used to. Using the bread knife, he deftly cut the string, removed the muslin cover, then a layer of greaseproof paper to reveal the jam underneath. Then in a slow deliberate voice he uttered his first words since we had arrived. Pointing to the bread, butter, and jam, he said proudly, "Bara, menyn, a jam.

He went and sat down at the table opposite us, though we were not quite sure just what to do next; but to Uncle Jack it was obvious as he put his fingers to his mouth indicating that we were to eat, he uttered one more word "Bwyta". We understood now exactly what he meant and did not need telling twice, as we tucked in to the food put before us. The bread was heavy, coarse and doughy; the salty butter glistened with droplets of water; and the jam, which had a thick crust of sugar on the top, was made with wild strawberries. It was a rare bread and jam feast, and although this formed a major part of the farm diet, I never tired of the strong and contrasting flavours of the salty butter mixed with the sharp fruits in the sugary jam.

I soon learned that life on the farm was physically hard with long hours; particularly in those days when there was very little machinery available; or in my uncle's case affordable, to ease the burden of heavy manual work. They did not a possess tractor. For the ploughing and carrying they had to rely on the magnificent Shire horses, and the milking was done by hand. There were many back breaking and repetitive tasks that needed doing, and today, we three boys were going to be introduced to one of these in what was to be our initiation into the life of farming.

We had arrived at the farm at approximately half past two, and at half past three after we had eaten and rested awhile, Uncle Idris decided that it was time to resume the day's work. Mammy called us to her, saying that we were all to go with my uncles to one of the top fields, where there was some recently cut hay that needed turning. The bright August sun had been out for well over an hour now, and looked like it could continue for the remainder of the day. She explained to us as we followed Uncle Idris out of the house; that the hay should have been gathered in by now; but they had experienced extremely wet weather that summer which had caused problems and delay. Most of it to had been cut and stored, but there was still about a quarter of the crop still lying on the field and was now in a soggy condition. It needed to be dried out before it could be stored; and for this, it required a couple of days' good hot sun and constant turning.

We trooped through the farmyard past the steaming dung heap, which was alive now with swarms of beetles and flies of different sizes and shapes. Uncle Idris was marching ahead making for the barn, whilst we followed behind, with Uncle Jack just ahead of us. He was constantly looking back as if to ensure that we were still following. He seemed pleased and delighted with our presence, as a lonely child I expect, would have enjoyed the company of other children.

At the barn, in one of the corners was an array of pitchforks, most of them well over 6 ft long. Daniel was given one of these, and Mammy selected a smaller one for Harry, and the smallest of all for me. True to form Harry rejected his, insisting that he could use a full-size pitchfork, to which surprisingly Mammy gave in without any argument. So now suitably armed we made our way up to the top field, and as we walked uncle Idris began to call out, "Mario, Mario".

We were in the field immediately behind the barn, where a dozen or so black-and-white cows; they were Friesians Mammy told us, were gently grazing the long lush summer grass. There were also two smaller dark-brown cows. These were Jersey cattle she said, and they produced very rich creamy milk, which was added to the main yield to thicken and fatten it.

The terrain got gradually steeper as we approached yet another five-bar gate, before it levelled out and formed a small plateau that was the top field. It was quite large, and half of it had been cleared; the stubble was already beginning to disappear under the new growth of grass and clover. The other half was covered with rows of newly cut hay, and it was this that we had to turn with the pitchforks.

There was no special skill involved, but still Mammy demonstrated just what we had to do, by walking backwards along the rows turning the hay as we went. The knack was to turn over the hay and avoid snagging the long sharp throngs of the pitchfork in the ground. Should this happen the implement would spring from your hands, and fly off in any direction whilst showering all and sundry with muck and bits of hay. I was I am afraid, guilty of doing this quite frequently. I found it difficult to handle the pitchfork, which grew increasingly heavier as we progressed along the lines of hay. Mammy though, soon rediscovered the skill she acquired when she was a child, and effortlessly managed the pitchfork, turning the hay in an easy rhythmic style. I made sure that I kept close to her, only going through the motions really, and resting as often as I could.

Daniel was alongside Uncle Jack, working steadily and methodically as he always did, and Harry surprisingly; was working with great enthusiasm alongside Uncle Idris. Heavy manual work seemed to suit him, and I can honestly say that for most of the time, on the farm, he was a far different, much nicer person.

Uncle Idris would stop work now and then, and shout in various directions for the elusive Mario, but there was no response. He was getting increasingly agitated, muttering and cursing the man in his native tongue; until finally throwing down the pitchfork he stormed off in the direction of the farm angrily shouting "Mario, Mario", as he went.

I asked Mammy, "Who is Mario, Mammy." "Mario" she said in a very disapproving voice, "is an Italian prisoner of war who is supposed to be helping with the work on the farm. Your Uncle Idris is very annoyed, and has gone off to find him".

Then, no sooner had my uncle disappeared from view down the slope towards the farmyard, when suddenly as if from nowhere, appeared a huge barrel-chested young man. He was dressed in a dark grey soldier's uniform; with the letters POW written in large black print on a white patch, which was stitched onto the back of his jacket. He walked up to where Uncle Jack was quietly working away, gesticulating with his arms and shrugging his shoulders, babbling away in a strange language and wearing a hurt boyish look of innocence on his face. Uncle Jack knew that his brother was furious with the young Italian; but he did not show it; he just shook his head and smiled, pointed to the pitchfork that Uncle Idris had just discarded, and motioned that he should pick it up and get on with some work.

We were then treated for the next 20 or 30 minutes, to a solo singing performance the like of which I have never heard since. The young man's eyes twinkled as he smiled at us. Giving a little bow to Mammy, he picked up the pitchfork and with great gusto began to dig at the hay, then immediately burst into song. I did not understand the words, but the language of music is universal, and I appreciated the soldiers marching songs that he began with, and the serenades and love songs that followed.

All too soon, the performance was brought to an abrupt end, by the reappearance of my Uncle Idris, who was accompanied now by another man who was also wearing a uniform; a British army corporal. They were deep in conversation as they approached us, my uncle especially demonstrative, by shrugging his shoulders and wringing his hands. Whether it was the sight of Uncle Idris, or the corporal, I did not know, but Mario's singing ceased immediately. His change of mood was sudden and dramatic; the proud robust tenor who was happily entertaining us seconds before, became a crouched and sullen figure; his head bent forward and eyes fixed firmly on the ground as he wearily prodded at the hay. The corporal broke off his conversation with my uncle and shouted, "Right, come on Mario you lazy Iti sod".

I am sure that the expletive would have been somewhat

stronger, if the corporal had not noticed the presence of Mammy. Mario looked up in response, a questioned look that asked; "are you calling me, I do not understand". The corporal shouted once more, and this time there could be no mistake as he pointed directly at him. "Yes Mario you, come-on it's time to go".

This seemed to get through to the young Italian, and his face lit up, he understood; he dropped the pitchfork and obediently ran over to the corporal. He now stood to attention and saluted, and the corporal could barely hide the smile that showed on his face as he said. "Come on you soft sod". As he turned to walk back to the farmyard he called across to my uncle, "We'll be back in the morning at eight".

There was a small prisoner-of-war camp on the outskirts of Ammanford, and the prisoners were taken by lorry and dropped off at the various farms in the district between 7 and 8 o'clock in the morning; then collected and returned to the camp between 4 and 5 o'clock in the afternoon. Because of the demands of war and the call up of the nation's young men, there was a terrific shortage of manpower on the land; particularly at this time of the year at harvest time, when in normal times a lot of casual labour was used. The Italian prisoners of war were a valuable source of manpower, but it was my uncle's bad luck, so he thought, that he had been allocated Mario. As the army lorry departed from the farmyard; we could hear once more in the distance the rich vocal tones of Mario and his comrades, as they sang in unison glad to be reunited once more after another sorrowful day in captivity.

The day's work had ended for Mario, but not for us; there was still half of the hay yet to be turned. Uncle Idris and Mammy were discussing something in earnest, then he and uncle Jack left us and made their way back to the farmyard. I understood nothing of what was said as their conversation was entirely in Welsh, but then Mammy called to Daniel. "You and Harry keep turning the hay, it's milking time now and I'm needed with the cows".

She must have realised that I was struggling with the pitchfork, and getting tired as she took hold of my hand saying, "You come with me bach. You can help with the cows too". Just what help I could provide I had no idea; but I was thankful to her that she allowed me this welcome respite from using the pitchfork and turning the hay.

Uncle Idris was already in the bottom field behind the barn, and with the aid of the dog was moving the cattle towards the open gate leading to the farmyard. Mammy explained that it was a job that could not be rushed, as it was the worst possible time, just before milking, to startle and panic the cows into a minor stampede. She said that it would adversely affect the yield and quality of the milk. Some of the cows I noticed seemed more willing than others, in making their way through the gate over to the cowshed. But once more Mammy explained that there was a kind of a hierarchy in the herd, that the senior cows would be leading the way and milked first. Sure enough, I watched as they took their rightful places in the stalls in the cowshed; and I witnessed this on all subsequent occasions.

Uncle Jack had brought buckets of fresh cold water from the well, and had filled the pipes in the cooling shed. Everything was now ready for the milking to begin, and I watched with fascination as Mammy sat on the three-legged stool; pushed her shoulder hard against the side of the cow and began the rhythmic pulling and squeezing of the cow's teats to extract the milk. The bucket, which she held steady between her legs, quickly filled as the streams of milk poured into it; the sound changing from the first hollow tinkling to the deep thudding splashes as the level rose.

Watching the milking being carried out by hand is an almost hypnotic experience, the serenity of the cows chewing away at the cud and the regular pitter-patter of the milk hitting the bucket. The rest of the afternoon quickly flew by; and it seemed no time at all when the milk had been cooled, put into the churns and loaded on to the horse-drawn cart. Daniel and Harry had finished turning the hay, and had joined us. Then the three of us piled on to the cart, and with Uncle Jack leading the horse we made our way down to the main road. It was there that this man, with his child-like nature and personality; demonstrated his great strength; by lifting with ease the fully laden milk churns from the cart on to the platform, to await collection that evening by the co-operative milk lorry.

So our first day on the farm had rapidly come to an end, and the three of us, even Harry, showed signs of great tiredness and a desperate need for sleep. With the day's work done, we trudged back to the farmhouse, as the sun began to set; in a faintly tinged red sky; that warm summer's evening. Mammy had prepared what was for us a sumptuous supper, thick slices of doughy bread and chunks of farmhouse cheese. We washed this down with cups of fresh warm milk from that evening's milking. With great smiles of satisfaction, she watched as we devoured the food, then without any arguments from us she packed us off to bed.

There was however one last surprise that awaited us that evening, when we discovered that Daniel and I were to share a bed, which was colossal, with Uncle Jack. Harry, because of his bed-wetting problem, was to sleep on his own. It was 8 o'clock on a beautiful summer's evening but this was Uncle Jack's normal bedtime. He was well aware that we were to share his bed that night, but he insisted on sleeping on the inside close to the wall. He settled himself down facing the wall with the blanket pulled tightly over his head, and within seconds he was sound asleep. As we got into the bed alongside him, Mammy quietly explained that he always slept like this, always on the inside of the bed, where he felt safe and secure during the hours of darkness.

## CHAPTER 17

# MARIO AND THE CIDER

Life on the farm, I was soon to learn; was dictated by the never-ending cycle of milking the cows. Once before 6 o'clock in the morning, and again in the late afternoon. The first job of the day, summer and winter, was to tend the cattle and get the milk into the churns and down to the main road. As I woke that first morning, greeted by great shafts of warm sunlight pouring into the bedroom, I found myself alone in the bed. Uncle Jack had risen noiselessly hours earlier, to carry out his first duty of the day, to make a cup of tea for himself and Uncle Idris, and for this one day Mammy. Breakfast would be taken later after the cows had been milked.

Daniel and Harry had also risen much earlier, and had helped with the latter stages of the milking, had breakfast and were already on their way to the top field by the time I got up. My limbs and back were aching from my involvement with the pitchfork the day before, and I really would have remained in the warm comfortable bed, if I thought I could have got away with it. Anyway I felt an urgent need to attend to the call of nature; which made it imperative that I quickly got up; scrambled into my trousers and boots, and forgetting about my aches and pains dashed downstairs. I had no idea where the lavatory was, as the day before when I wished to relieve myself, I copied my uncles as did Daniel and Harry by peeing in the nearest ditch.

Luckily for me Mammy had remained in the farm-house, and knew exactly what I needed as I burst into the living room my hands clasped to my bottom, and the funny jig I was doing dancing from one leg to the other. This, with the pained look on my face said it all, "Where's the lav Mammy".

Before I could repeat the question she had scooped me up in one of her strong arms; carried me out of the house, across the farmyard, up some steps at the side of the cowshed and there at the back were some smaller white-washed buildings. The smallest of which was set apart from the rest and furthest away from a cowshed; this was the lavatory. Fortunately for me it was not occupied, and the door was open as Mammy in one swift movement; honed to a fine art from years of practice, had my trousers down and sat me on the cold wooden seat in the time it would take to blink. She tut-tutted, as she stood back and watched the relief on my face as the floodgates of my bowels opened. "Dew Dew, Handel, cutting it short again are you".

I took a little time to compose myself, as I was slightly out of breath due to the exertions of the last couple of minutes; when I gradually became aware that there was an extremely cold draught blowing against my exposed bottom, and I could hear the soft tinkling of running water coming from the same region. I began to realise then that this was no ordinary lavatory; it was in fact a two-seater, and I was glad that Mammy had sat me on the one I was now on, and not the one that was immediately alongside me; which was designed for a much greater girth than a smallish six-and-a-half year-old boy.

The lavatory seat was made of two planks of close grained wood, which was practical and necessary; to avoid any close encounters with wood splinters, causing damage to that delicate part of the body which came in contact with it. The surface of which had become highly polished with the years of usage. I can imagine someone who just did not quite fit over the smaller hole, receiving a mind-boggling frightening experience, whilst precariously clinging on grimly when obliged to use the larger one. Particularly when I noticed that the entire structure of the lavatory, was built over a small, running brook, which carried away the effluent to the river in the valley below.

Leaving me to regain my composure, Mammy went back to the house but not before reprimanding me. "Now hurry up Handel, no daydreaming mind, there's a lot of hard work to be done today, and you need a good breakfast".

When I returned to the farmhouse I could hear the sizzling of an egg being fried, which Mammy soon put before me with some thick fatty and very salty Welsh bacon. As I was tucking into this she began cutting some more of the doughy farm bread and telling me, "You need plenty of good food to do farm work Handel, especially breakfast. So you make sure you are up early tomorrow and have a good breakfast with your uncles".

She buttered two slices of bread and piled on some of the jam, then poured some milk into a large cup saying, "Eat the bread and jam Handel, and drink up all the milk". Mammy was demonstrating to me that when I had the opportunity to eat good food, I was to graciously accept it. She was a strong advocate of building up strength in the good times, to weather the lean times that would surely come.

Satisfied that she had filled me up with as much food and milk that I could take, she said, "Now then bach, there's one special job that you must do every morning after breakfast. Come on and I'll show you".

She led the way out of the house across the farmyard and up the steps at the side of the cowshed, where she had hurriedly carried me earlier. The whitewashed buildings that we passed on the way to the lavatory, were in fact stores filled with bags of cattle feed and grain. One of the bags of grain was open, and resting on the top was a large metal scoop. Mammy picked this up, and pushed it into the grain filling it to about three-quarters full, then carefully shaking off any excess back into the bag to ensure there that not one grain fell on the floor. "Right, Handel", she said, "this is for the chickens, it is to be scattered about the farmyard and the fields close by, and you do this every morning after breakfast".

She handed me the scoop, which I found necessary to hold with both hands, and warned "Don't spill any now, not in here, and follow me".

So began the daily ritual of feeding the chickens, the one task that I can honestly say I really enjoyed during my stay on the farm. The grain was just a supplement to the chickens' diet, which was mainly acquired by scratching, and pecking, at the abundance of insects and creatures that populated the farmyard and surrounding land. By scattering the grain over the widest possible area, it encouraged the chickens to spread out and forage for their food.

We had only gone two or three paces away from the grain store, when the first inquisitive chicken discovered us, and began furiously clucking and jumping in anticipation of the feast to follow. Within seconds she was joined by a dozen others, which started off a chain reaction with a hundred or more chickens all screeching, and clamouring, in headlong flight towards me. With all the commotion going on, it was a little frightening at first, then Mammy, showing me the way shouted. "Come-on Handel, run at them".

She laughed as she ran back down the steps with me following; scattering the chickens, which then began lining up behind me; picking up the grain that was already falling from the scoop as I ran. It was like running the gauntlet of a horde of mad demons, as we raced down the farmyard, with feathers, and chickens, flying everywhere. By the time we got to the barn half of the grain was gone, and the chickens were beginning to thin out as they found and became engrossed with eating it. Now that the scoop was lighter, I was able to hold it in one hand and Mammy yelled above the din. "That's right Handel take a hand full, and throw it over the hedge into the field".

We then walked around the perimeter of the farmyard, throwing and scattering the grain over the hedges and onto the tracks and fields.

It was fun feeding the chickens and I looked forward to this time of the day, and the job that immediately followed it collecting the fresh eggs. With the chickens fully engrossed in feeding, it was a good time to go raiding their nest boxes; which were generally quite full after a night's laying. Mammy got a large wicker basket from the dairy, and we must have collected 30 or 40 eggs that first day. She said that the chickens would continue laying eggs throughout the day, and I should visit the shed again in the late afternoon, and collect any further eggs that had been laid. In the old days, when Mammy lived at the farm, the surplus eggs would have been taken to market, but now they were sold to an egg merchant who called at the farm twice a week.

With the fun jobs finished, it was time to resume more mundane and backbreaking tasks, such as turning the hay. It was not yet 9 o'clock and the promise of the bright early morning, was developing into a gorgeous hot summer's day. Mammy said that I was to join my uncles and brothers up at the top field, but that she was not going to join us this morning. As a special favour for my uncles, she was going to cook a roast dinner with all the trimmings. It was going to be a rare treat for the two bachelors to have their sister cook them a proper meal.

With all that had been going on that morning, I had completely forgotten about the young Italian prisoner-of-war, Mario; who was now working alongside Uncle Jack and Uncle Idris, and my brothers, when I arrived at the top hay field. Unlike the day before when he had first joined us, and was full of bravado; entertaining us with his singing, today he was showing no particular enthusiasm for the work. Turning the hay with slow, lethargic movements; his face morose and sullen; it was hard to believe that this was the same man that could sing with a voice so rich in tone and volume. As I approached them Harry broke the silence by shouting," Come-on mun 'andel where've 'u been all mornin'".

He was deriding me again, as he knew that I found the work of turning the hay hard and tiring, whereas he found it easy and rewarding. Well I thought, I had been working too, and I shouted back at him, "I've been 'elping Mammy feeding the chickens".

Too late, I realised that I had said the wrong thing when he retorted and laughed, "Mammy's boy, feedin' chickens is girls work, you big sissy".

I was rescued from this slanging match, that I knew I

could never win, by Uncle Jack who called me, "Dere", he said, as always just the one word; he was smiling and holding aloft in his hand the small pitchfork that I had used yesterday. I was grateful for this and ran over to him. He handed me the pitchfork and then pointed to the ground close to his feet, indicating that I was to work alongside him. Like all childlike and innocent people, he was keenly aware and could sense good and bad vibes, and I realised there and then that I had an ally in Uncle Jack.

The brilliant morning sun was doing the work that was required of it. The damp hay was quickly drying out, as Uncle Idris, every now and then, would take some and slowly press and rub this in the palms of his hands. The grunts and nods of approval from him increased as the morning progressed, as we continued turning the hay; eagerly awaiting each of his samplings, until just before midday we were rewarded with the final grunt of satisfaction that the job was done. As long as it did not rain that afternoon, the hay would be ready to be gathered in and stacked in the barn.

Roast pork with sage and onion stuffing, boiled potatoes and broad beans, with lashings of thick fatty gravy. This was the treat that was waiting for us when we returned from the fields, for our main meal of the day. Mammy had promised my uncles a good roast dinner which they ate with relish, and even Mario who until then had not shown any great enthusiasm for welsh cooking, seemed to enjoy it. Although he still remained silent and a little sullen at the table. Mammy's apple tart and thick jelly-like custard seemed to have been a revelation to him, as he devoured this ravenously. It must have come as a terrible shock to him when he discovered later that afternoon, that Mammy was returning to Swansea, and that the following day, once again, we would be reverting to

Uncle Jack's cooking.

With all the excitement of our first days at the farm, I had firmly put out of my mind the thought of Mammy returning home that day. It was going to be a terrible wrench for me she knew, when the time came for her to leave. So after dinner when my Uncles had their customary afternoon nap, she took Daniel, Harry, and myself, into one of the small fields at the side of the house, which was known as the garden. Mario had quickly disappeared as soon as dinner was over. The field was completely enclosed on all sides by hedges, and was really a vegetable garden. The farm was self-sufficient for most of its food, and growing here were cabbages, peas, broad beans, swedes and soft fruits like redcurrants, blackcurrants, and gooseberries.

"Come on boys" she said as we followed her through the small wicket gate, "you can help me pick some fruit and vegetables, I'm not going home empty handed".

She had brought her carrier bags for the vegetables, and some brown paper bags for the fruit. Then for the next hour or so we had quite an enjoyable time, as she showed us which fruits were ripe and ready to be picked, and which vegetables to select. We filled the carrier bags full of the garden's produce, but not the strong synthetic rubber bag made from the old barrage balloon; she was keeping this for some bacon, ham, eggs, and butter, which she also intended taking back to Swansea that night.

As we walked back to the farmhouse from the garden, we could hear the sound of singing coming from the field down by the river. Mario had emerged once more from where ever he had spent the last hour, and was now indulging in his favourite past time, lustily singing like the birds, celebrating the summer's glorious sun.

That afternoon, Uncle Idris harnessed Sal the Shire

horse to the large cart, and off we went to the top field, to bring in the hay that was now ready to be stacked in the barn. Once again Mario was missing, and like the day before Uncle Idris was getting himself into a sweat; calling his name and cursing him, but knowing full well that Mario would appear only in his own good time. It was like a game of hide and seek. We began the afternoon's work, then Uncle Idris went off in search for the young Italian; who about ten minutes later, suddenly materialised from out of nowhere with a huge grin on his face. He picked up his pitchfork and joined us in loading the hay on to the cart, and immediately burst into song. Like the day before, and as if to get him-self into the right mood for work, he started off with a rousing marching song. He was just starting on the first of his serenades, when we spotted Uncle Idris marching furiously back towards us, he was shaking his fist and shouting at Mario, but now in English. "Where've you been you lazy swine, the corporal will hear of this". He then reverted to Welsh, continuing ranting and raving at the young Italian until he had expelled his anger. It is much easier to express your wrath with words that come naturally to you.

The transformation in Mario was once again sudden and dramatic, with the reappearance of my Uncle. Gone was the robust hard-working joyful singing young man, and replaced by one that was hunched shouldered, sullen and silent. Yet I did not believe that it was my uncle's exasperation and display of anger that caused this sudden change in his personality, it was far deeper than that. His resentment of Uncle Idris had its roots in something else. I was later to find this out, a common human error; a misunderstanding brought about when peoples of different cultures meet under the dreadful circumstances of war.

Twice we loaded the cart that afternoon, packing the

hay as tight as we could by stamping and pressing on it; cramming in as much as we could before taking it down to the barn. Things were beginning to get rushed as milking time was rapidly approaching, but the hay had to take priority whilst the weather held. Mammy was also returning home that night, and my uncle had arranged with the corporal the previous day; that when he came to collect Mario he would give her a lift to Ammanford in time for the 6 o'clock bus to Swansea.

All too soon that time arrived, and at 5 o'clock she said goodbye to her brothers and taking Daniel, Harry, and myself, to one side she warned. "Now promise to be good boys, and be obedient to your Uncle Idris. Daniel you watch over Handel, and mind you, Harry, you work hard boy, and no mischief ".

I could sense then that she was a woman close to torment at leaving us; but she was only too aware that she had other children; two tiny tots still only babies, in the care of her two daughters who were really still children themselves. She picked up her carrier bags loaded now with goodies from the farm, and walked down to the Army truck that had reversed up from the main road, and sat alongside the corporal in the cab. She hadn't forgotten me as she waved goodbye and shouted, "Handel stay close to Daniel, and don't forget to feed the chickens".

This was the first time in our young lives that we had ever been parted from her; and I am convinced that Mario and his companions, who were watching from the back of the truck could sense the sadness of the occasion. As they too were young men parted from their mothers. I felt an emptiness: a void had entered and stolen my soul, as the army truck disappeared from view, and the young Italian prisoners of war sensitive to our feelings quietly sang a song of lament.

For the rest of the day, the couple of hours that remained after Mammy had departed, a state of lethargy or melancholy hung in the air. My uncles completed another day's milking, whilst we helped by bringing water from the well, and I remembered to check the chicken shed and collect the eggs before the chickens went to roost. There was a silence about the place, and I was already beginning to miss the background din and atmosphere; that comes with living close to a town and centre of industry. It takes a special breed of people to farm the land, particularly in the remote and isolated farms amongst the hills of Wales. Mammy confirmed this later on in life when she swore; that for all the troubles that living in the town brought, she was adamant that she would never return to life on the farm.

But for all that we were never idle, there was always plenty to do between the monotonous tasks of the twice daily milking. Apart from feeding chickens and collecting the eggs, I was given the job of picking the soft fruits as they became ripe. Daniel and Harry were given more manly tasks; like helping my uncles cutting and trimming the hedgerows, or helping Mario down in the wood, who was cutting and stacking logs ready for winter. The main task, however, was harvesting the potatoes, and in doing this we proved to be of great help to Uncle Idris. But, there was one job, which I found to be fascinating, and had a peculiar interest for me. That, was digging clay from the riverbank, which was then mixed with small coal, and transformed into what was known as pala. Whilst the mixture was still wet it was cut into slabs, about the size of a house brick, then stacked and allowed to dry out. It was in very economical form of fuel, the clay cost nothing apart from the work of digging it out from the riverbank, and the small coal was obtained cheaply from the local drift mine, of which there were many in the area.

Uncle Jack did all the cooking, and his meals were monotonously predictable. Breakfast was always thick slices of fatty Welsh bacon and eggs, and supper bread and cheese or jam. The only meal of the day that had some variety was dinner. It consisted mainly of meat; boiled ham or bacon, or roast salt pork, and boiled potatoes and vegetables. Any leftovers would be eaten cold the following day, and bones and scraps boiled again with vegetables to make Cawl. Still it was wholesome food, and no one complained after a hard day's work in the fields; apart from Mario, whose looks of disgust ranged from mild when it was roast pork, to absolute horror when presented with a bowl of Cawl.

We were fortunate that the weather was mainly hot and sunny, with only an occasional light shower of rain. We were at the farm for nearly three weeks, which slipped by quickly; as we rose early, worked hard all day, and slept well at nights; giving us, or at least me, little time to think of Mammy and become homesick. There was just one period of the day when we could rest and relax, away from the demands of the farm work, and that was the hour or so after dinner when Uncle Jack and Uncle Idris had their afternoon nap. We took heed of Mammy's warning to keep quiet at this time of the day, and away from the house so as not to disturb them. Mario did his usual trick of disappearing; only to re-emerge after roughly half-an-hour in one of the fields or down by the river, giving vent to his favourite Neapolitan airs.

Daniel and I were content to sit in the garden lying on the grass and soaking up the warm early afternoon sun, whilst Harry; who remained with us for most of the time, was fidgety and couldn't keep still. He enjoyed the farm work, particularly working alongside Mario, who although he always remained silent when Uncle Idris was around, was beginning to express himself in his native tongue. He was expansive and demonstrative; waving his arms about and pulling faces, which he knew would amuse us, and that included Uncle Jack; whose serene and smiling face would brighten up into a broad grin when Mario got up to his antics. But as soon as Uncle Idris reappeared, his character and mood changed dramatically, becoming once more the oppressed and disgruntled prisoner-of-war.

I liked and appreciated Mario when he was happy and singing, pulling faces, and expressing himself in Italian; for it lightened the atmosphere of the farm, and was entirely opposite to the dour and constantly worried personality of Uncle Idris. Although we could not understand one word of what he was saying, I'm convinced to this day that he was taking the rise out of his British captors, and Uncle Idris in particular. But to Harry, Mario was someone to be admired; he was taking on the mantle of a hero. He wished to be with him constantly, and began seeking him out after dinner. At first he would find him once he had started his afternoon singing session, drawn by the Italians powerful voice. But there was always that gap of about half-an-hour in the time after dinner, when Mario would quickly disappear then re-emerge again and begin singing. This intrigued Harry, who was determined to find out exactly where the Italian was, and what he was up to during this time. So he decided that we would follow him, and one morning after breakfast he told me of his plan. These were my instructions. "Right 'andel, just before Mario's finished 'is dinner, you pretend you're going to the lav right, then 'ide outside the 'ouse and see where 'e goes. Then I'll come out and we'll follow 'im".

He could see from the perturbed expression on my face, that I was not particularly enamoured with his plan. But any doubts I had of carrying it through, were banished from my head for good when he held up his curled fist close to my chin, and for good measure he added in a threatening voice, "Don't-tell-Daniel: right".

For dinner that day Uncle Jack had prepared Cawl. So Mario would not be hanging around the dinner table for long today. I had to try and judge just when he had had enough of the soup to satisfy his hunger, so I could make my excuses and leave the table. Besides watching Mario, I was determined that I was going to get down inside me as much of the food that I possibly could. Harry who was sitting next to me had the same idea, and we both tore into the hot soup; sucking at the liquid and juggling around in our mouths the potatoes and vegetables between tongue and teeth; in a desperate effort to cool the food before swallowing. Normally Uncle Idris ignored us at the dinner table, which he did for most of the time anyway, but today the disgusting noises that Harry and I were making brought a reprimanding response from him. "Gan bwyll boys, Gan bwyll". I was only halfway through the meal; when I could see that Mario was beginning to lose interest, and prompted by a sharp dig in the ribs from Harry I rose to my feet and blurted out, "I'm going to the lav".

Apart from Harry who was staring at me with menace in his eyes and mouth set firm, no one else took a blind bit of interest; they just calmly kept eating the soup like cows chewing the cud.

I left the room only just in time as I heard some movement behind me; it was Mario who felt that he had now satisfied his hosts sufficiently with his presence, and having had enough of the Cawl he too would leave the table. I had little or no time to think as to where to hide outside the house; I just kept running across the yard and up the steps towards the lavatory, quietly praying that

Mario was not following me. I was never any good in the art of deceit and just kept on running, my heart pounding, until I reached the lavatory, entered and slammed the door behind me.

I was beginning to panic now, and this increased when I thought of what Harry was going to do to me, if I did not discover where Mario had gone. I waited for what seemed an age, but was probably no longer than thirty seconds, then out of panic not courage I left the lavatory and tip-toed back down the steps to the farmyard. There was no sign of Mario, but I could see Harry by the cowshed, he was walking crab-like down the yard keeping close to the building, in the direction of the barn.

Now the barn was the one area or building, that Uncle Idris had strictly forbidden us to enter unless he was with us, under a penalty even worse than death. Mammy had backed him up strongly on this, explaining that there was dangerous machinery and tools kept there. It was the biggest building on the farm, almost as large as the house, but it was strictly out of bounds. Like the rest of the farm buildings the doors had no locks, just latches and bolts, and I was horror-struck now as I watched Harry approach the barn and disappear behind the large double doors. I could only assume that he was looking for me, and as much as I was reluctant to disobey Uncle Idris, the fear of crossing Harry compelled me to follow him. My Uncles I knew would be settling down for their afternoon nap, and there was no sign of Daniel; then before I really had time to think about the consequences, I was standing outside the barn doors and peering into its murky gloom. The only light that ever penetrated the place was either from the open doors, or from a single grime covered window, at the far end. Near the door was the heavy wooden cart and some pieces of machinery, then some bales of straw and bags of cattle feed.

At first I could not see Harry, and not knowing what else to do I meekly called out, "arry, 'arry where are you".

I must have startled him, something I thought I would never be capable of, as I saw the sudden movement of his head, as he turned round to face me simultaneously uttering," shush". He was crouched down at the side of the cart, and was now gesticulating and furiously waving his arms about, but in the poor light and being apprehensive I was unsure of just what he wanted me to do. For a couple of seconds we both remained still and quiet, but then the silence was broken from a most unexpected source. "Aye boys", it was Mario, I could just make out his shadowy silhouette standing at the far end of the barn. He called us, "Come boys, come, it's okay, see what I got". The shock of seeing Mario; I now realised that Harry had followed him into the barn; and hearing him speak English seemed to remove any fears and apprehension that we felt. Harry stood up and ran towards him calling me to follow. "andel come on it's okay". But before entering the barn I looked back towards the farmhouse, but there was still no sign of Daniel. I would have dearly loved to see him and have him with us now.

When I got to the far end of the barn Mario was sitting on a bale of straw with his back to the wall, and alongside him in the corner was a huge wooden barrel with a small tap at the front, resting on two stout wood blocks. Harry was standing in front of this, his hands on his hips, with an inquisitive look on his face. Mario got up, and in his hand he held a small metal cup, what proved to be a $1/2$-pint milk measure. "Siddown boys", he said grinning, then he gathered together some of the loose straw that was strewn on the ground with his feet, and we sat down. "You amazed eh", he said, as he shrugged his shoulders, and there was pride in his voice, "I spica da eengleesh, I tell you boys, I spica da fuckin good eengleesh".

He stooped down in front of the barrel and placing the cup under the tap he turned this on, and out slowly trickled a stream of dark golden liquid. When the cup was nearly full to the brim, he turned off the tap and putting the cup to a his mouth sucked in a great draught of the fluid, grimaced as he swallowed it then gave out a great sigh of satisfaction. The smile returned to his face as he handed the cup to Harry saying, "itsa good, itsa juice, itsa juice of da apple".

Harry did not need a lot of encouragement as Mario added, "Go on dreenk, itsa nice".

The cup was now about half full, and I could smell the pungent aroma of rotting apples, as Harry put it to his lips and copying Mario sucked loudly at the liquid, swilling about in his mouth before swallowing. Not saying a word, he handed the cup to me but I could see that his eyes were beginning to water, and that he was having a little difficulty in breathing. I took the cup, which was now about a quarter full, but would not dare to drink from it until I had seen the final effect it had on Harry. Mario laughed as Harry eventually managed to catch his breath, his chest and shoulders heaving as he gasped at the air then blurting out, "Cowing 'ell mun, that's strong".

Now that Harry had recovered I knew that it was my turn next to try the drink, they were both waiting and looking at me in expectation. But Harry could not wait long before saying, "Go on 'andel you sissy, 'ave some".

I could not lose face in front of Mario, but I was determined that I was not going to make the same mistake as Harry. I took in a deep breath first, then putting the cup to my mouth I sipped at the liquid; its sharp pungent flavour exploded on my tongue awakening taste buds I never knew I had, then stinging my throat and allowing it measurably to warm my stomach as I slowly swallowed it.

I was glad that I took my time with the drink as I could feel a strange glow inside me, as the warmth of the juice slowly spread from my stomach to the rest of my body. Unlike Harry whose nervous system must have been shocked to a state of near paralysis, by the way he had downed the liquid in one swift gulp. Mario took the cup from me, and slinging away the dregs he said, "it'sa nice aye, we 'ava some more".

He filled it up again and took another hefty swig, then another, and in two swift gulps he had emptied the $1/2$-pint cup. Then he sat back down on the bale of straw, his mouth agape with staring eyes; I wondered what was happening to him, I could faintly hear the liquid churning and rumbling in his stomach; then it got louder and louder, before finally exploding in a gigantic belch from his open mouth. Harry and I burst out laughing, a mixture of mirth and relief on my part. Mario joined in the laughter as he got up and swaggered once more to the barrel for another cupful. He took a couple of sips savouring the liquid this time, before handing the cup to Harry, "dreenk" he said, as he sat down once more.

Harry had got over the initial shock to his system, and eagerly welcomed the cup as it was given to him, but now following my example he took his time and drank the juice slowly. He drank more than half the contents before he handed the cup to me, and I having experienced the soft glow and feeling of warmth inside from the first drink gladly finished it off. Our eagerness and the apparent pleasure we got from the drink seemed to please Mario. "You lika the juice aye", he said, getting up again and refilling the cup.

He was getting a little unsteady on his feet now, as he

stood in front of us gently swaying and spilling some of the liquid from the cup, which this time he had filled to the brim. Steadying himself, he took a sip then pointing then at the barn doors in the direction of the farmhouse, he said slowly and deliberately, "You uncle eeza preek."

He took another swig of the cider, and went on, "you wanna know why I don spica da eengleesh to you uncle, aye. I tell you why boys, eeza preek".

The cider was not only beginning to loosen his tongue, but also the control of his legs, as he handed the cup now half full to Harry, then suddenly staggered backwards and almost falling sat down on the bale of straw once more. He slouched there silently for a couple of seconds, his back to the wall, whilst Harry and I finished off the remaining contents of the cup.

His tousled curly hair was becoming bedraggled, stroking his fingers through it as he became more agitated, and his already ruddy and sunburnt face almost crimson. Then putting his hands on his knees in an effort to steady himself, he leaned forward and with caution in his voice as if he were divulging a heart felt secret he said. "I got family in Noo York, I leev for seex months, een Ameriga".

He paused to gather his thoughts then raising his voice said, "I go back home to Italia, and dat fuckin Mussolini he grab me for da fuckin arrmy".

Momentarily, he held his arms up in front of him, his eyes pleading in disbelief of the injustice meted out to him, before quickly restoring them to his knees to prevent himself from keeling over. Slightly shaking his head from side to side he said, "I no lika da fucking arrmy, I no lika to fight". He paused briefly and his eyes brightened up as he joyously said, "I lika to seeng, I lika da girls, I lika to maka love, I wanna go back to Ameriga".

Then his mood and tone changed, he was sad again. "I

no lika dees Wiles, eeza cold, eeza wet, I lika da sun." In frustration now he raised his voice, "I lika to eat da pasta, da spaghett, I no lika da soup, da fuckin Cawal". The thought of the cawl reminded him once more of Uncle Idris, "an you fuckin uncle, preek, he no spica da eengleesh, he only spica da wilesh."

He tapped at the palm of his hand with his forefinger, to press home the point that he felt insulted. "He meetsa weeth da postman, day spica da Wilesh, he meetsa weeth da caporal, day spica da Wilesh, he meetsa weeth da egg man, day spica da Wilesh. Everybody he meetsa weeth he spica da Wilesh, and you funny uncle, he no spica da eengleesh or da fuckin' Wilesh".

Sighing with exhaustion, but relaxed now he leaned back against the barn wall, he closed his eyes and began to sing, the tender words and melody, were filled with melancholy. He must have been thinking of his home. The strong cider had nearly completed its grip, not only on Mario, but on Harry and me as well. I looked across at my brother whose eyes appeared to be getting heavy, and his head was already beginning to droop. Mario's song, I think, must have been a lullaby; as my head began to swoon, and my body floated up and away out of the barn across the fields and his image got smaller and smaller and his voice quieter.

Once again the only words I could understand, of the tirade of expletives and abuse emanating from Uncle Idris when he discovered the drunken scene before him was Iesi Annwyl of Nazareth. The noise he created as he shouted was ear splitting; yet strangely the words he spoke seemed to emanate from a great distance. I forced my eyes to open through the foggy haze of a rudely broken sleep, to be welcomed by the worried face of Daniel who was standing over me, and a blur of waving arms alongside him that was

Uncle Idris. He got his arms around me and pulled me to my feet, and at the same time was kicking Harry, who was now on his haunches, up the backside.

He chastised us both, "Come on get up, and get out of here", he said as he half dragged and half walked me out of the barn, with Harry staggering along behind us.

I could still hear Uncle Idris ranting and raving, but it seemed he was having very little effect on the drink-induced, unconscious Mario.

Daniel thought it best, and I believe it was very wise of him, to get us out of Uncle Idris's way until he had calmed down a bit. How he managed it I am at a loss to understand, but he got us to the relative peace and security of the kitchen garden. We had been in the barn for over two hours. Daniel and my uncles had searched the farm and the surrounding fields, when it was time to resume the afternoon's work, only to discover that we were in the last place they thought of looking.

The afternoon sun was bright and hot, and I felt sick and giddy after emerging so quickly from the gloom and cool dark interior of the barn. I was lying flat out on my stomach with my head resting on my arms, and my eyes firmly closed. In this position with my body pressed close to the ground, and fingers clinging to the grass, I felt I had some control over my limbs. But the feeling of nausea remained with me. My brain and senses were not at all functioning properly, as I had all kinds of mixed-up thoughts and feelings swirling about in my head and body. I was desperately tired but did not want sleep, my throat was parched but my stomach retched at the thought of water, and I wanted to cry and call-out for Mammy; but my pride would not let me. I was experiencing my first hangover.

After about half an hour, Daniel decided that we had

had enough time to recover. He leaned over and shook me saying, "Right 'andel get up, we've got to get back to the potato field, and you Harry get up. Uncle Idris is very angry with you. If he tells our Mammy what you've been up to, you'll get a real hiding".

I had already thought of that, but at that moment I would have gladly swapped for the hiding as long as I could have Mammy. My arms and particularly my legs felt like lead, my eyes closed tight, I did not want to move; but Daniel persisted as he leaned down once more and getting me by the arm slowly pulled me to my feet.

"Come-on start moving 'andel", he said, as he first steadied me then got hold of my hand and began walking, pulling me along with him.

Feeling wobbly on my feet, reluctantly I followed him. My eyes were open now and I could see Harry who was already making his way out of the garden, his powers of recovery were much greater than mine.

When we got to the potato field both my Uncles were already there, busy filling the buckets then emptying the potatoes on to the cart. I felt slightly better when I arrived, the walk up the hill had released some of the tension within me, and I felt more relaxed now. But I still had a splitting headache, and I was full of wind. Ever since that day I have been very wary of anything to do with apples, as they seem to react unkindly with the chemicals in my stomach, churning and producing foul and violent explosions from my mouth and nether regions.

We worked in silence for the remainder of the afternoon, but there was no sign of Mario. Uncle Idris was his usual dour self, but at least he was calmer now than he was earlier, and even Uncle Jack seemed to disapprove of us, as he looked unhappy and downcast. Then at about half past four, we heard the whining engine and gear crashing of the army wagon coming up the farm track from the main road. The corporal had come to pick up Mario. Uncle Idris's reaction was immediate and fast. Muttering to himself he abandoned the potatoes, and marched off furiously, almost running across the field and down the hill to the farmyard. Uncle Jack, although slower to respond, was now following him.

Harry called over to Daniel, "what's 'appened to Mario, where is 'e".

Daniel shrugged his shoulders but before he could say anything, Harry was making a beeline for the gate. Without thinking of the consequences Daniel and I both ran after him, we to were intrigued to find out just what had happened to Mario. The last time I saw him, he was in a stupor and sprawled out on the bale of hay, and incapable of doing anything.

Down in the farmyard, Uncle Idris was engrossed in an animated conversation with the corporal, and Harry was hiding in the hedge overlooking them; where Daniel and I joined him. Uncle Jack was walking up to the house and went inside; then in less than half a minute he emerged again; but was now carrying a bucket which he handed over to the corporal, who then disappeared into the barn. After a brief interlude, there was a shriek and a scream, which was followed by a string of four letter words in the mixed languages of Welsh, English, and Italian. We could clearly see now just what the bucket was for, as Mario came bounding and stumbling out of the barn with his head and shoulders soaking wet. He was greeted with shouts of derision and laughter from his fellow prisoners; they already knew that he was helping himself to the cider, and had guessed what had happened.

Following him was the corporal who shouted. "That will teach you to drink, you young Iti bastard, now get into the bloody wagon".

Everyone was laughing including the corporal, but not Mario, or Uncle Idris who could not see the funny side of it at all. He was probably thinking of us, more concerned for our safety and welfare than the loss of the cider; and possibly the verbal wrecking he would get from Mammy if she found out what happened. She was still his oldest sister, and he may have well remembered how formidable and vitriolic she could be when roused.

The army lorry reversed and retreated back down to the main road, with the usual rousing chorus from the Italian prisoners of war; but without Mario's strong tenor voice today, fading into the distance. We did not realise it then, but that was the last we were to see or hear of Mario. Uncle Idris had finally lost patience with him, and had told the corporal that for the time being he did not require any further help, especially from young Italian prisoners of war. I hope that Mario survived the war, and returned to his warm, sunny homeland, to eat pasta and spaghetti, and to sing and make love; and that he achieved his ambition of returning to America.

The last days on the farm, seemed drab and dreary without Mario, although the weather remained fine and sunny which enabled us to harvest the remaining potatoes. I was extremely happy when Mammy finally came back to collect us, as were my brothers. Working on the farm had lost most of its appeal for Harry too now that Mario had gone. We said goodbye to Uncle Idris and Uncle Jack, our time on the farm had come to an end. Sad as I felt at leaving Uncle Jack, I could not wait to get home to the Hafod and Maggie, Molly, and my two young brothers. It is true that you never miss what you have never had, but I had brothers and sisters at home, and missed them almost as much as I missed Mammy. We were a family, a living vibrant being, and I was embodied in it. Even though we had few worldly possessions, and suffered want, hardship, and emotional upsets; these experiences had moulded us, helped with the fortitude of Mammy, into a strong bonded unit, that some others as time passed by would look upon with envy in their hearts.

I was just thankful that Daniel, who seemed to suffer more than most, but accepted life's ailments without complaint, was with me at the farm. For I do not think that I could have coped or even survived without him.

## CHAPTER 18

# THE DARK BEFORE THE DAWN

The autumn of 1942 and the winter that followed, was a time of great hardship for our family; some of the most difficult months we were to experience during or even after the war. It was a particularly turbulent period for me, and, strange as it may seem for puss the cat. Some of the events were no doubt because the country was now into the extreme depths of war, and the shortages of some food and fuel were beginning to take their effect. Other matters, concerning puss the cat and myself would probably have happened anyway. It was as if the fates conspired to test the strength of character, the fortitude, the will and determination of the country, our family, and me specifically.

Our working holiday on the farm, meeting my uncles and Mario, seemed a lifetime away as the summer rapidly drew to its close, and it was back to school once more. My funny little pal Dinky Miles had also been away for most of the summer holiday; across the water, he said echoing his mother's words, to his father's hometown of Weston-super-Mare. He told me of his great adventure, travelling by train over a hundred miles, which took him and his mother the whole day. I said that it took us most of the day to get to the farm, but that I did not think that it was as far as Weston-super-Mare. I told him of my uncles, and especially of Mario and his singing and pulling funny faces; but did not mention the episode involving the cider as I still felt a little ashamed of that; and besides it was a secret and best forgotten. Everyone agreed: Uncle Idris, Daniel, Harry, and me that we did not want Mammy to find out.

We were spending more time now playing in the park, on the swings and roundabouts and a frightening contraption we called the Jerker. This was a giant swing consisting of a stout plank of wood suspended between two metal stanchions; which could accommodate up to half a dozen small children who needed to hang on for their lives, whilst being jerked from a standing position to ever increasing heights by two older children; usually girls, one standing either end. For the adults, there were splendid tarmac tennis courts, a bowling green, and a football field for the older boys. Although I recall what the town's Parks Department tried to pass off as a football pitch, was probably made up from the contents of the nearby tip. No grass ever grew on it I am sure. Its ash and cinder surface would have been more suitable for a motor-cycle speedway track.

There was an area at the centre of the park that was permanently fenced off, which displayed flowerbeds and shrubs, and only the Park keeper, or Parky as we called him, was allowed to enter. Of course, that meant it was a challenge to us to dare to be seen in this prohibited area, when Parky was a fair enough distance away before spotting us and giving chase. Then we fled in the direction of the tip, usually beating him to the heavy wrought iron gates, painted as were all council fences in magnificent prescription green, then tearing across the street and square to the refuge of the tip.

There was no way he could get us once we had reached this safe haven. If however, the boy being pursued was unlucky enough to stumble as he fled, for it was always a boy, girls were expected to behave; he would feel the full weight of Parky's hand across the back of his head; before being frogmarched to the park gate and get the front of his boot up his backside as he was kicked through them. Although it was a kind of challenge between us, and the Park keeper, when we entered a fenced off area, we kept strictly to the grass and the bushes. It was taboo and unthinkable that we damage the flowers and shrubs. There were always exceptions to the rules, but on the whole most of the children, poor and needy as we were, believed in a code of conduct and a certain set of values. Strangely the only flowers I can remember being on show there were wallflowers; I suppose that was all that could be expected, given the time and resources available during those dark and turbulent times.

September came and went, I resumed my daily routine of running messages for Mammy and some of our neighbours, settling effortlessly back into school. There was a new girl in our class, another Rosie; but was very different to Rosie Smith, in looks and character she was the complete opposite. She was as pretty as Daisy Davies, and like her had good quality clothes, but was much more out-going and extremely talkative. Whereas Daisy Davies looked and acted like a china doll, Rosie O'Neill or McNeill, I was never quite sure of her correct name, was a very lively and bubbly little girl. She had an older brother, Billy, who was in the same class as Harry in the boys' school. He was not as outgoing and assertive as his sister.

He was a bit of a loner, a deep brooding kind of character; who measured his words carefully when he spoke, and Harry was greatly intrigued, by this boy whose family suddenly appeared from nowhere. There were just the three of them, Billy, Rosie and their mother. Where did they come from? where was the father? had he too been a casualty of the war like our father? Harry got as close to him as he possibly could, closer than most, but try as he might he never extracted the information he was after from the newcomer. But, there was one thing that he was certain of; his name was McNeill not O'Neil as his sister Rosie sometimes called herself.

As ever the world and life still looked unkindly on poor little Rosie Smith. She did return to school after the holidays, and attended for most of the late summer and early autumn, but with the closing in of winter the periods of absenteeism grew longer and longer. At the time I did not give a lot of thought to this or pay particular attention, Rosie was a sickly child and missed a lot of school. Even when she did attend she always kept herself in the background, and huddled near the school entrance during playtime; a forlorn little figure afraid to mix with the other children probably out of fear of being shunned by them. Sometimes, on the rare occasions when I was on my own, which was usually on my way home from school; she would run after me and walk with me part of the way. I always felt a little embarrassed then, not knowing what to say, it was just, "ello 'andel, ello Rosie", silence, "so long 'andel, so long Rosie".

It was whilst I was on my way home one dinner-time; walking up the gentle slope of Odo Street from the Infants School, my hands dug into my trouser pockets to protect them from the first chill winds of autumn; that the first of the unfortunate events happened, the start of the traumatic time that lay ahead. The infants were always let out a little earlier; to enable us to clear the school, before the older boys were unleashed into the street and surrounding area like caged animals set free. But today someone had got the timing wrong. I had got halfway up the slope, when suddenly the double doors of the boys school main entrance burst open; and out poured a deluge of rampaging 14 year-olds with only one thought in their heads, food. In headlong flight and gathering pace as they stampeded down the hill; I did not stand a chance as I pressed myself close to the school wall. Then the first of the flying arms hit me in the stomach, and as I went down with the pain; I was hit again, this time knocking my head back and smashing it against the wall. My body and legs being trampled on after that, proved to have to no long standing ill effects or injury; but the main damage, the bump to the crown of my head was to cause me great pain and many problems later on in life.

I was dazed and my head was bleeding profusely when I was rescued by a couple of boys following the first onslaught, and taken to the local doctor. This was to be my first meeting with the eccentric and no-nonsense, chain-smoking, whisky-drinking Irish lady, Dr Nancy Evans, and her strong well-built assistant Ivy. It was also my first experience of the substance ammonium carbonate, or better known as smelling salts, which she used to bring me back from my semi conscious and faint condition. This did not help my already shocked and frightened state of mind nor my nervous system; as I wriggled and squirmed trying to free myself but to no avail; from the iron vice-like grip of Ivy who was holding me down. She only relented and relaxed her hold on me; when I conceded defeat to her superior strength, and flopped in her arms like a plate of jelly.

If I had known what was coming next I would have put up a much better fight and not given in so easily; as the doctor satisfied now that I was a more willing patient proceeded to tend to my head wound. Softly and gently; murmuring and mumbling through the smoke and half closed lips that held a half burnt cigarette; she parted the blood-congealed hair with cotton wool and water, to expose the damage to my scalp. The cold water eased the pain of my sore and aching head; but it was a trap, I had been lulled into a false state of ease and relaxation. I should have realised and been aware; as the doctor had finished cleansing the wound, that Ivy's grip of my arms was getting rather firmer and then came the sting. My eyes filled with water and I was left gasping for breath; as I expelled the most blood curdling "Ouooch"; as she placed the tincture of iodine soaked lint on to the open wound. Anyone who has had similar treatment from the little brown bottle will sympathise with me, when I state that the whole experience left me a sobbing quivering wreck. As Dr Evans finally applied the bandaging around my head, there was a knock at the surgery door; it was Mammy who had been told what happened and had come to get me. It was the first time that the doctor spoke during the whole of the harrowing experience, as she responded to the look of alarm on Mammy's face. "To be sure now, he's a brave little lad, and he'll soon be on the mend".

The words spoken in her lovely Irish brogue; seemed to melt away any fear or anxiety that remained with Mammy; she liked this lady physician's style, and from that day on Dr Nancy Evans became our family doctor.

Once the initial shock of the injury to my head, and subsequent treatment by the doctor had eased the pain, the hardest part of my ordeal; was having to miss the rest of the day's schooling. The doctor had advised Mammy to keep me home for the rest of the day, and to keep an eye on me as, "Head injuries are funny things".

Well I survived and did mend after a fashion, and came through that and subsequent days without any adverse effects. Although on my return to school the following day still wearing the bandaging, I was the subject of great mirth and hilarious laughter from the rest of the children. I was extremely glad and relieved when the lint dressing and bandaging were removed, and the crude remarks and taunts of "andel is a nutter", and "ee's an 'ead case", ceased.

There was no follow-up visit to the doctor in those days; if you looked alright, and you acted alright, then you were alright. But unfortunately, I was not. My recovery seemed to go well, the scab formed on the wound, and in time withered and came away. Then I discovered, I cannot remember exactly when, it could have been weeks or even months later; that a soft jelly-like lump the size of a shilling piece had formed on the crown of my head where I had been injured. I was not sure whether this was supposed to happen; was this normal; did everyone who had received a bump to the head end up with one of these special lumps. All my body parts seemed to be functioning normally, I was not in any pain, so I just decided to accept the situation and say nothing. No one would discover it; I was blessed with a good crop of wiry hair, and on Saturday nights, bath night, I bathed myself and washed my own hair. Although the barber might spot it when haircut time came around.

With time I did forget about it and not even Mammy or the barber discovered it, but my pal Dinky did. We were fooling about one day on the waste ground near the tip, in a deadly sword fight involving Robin Hood and the Sheriff of Nottingham; then a blow to the side of my head from the stick he was wielding drew blood. It was not a lot, just a minor scratch, and as I went down feigning death, he rushed over to me apologising. "I'm sorry 'andy, I'm sorry".

I did not doubt his sincerity, but I also believed that he was eager to inspect the damage he had done. His hands and fingers were all over my head probing and prodding. Then he found the lump. "Ay 'andy", he said, he pressed the lump with his thumb, "oo-wer what's this lump on uwer 'ead".

He pressed it again and repeated the sound signalling his disgust, "oo-wer". It was probably just my imagination, but I could feel the blood coursing through the veins in my head, and I felt embarrassed and ashamed. I got up from the ground and pushed him down, "Gerroff mun Dinky", I yelled at him, "and leave my 'ead alone".

Fighting back the tears I turned and ran down from the tip, across the road and the square, then kept running until I reached the playing field in the park. I could hear Dinky's plaintive calls, "come back 'andy mun, I din't mean it, I din't mean it".

Within days we made it up and Dinky promised that he would not tell anyone, but of course he did. He was absolutely fascinated with this strange squeezy lump on my head; I became quite a celebrity in the school playground, especially with the girls as they would beg, "Let me feel your lump 'andel".

If I consented they would tentatively feel through my hair until they found it, squeeze it with thumb or finger, then run off screaming with a mixture of fear and delight.

That was the funny side of it, but it did cause many problems later on in life; and when I was 16, I had to undergo major surgery to have the thing removed. As a result I was left with three deep, long jagged scars, and fifty seven stitches, some of which are still embedded in my scalp to this day. It became a nightmare to visit the barber's; if one or more of the stitches got caught up in his comb or scissors, resulting in a bleeding head and one annoyed barber.

Puss the cat became another casualty about this time. She was never a very friendly animal, mostly aloof and indifferent; except when seeking scraps of food; doling out any acts of affection in very small doses. Mammy never allowed Puss to stay inside the house during the night; summer or winter, the last person going to bed at night, was expected to put the cat out. She strongly believed that cats were creatures of the night, and that they did their necessary hunting then, keeping the area clear of vermin. The only drawback to this was that when she was in season, she attracted all the tomcats for miles around; with their wailing mating calls from base to baritone and up to tenor; producing a chorus that jarred the nerves and shattered the ears of our long-suffering neighbours.

So we were more than a little surprised, when one night we discovered that Mammy had put down some old newspapers and rags under the kitchen sink, and allowed Puss to remain inside the house. She was even given a saucer of milk, which was a rare luxury. "The cat's not very well", she said, "she's sick, she needs rest so leave her in peace".

Two days later we still had Puss the cat, but now four kittens as well. They were scrawny little things, all huddled together in the curve of their mother's body. We were all very excited at the prospect of having four kittens to play with, but Mammy said that we could not keep them. "Ask your school friends if they want a kitten", she said, but then warned, "you make sure that they ask their mothers first mind, and they'd better be quick for they won't be here for long".

I told Dinky about to the kittens, and he said he would love to have one, and so did most of the children in my class. When I got home I told Mammy that a lot of the children wanted a kitten, but I asked her could we keep just one for ourselves. She did not reply to this, she just said, "Well, if they really want a kitten, then their mothers must come with them to collect it".

Maggie, Molly, and Daniel, seemed to lose interest quickly, after the initial surprise of the kittens arrival and refused to discuss them with me. So I sought out Harry who was mucking about on the tip, he was throwing lumps of hard clinker at an overhang trying to create an avalanche. As usual he ignored me as I approached and stood near him, but then he stopped his throwing when I mentioned the kittens, and told him of all the children who wanted one. But I was not prepared for his reply, and he shocked me when he said. "They won't 'ave the kittens mun, their mothers won't let them 'ave one, best thing to do is drown 'em".

He waited for his words to sink in, then laughed as the look of horror crossed my face. "That's what they all do mun", he said, revelling now in my torment. "They put 'em in a sack with a stone", he laughed out loud again prolonging my agony, and as he ran off he shouted, "then they chuck 'em into the canal".

Harry, I knew, would say anything to make me feel bad, and I did not believe him, but the thought of the kittens ending up at the bottom of the dirty old canal made me feel sick. I ran home to Mammy, and told her just what he had said seeking reassurance that this would not happen.

"No, no, bach", she said soothingly, putting her hand on my shoulder, "I promise you that they won't go into the canal". Then changing the subject, too quickly for my liking, she said, "now bach I want you to run down to the shops and get me some potatoes".

She delved into her bag and produced a sixpenny bit, and hurrying me said, "Get the bag, and go now quickly before it gets too dark".

At school the following day, Dinky said that he was sorry; but his mother said no, he could not have a kitten, and most of the other children did not want to talk about them. Rosie O'Neill still seemed quite hopeful, saying her mother was thinking about it, but Rosie Smith who I was pinning my hopes on most after Dinky, was once more absent.

When I got home at dinnertime I told Mammy that Dinky was sorry, but his mother said no. Rosie O'Neill's mother was still thinking about having a kitten, and I was sure that Rosie Smith would still want one too. She was busy with the frying pan over the fire, cooking scallops, big rounds of potatoes fried in deep fat. Her only reply was, "Well we'll see, we'll see, now quick bach go next door, Mrs Evans wants you to run down to the shops. I'll keep your dinner warm for you".

I got three halfpence for running the message, and Mrs Evans said she wanted me again that afternoon after school.

Between Mammy and Mrs Evans I was kept running errands until well after dark, and exhausted I thankfully climbed into bed that night; but not before Mammy informed me that Mr Evans was kindly taking the kittens down to the Copper Works; where they were needed to catch all the mice. At the time I accepted this without question, as I had seen many cats prowling around the works and the banks of the canal that was near it. "So you see bach, they haven't gone into that dirty old canal, so don't you listen to Harry now". So I refused to listen to

Harry, and did not believe him when he said, "You are stupid mun, Mammy drowned the kittens in a bucket out the back, and Mr Evans buried 'em in 'is garden".

Gradually I accepted the harsh realities of life, and did not make a fuss or ask questions the next and subsequent times that Puss the cat had kittens. Having pets doctored or spayed in those days was for well-off people only. It was a common occurrence I discovered, as I got older, that if we saw a sack at the bottom of the canal, the river, or floating in the docks, you could bet your last penny that it contained unwanted kittens or puppies.

Winter seemed to come early that year, leading up to an extremely bleak and miserable festive season. There were no sweets or chocolates at Christmas, nor oranges; but we did have some apples and nuts. Coal, although not rationed, was scarce, or at least in our house; the most likely reason could have been a scarcity of cash, and we turned once more to the abundant resources of the tip; scavenging half burnt lumps of coal and coke from amongst the ash and cinders, as well as gathering firewood.

It was on one such expedition to the tip, one late cold and grey Saturday afternoon just before Christmas that Harry and I, were joined by Rosie O'Neill's brother Billy, or Jock as he now insisted on being called. Harry was intrigued by this lanky surly newcomer, and had persuaded him to come with us. I do not think that it was a question of need on his part, or his family, to scavenge, as was our lot, as they seemed to want for nothing. They lived in a house similar to ours, but overlooking the park, which signalled a certain degree of affluence

One of the most productive areas for scavenging, was to the left of the old white cottage and corrugated iron garages or sheds; where the Jones Brothers or their predecessors had cut a swathe on the edge of the tip revealing some of the older waste of ash and clinker. Harry began in earnest; he was out to impress his newfound friend; demonstrating his expertise in locating just the right sort of fuel we were after. He would select a good-sized lump of coal, and holding it up before him like a jeweller inspecting a rare and precious diamond he would say. "See Jock, this is what we are looking for mun, find some like 'is and put 'em in the sack".

The boy was not impressed, he just grunted and scuffed away at the ash in front of him with his shoe. Harry and I continued digging away and gradually the sack was beginning to fill up. We had learned from past and painful experience; that we could just about manage to carry the sack and its contents, when it was about half full. With two of us picking, it would normally take us about an hour to get this amount and finish. Jock I could see had no intention of helping; he just slouched around with his hands in his pockets, and eventually wandered off in the direction of the old cottage and the sheds. Harry had not given up all hope of getting some work out the boy and shouted after him. "See if 'u can find some sticks mun, we need some firewood as well".

He did not reply or even look back, and I thought then that we had seen the last of him for the day. Oh how I wished that that had been the case.

The sack was just about half full, getting to the point when we were thinking about finishing, when Billy McNeill returned. He was carrying two pieces of wood which he handed to Harry, "Are these any good", he said.

They were not the normal bits of wood that we gathered from the tip, half rotten and weathered with age, but pieces of planking, painted black. "Yes mun, Harry replied, "these are great mun, where did 'u get 'em from".

The boy did not answer, he just turned and walked back in the direction of the garages from where he had just come. Harry shouted after him, "ang on mun Billy, wait for us mun".

Billy stopped walking, turned and looked back at us but did not say or do anything; but to Harry this meant that he was prepared to wait for us, at least for a while. "Come on mun 'andel", he ordered, "grab 'old of the sack".

I did as I was told and grabbed the neck of the sack, he got hold of the other end, and we scuttled off after him.

It soon became clear, just where Billy had got the bits of wood from. There was a row of five garages, constructed mainly of corrugated iron, on a wooden frame. The middle one was the only garage to have a small fixed window. The glass for this was framed inside some wooden planks the type used for flooring, which had been bolted on to the corrugated iron. It was this planking, which Billy had attacked; splitting away the two pieces that he had given to Harry, which were now inside the sack. Without thinking, and not to be outdone by his newfound friend, Harry attacked the wooden frame, but try as he may he failed to dislodge anything greater than small splinters. Billy McNeil just stood by and watched, his face as expressionless as ever; but I am sure inside he was gloating, as I admit I was, by Harry's pitiful attempt to emulate him. Finally frustrated by his lack of success; I was not surprised when his anger spilled over as he cried out. "Right stand back, I'll get the cowin' thing", and picking up a hard lump of clinker threw it at the window smashing it into small pieces.

The noise of the glass being shattered sounded like a thunderclap, probably emphasised and enhanced by the impact on the empty hollow garage.

Harry I could see by venting his outrage on the window,

now felt a lot better; but the cool and calculating manner that I associated with Billy McNeil had vanished, and in its place there was now a very scared and frightened little boy. For a second he was transfixed to the ground where he stood, his eyes wide and mouth agape, shocked by the sudden savagery of Harry's action. He was literary dumbstruck as he sucked in a great gulp of air, turned on his heel and fled without looking back, across the road, heading for the safety and shelter of his home. Without any mercy Harry yelled after him, "Run rabbit run, come back by yer mun you cowin' sissy".

Unlike Billy McNeil at that time I was not particularly worried about the consequences, and certainly not shocked by what Harry had done. Although the garage was not far from our house, I did not believe then that Mammy would find out, and that was my only concern.

But Mammy did find out, from the two policemen who called at our house later on that evening. One of our neighbours had seen what had happened that afternoon, and had reported the matter to the central police station in Swansea. Mammy was not dealing with Sergeant Clifton now, who would have done his utmost to resolve the matter and keep it unofficial; but would now be subject to the full rigour and might of the law. We had to attend the Central Police station the following day, along with Billy McNeil and his mother. It was a problem that we all could do without at any time of the year, but not now particularly just days before Christmas.

Harry and I got the inevitable good hiding from Mammy that night, and I cried myself to sleep, not from the effects of the physical chastisement; but from the shame I felt that I had brought on Mammy and our family. Everyone would find out about the police officers' visit to the house, our neighbours, schoolteachers, the vicar, all of the very people Mammy had set out to impress in our new neighbourhood.

The following day, fitted out in the best attire that the family could manage; I was dressed in Harry's navy-blue jacket and trousers, which was still a bit large for me, and similarly Harry had on Daniel's best suit. These were the clothes that they first wore at my father's funeral, and had been kept since as their Sunday best. We caught the number 73 bus to High-Street Station, and then walked from there to the police station, which was situated in Orchard Street. Billy McNeil and his mother were already there. Mammy and Mrs McNeill were totally ignorant of the law, but as I recall there was no one present to represent them. Harry and Billy were charged with criminal damage to the garage window, and would have to appear before a juvenile court at a date to be fixed after Christmas. The thought of this hanging over us throughout the festive season; cast an even darker cloud on what was already proving to be the most gloomy and dismal Christmas of our lives. The only bright spot of the day as far as Mammy and I were concerned, was that I was below the age of criminal responsibility, and that I would not be charged.

Apart from having no sweets, chocolates, or oranges in our Christmas stockings that year, the greatest disappointment of all and what seemed to sum up the whole wretched time, was that Mammy failed to get a chicken for Christmas dinner. If you missed out then it was an extremely long time, an eternity; to wait until next year for the pleasure on Christmas morning of the house filling with the aroma of the fowl with bread and thyme stuffing roasting in the oven, and finally tasting the succulent white meat. Alas it was not to be that year, we had to make do with what Mammy called a furry chicken instead, a rabbit.

With the coming of the New Year, things did not get any better. News had reached the school of our misdemeanour involving the police. Harry was hauled before the boys school headmaster, and given a good dressing down regarding the shame he had brought upon the school's reputation, and not least the shame and worry he had brought upon Mammy. I had a similar dressing-down from the Infants headmistress. My worst fear was the other children in my class discovering my guilty secret; for I felt sure that they would all know, or would soon know when Rosie O'Neill and her tongue were let loose in the school playground. Strangely this did not happen, she seemed blissfully unaware of the problem confronting her family and ours, concerning the impending court appearance of her brother and Harry. I did not tell anybody, not even Dinky. No one seemed to know and if they did, they showed no interest in it. I had been fortunate that with the intervening Christmas break, people had other things on their minds, their own lives to lead, with the struggle to meet the needs of the festive season, which was turning out to be pretty grim for most of them.

I seemed to be coming out of this trying period quite well. I had settled back into school easier than I expected, and at the end of the month, on the 30th of January, I had my 7th birthday. As a treat Mammy took me to the Manor Cinema, where we saw an old American war film called The Real Glory and starred Gary Cooper. I cannot remember much about it now, but at the time and for many years after, I considered this to be the greatest film ever made. Some of the things you remember as a child seem out of all context to the life you lead; it was perhaps a brief interlude when I was able to escape from the pressures of life and anxiety and the inter reaction with other people. It was probably that evening at the cinema, that the care and heavy burden was lifted briefly from Mammy, allowing her temporarily to forget her struggles and hardships for a few hours and to smile.

But the cruel winter had not finished with us yet. During the whole of 1942 we had only received just the one air raid in July, and it looked increasingly likely that Hitler and the Nazis had forgotten all about us, and our town of Swansea. But then almost two years from the date when our house was bombed and my father killed; the Luftwaffe returned with a vengeance for one last spiteful attack on 16th February 1943. It was a sharp reminder to us that the war was still a physical reality, that people were being killed all over the world, and we were still part of it with a long way to go yet. The raid was particularly savage and many high-explosive bombs were dropped, resulting in a severe loss of life with over thirty people killed and many more injured.

Ironically it was just after this, the last raid on the town; that the council decided to erect in the front room or parlour of our house, a super-duper brand-new indoor air raid shelter. It consisted of a heavy steel plate; that was bolted onto the wall of the room on two sides at a height of about three feet, with a strong metal grille at the front, forming what was really a gigantic cage. I cannot remember the exact dimensions, but it covered approximately half of the room. For many months after that last air raid; although we did not know it was the final raid at that time, we were expecting the German's bombing campaign against us to resume once more in earnest; the five of us boys slept inside this contraption to be joined by Mammy and my two sisters in the event of the air-raid warning sirens being sounded. We could all just about manage to squeeze in like sardines in a tin, if we lay head to toe; and Mammy holding Eddie while Maggie held Walter. If we had had a direct hit, underneath that very thick steel plate; I should think we would have been flattened like pancakes, and all I can think of now is thank God it was never put to the test.

Then came the day that we had all been dreading, when Mammy received an official summons from the Juvenile Court that she was to attend with Harry; so that judgment might be determined for the offence of wilful damage to property. She had not made contact with Mrs McNeill since that day at the Central Police Station, but thought it would be wise now to speak to her if only for mutual support. From Mammy's reaction after visiting her, the response from that lady was somewhat cool to say the least. Perhaps it was only natural that she blamed Harry for the trouble they were in, as it was he who actually smashed the glass; but one thing was agreed; that neither lady would broadcast the issue, to avoid being the subject of any local gossip, and that they would accompany each other and their respective miscreants on the day of the court hearing.

The verdict pronounced upon Harry and Billy McNeil was that their crime would be recorded, with a severe warning that much nastier things would happen to them if they were ever hauled before the court again. There was a much lighter atmosphere at home that evening, when Mammy and Harry returned. The boys had got off lightly, as there had been talk and fears by Mrs McNeil and Mammy of Probation or even Borstal.

Rosie O'Neill failed to turn up for school the next day, and I mentioned this to Mammy, who casually responded by saying that Mrs McNeil had decided to leave the Hafod and was returning to London. I found this to be rather curious and wondered if it had anything to do with the recent problem involving the police. But question her as I did for a suitable answer, Mammy pleaded ignorance as to why the family had departed so quickly, and that it was "none of our business".

Once again it was only many years later when I was able to understand how complex life can be, that Mammy explained the reason for their sudden departure. It also cleared up the mystery and confusion regarding the family's name.

That day after the court hearing, and greatly relieved by the verdict; Mrs McNeil had confided in Mammy on their journey home. The family name was really O'Neil, and she and her husband had left their native Ireland before the war, as did many of their countrymen to seek work in England. Tragically, Mr O'Neill who had found work in the docks in London had been killed in an accident, and instead of returning to Ireland, she decided to stay in England where both of their children had been born. She had settled there, and had made friends in that part of London where they lived. It was a struggle bringing up the two children on her own; but her husband's employers had accepted liability for his death, and the loss she had suffered was made more bearable after she was paid an adequate sum in workmen's compensation. So she thought that with time, she and her children would have a good future.

But then the war started, and the bombs began to fall on London, and people's tolerance and goodwill were put to the test. Hate and prejudice breed and manifest themselves in these foul conditions. Rightly or wrongly, Ireland had not entered the war on the side of Great Britain, and some of the native Londoners turned on those that they thought were alien or foreigners. Mrs O'Neill had become the target for much of this hatred, and finally driven by despair, had left the capital city and decided to move to where she thought would be a more friendly environment, in Wales. She also decided to change the family name from O'Neil to McNeill, and pretend that they were Scottish. This had imposed a terrible strain on her, but more so on her son Billy, who had done his utmost to keep up the pretence. But, the trouble with the police was the final straw. She realised now that the burden she had placed on herself and her children was too great, and she had decided to return to her native land.

The last thing to happen, as that dreadful winter came to an end, and was for me the most tragic event of all, was the death of little Rosie Smith. The poor child never returned to school after the Christmas holiday, having been struck down once more with one of her recurring ailments; but this time sadly she never recovered. The headmistress announced her death during morning assembly, and the Lord's Prayer that day was dedicated to her. I did not feel any sense of loss at that time, although I knew that perhaps I should have. I am aware now, after shedding the shell that I developed as a child for protection and self-preservation; that Rosie valued my friendship, and for those brief moments that she was in my company I brought some joy into her wretched life.

## CHAPTER 19

# GROWING UP

By the early summer of 1943 all the trauma and woe of the previous winter was far behind us, and there was only one topic of conversation now, the phrase on everyone's lips was, "the Yanks are coming". We had already seen the gigantic Flying Fortresses passing overhead at the end of their Atlantic crossing, en route to their bases in the South and East of England. But now all the local news and gossip was that a large number of American troops were coming to Swansea, and they were already preparing sites on the outskirts of the town as bases. This year of 1943 was going to be a big year for the country, when at last the progress of the war was going to turn in our favour. It was also a big year for our family, as there were many changes about to take place.

Walter was five years old now, and it was time to take his place in the Infants School. He should have started in January, the first week after the Christmas holidays. But it had been a miserable winter with food and fuel shortages, and in those circumstances it is always the weak and sickly who suffer most. Without a doubt Walter certainly came into this category. So it came as no surprise to us that the very thought of starting school, was not at all welcomed by him, and he had already decided well in advance that he would have no truck with it. As I have already mentioned he had come close to death through sickness on at least two previous occasions. My earliest recollections of him, if he was not being nursed by Mammy or more often Maggie; then he would be wrapped in a blanket and propped up on the couch, or lying in bed. For all his weakness and poor condition, his tenacity to cling on to life was summed up by constantly reminding us that he was still living, with his remorseless moaning and grizzling.

He was unashamedly picky with his food, and I have seen Mammy nearly driven to despair at times; when she would have to turn around and prepare something different for him, if what the rest of us were having was not suitable to his palate. He seemed to survive on a diet of toast and scallops. The bread was more often than not plentiful and that was not a problem; that, was having to toast it in front of the fire, and finding something to put on it. Butter was his preferred choice, but that was on ration, as was margarine, jam, treacle, and cheese. If none of these were available; then he would have to put up with dripping or lard, then the moaning and the grizzling would be turned up to full throttle; as a reprisal to the family for the shameful treatment being meted out to him. But scallops, was his favourite food, and even then they had to be cooked just right. The potato had to be sliced much thinner for Walter, and fried in a pan of hot fat until they congealed and almost burnt black on one side, before being turned and almost cremated on the other side. Once again the grizzling would cease only if the scallops were cooked to perfection, if that was not achieved then the moaning and grizzling decibels would be commensurate to that level of his satisfaction.

Walter was very much like Harry in appearance, with jet-black hair, sallow skin, and extremely dark brown eyes. They were his most appealing feature, very large and round sad eyes, with long black sweeping eyelashes. He always reminded me of an abandoned baby bird, struggling to stay in the nest, just a nudge away from the precipice and falling to the rocks below. One look into his eyes and you could see deep into his aching and weary soul, the torment of which appeared to justify his incessant complaint of his lot in life. It was this demeanour that cried out to people, "there but for the grace of God go you", this need for pity and sympathy oozing from him; that got him his own way and the attention he needed.

**************************************

I can probably best sum up just how resolute he was in getting his own way, and he was far more successful than even Harry in this, by describing what happened a little later on in life involving the school dinners. It was just after the war when school dinners were introduced, and our family because of our need, qualified for two free meals a day, specifically to go to the youngest children. So, for us, that meant free school dinners every day for Walter and Eddie. For Mammy and our family, where every morsel of food had to be counted and was precious, this was a gift from heaven. The school meals were adequate and palatable, and it pleased Mammy to think that her two youngest children would receive them. She knew that it would be a test of wills with Walter, but she was determined that this was a battle she was going to win. She should have known better.

It was essential that the teaching staff, we were all in the boys' school then, should be aware of the problem concerning Walter; and they were duly put on their guard to ensure that he ate the food put in front of him. Of course he had no intention of doing this, although he did take his place in the queue to be served with his dinner, and sat at the table. But that was as close as he got to the food. I can only assume that those in charge that day, believed that once he had taken his dinner to the table he had accepted the situation and relaxed their vigilance. Within seconds of this he had crept out of the boys' school hall where the dinners were being served, and had bolted out of the main school entrance heading for home, our mother, and his scallops. The same thing happened the following day, and for many days after. The teaching staff, the dinner ladies, and the even some of the older pupils were recruited to help but all to no avail. As soon as they were off guard he would be away. If he was spotted before he had left the school grounds, he would out-fox and outmanoeuvre them by wriggling and squirming out of hands trying to grab him, ducking and diving under tables and chairs; then stealthily melt away in the confusion and pandemonium that ensued.

Walter became a real challenge to the teaching staff and dinner ladies, who now in desperation turned for help to the school's supreme authority; the formidable figure of Mr Joe Morgan the headmaster. He was a mountain of a man, a modern-day Goliath. He was head-and-shoulders above the rest of the staff, a huge rotund man, with a girth to match his height. There was not a man, woman, or child, in the Hafod who failed to have respect for this man. But for all his imposing manner and stature, I can honestly state that we children did not fear him, well for 95 per cent of the time that is. The exception would be when he wielded his 5 ft long cane, meting out justice on unruly or disobedient youths. He was strong and stern, but an honest and fair man, and I never heard anyone complain, even the hardest of schoolyard villains, who felt the full weight of his cane on their backsides. Anyone punished by him, and that includes the writer, knew very well that they deserved the measure of force and severity of the cane that was cut across hands and bottoms.

So this was the measure of the man that was enlisted to tame Walter, the last resort, the saviour brought in to make the boy see sense and realise that school dinners were good for him. There was none of the normal banter and chatter that day, when the cowed figure of Walter, accompanied in close attendance by Mr Joe Morgan, entered the school hall and joined the dinner queue. The headmaster was rarely seen in the hall at dinnertimes, and an eerie hush and quiet descended on children and adults alike. It was unthinkable and unreal to see the great man here amongst them, so close, taking his place in the dinner queue, with one of his huge shovel like hands clamped onto Walter's shoulder.

All the children were well aware of the problems the adults were having, in getting my brother to remain in the school hall and eat his dinner; but never thought that they would go to such extreme measures as this. Walter had become the subject of much merriment and mirth with his antics during dinnertime, and had become quite a celebrity or even a hero with them. Bringing Mr Joe Morgan to deal with this scraggy and puny little boy they thought was grossly unfair; a very big hammer to crack a tiny nut.

They could see and sense a feeling of defeat and futility as the headmaster led Walter, his dinner plate heaped with the day's offerings in his hand, to his place at the table. There was no resistance at all, his head still bowed Walter sat down at the table, picked up the knife and fork in front of him and started to eat. Or at least he gave the impression that he started to eat, the other children acknowledged the defeat on his behalf, and solemnly turned to concentrate on obtaining or eating their own dinners. Mr Joe Morgan had solved the problem, or so he thought, and relaxed slightly the vice like grip on Walter's shoulder, which was just what the boy had anticipated. As he felt the weight and pressure of the head master's hand slacken, he just slid from the bench where he sat, and disappeared under the table to become lost amidst the legs and feet of the other children. There was utter pandemonium and confusion when the children, realising that Walter had tricked the headmaster, broke out in howls of laughter. Shrieking their delight, as he burrowed his way through the morass of legs, until finally he emerged, to a great cheer from the children, and scampered away from the hall down the steps and out through the main doors. Momentarily the headmaster had thoughts of giving chase; but realised that this would be futile with a man of his great bulk, trying to manoeuvre within the close confines of the lines of dinner tables. He was wise enough to realise that his charge was already on his way home to his mother, and that any attempt to recover the situation could only make matters worse. And it was vital, that he retained his authority and dignity in front of the children. So, he just joined them in their merriment; giving great guffaws of laughter almost admitting; he had been outwitted by the little boy.

There was to be no repeated attempt to induce Walter, by fair means or foul, to remain at school for dinner. Everyone agreed, that to continue with coercing him would probably do him more harm than good. He was not an unruly child or bad mannered in any way, and perhaps the best word to sum up his personality would be stubborn, or in Walters's case extremely stubborn. By his sheer tenacity he had defeated the whole might of the school authority, and had got his own way. Mr Joe Morgan withdrew from the contest with 99 per cent of his former respect still intact, and he settled for that. His solution to the problem was put to me the day following the fracas, when he called me into his study, and explained that it would be a pity to waste the free school dinner, and that I should take Walter's place.

Academically, not a great deal was expected of Walter, as through ill-health he had missed so much of his early schooling, and he did not show much interest in his school work anyway. It is therefore to his eternal credit that with time, despite his faltering start to life, he gained success as a qualified engineer, becoming quite robust physically to add to his already strong mental capacity.

*************************************

For Walter to start school and eventually leave the confines of his sickbed and the house to venture out into the world, must have come as something of a wrench for Mammy. She had cared for and nurtured him through long bouts of illness and sickness, and on more than one occasion had brought him back from the brink of death. But with the coming of Easter, at the end of the winter term, Mammy was faced with a very different problem. Maggie was 14 years old, and it was time for her now to leave school and start work. Mammy relied heavily on Maggie to help with the housework, and especially to look after the rest of us children. That could be a major drawback, with Maggie away at work for most of the day. But greatly offsetting this would be the very welcome extra income for the family, generated from her wages.

Starting work at the bottom, having to do all the menial tasks, being a general dogsbody and whipping boy for all and sundry; was the normal job for all new school leavers, and there was no lower life than the most junior member of the staff at the Star Supply Stores. This is where Maggie began her working life one early Monday morning, immediately following the Easter holidays. She would be aspiring to gain a position as a shop assistant, serving at the counter; which although not tremendously well paid, was a respectable job, which she and Mammy would be proud of. Any thoughts the rest of the girls working at the shop, whether shop assistants or the clerical workers had of lording it over Maggie, would be in for a rude awakening indeed. She could hold her own in any company, physically or otherwise. To get a clout around the head from her, or a lashing from her tongue was an experience few people would forget. I cannot remember any girl or boy being a match for her. Anyone daring or foolish enough to take her on would be swept aside with little effort, and normally they would not come back for any more.

I shall always remember the first time I saw her at her place of work, the job she was doing I had seen her do a hundred times at home. With a scrubbing brush, soap, and bucket of water, she was scouring the slabs of marble that most shops seem to have at their entrances in those days.

The fact that Maggie was working there, made no difference to my Monday routine. I still had the job of running there during my dinner hour with the cash to settle the bill for that week's goods. With vim and vigour, these words could not be more appropriate, she was attacking the floor; scrubbing furiously, and I just stood there not knowing if it was in order for me to speak to her or not. She was blocking the entrance to the shop, with soapy water swishing and swirling around, she did not look up but concentrated fully on getting the floor the cleanest it had ever been. Maggie could never do anything or any job by half; it had to be the biggest, the cleanest, and the best, whatever she did. She only acknowledged my presence when she had finished the area she was working on, and had rinsed it clean. Then she looked up at me, and with the same stern expression that was so reminiscent of Mammy said, "Don't just stand there Handel; either come in or go out".

She represented all the authority of Mammy, but somehow her voice lacked the warmth and softness that was so natural to Mammy. "'elo Maggie", I said, jumping over the pristine clean piece of floor she had just worked on, and joined the queue at the counter. Without hesitating she resumed the task before her, and I thought then, Maggie, will not be scrubbing floors for long.

Within a few short months, and as I had thought, she had won her right to a place behind the counter. She was still only 14 years old but looked ever so grown up now, dressed in a white smock and apron that was customary attire for counter staff. She had to endure so much strife and anguish in her young life, which had been particularly unkind to add to all the other problems, in having a younger sister who was considered much prettier and more pleasant than she was. But now a wonderful transformation was taking place, like a butterfly emerging from a cocoon, Maggie was developing into a strikingly attractive young woman. Her previously round girlish face now had length, with a strong jaw-line, straight nose, with high cheekbones, and her large dark-brown eyes were beginning to lose the agitated, sometimes hunted look of her childhood.

It was to be expected and only natural that Maggie and Molly would attract many of the local lads who had designs on them. They would begin to hang around the park or the square, where the older girls and the younger children would indulge in such games as hide and seek, or mob, as we knew it, hopscotch, and rounders. Most of the boys were older than Maggie, 15 and 16 year-olds who had already started work and had money in their pockets. But there was one particular lad who for some reason, had left school but had yet been unable to find a job. He seemed to hang around more than most, being particularly ardent in his endeavours at courtship. Perhaps his mind was more concentrated on the pursuance of love and lust, whereas a little more effort in seeking suitable employment would have stood him a greater chance of gaining Maggie's favours. Anyway for all his hard work and attention, she would have no truck with him. She used to call him "Willy Dodge on the Dole", and make us all laugh; and the only reason I can remember this boy, was because of this nickname she had for him.

In time Maggie did find the right boy, and got married when she was 20. Her mother-in-law who had no daughters of her own treated her like a princess, and was well-off enough to provide her with many of the material things in life, and the time to be attentive to all her other needs. This was in stark contrast to the way she had lived at home with us, Mammy had neither the money nor perhaps even more important the time to spend on her daughters. Maggie had experienced the brutality of my father, and the hardships the family endured much more than the rest of us. Much was expected of her by Mammy to help in running in the family, and in all fairness to her Maggie never stinted in her response. She was always at the front, standing side by side with Mammy, fighting the family's battles and putting everyone else's interests before her own. So I expect that she could be forgiven for allowing herself to be spoilt, indulging in all those pleasures that she had previously been denied, and for a while forgot about the mother who had fought and battled against the odds to keep the family together.

Although not as significant as the events happening in Maggie and Walter's life, but nevertheless a landmark for the family; was Harry joining the church choir, of which Daniel had been a valued member for well over a year now. At first he swore that he would never join, choirboys were sissies and dressed up like girls in their cassocks and surplices. But then he discovered that by attending choir practice on Wednesday evenings, the choirboys had a share of the Church's funds, which could amount to three pence or even more. If the choir was in demand for wedding ceremonies, then the reward could be even higher. For one particular wedding, Daniel had received the princely sum of one shilling, which no doubt gave food for thought to Harry. It came as no great surprise therefore to Daniel and my sisters, that Harry suddenly overcame all his reluctance to join the choir. Mammy probably saw it in a better light, always hoping but mostly praying, that Harry would become a better person as he got older and came under the influence of the vicar and the good people at the church.

When I first discovered that he was seriously thinking of joining the choir I was filled with fear and dread, knowing that God was a witness to the awful secret that I shared with Harry. I felt certain that he would be struck down dead if he even attempted to don the surplus and cassock, as God would never allow this to happen. Harry, had committed the most heinous of crimes, he had stolen money. This in itself was bad enough, as he had broken one of the Ten Commandments, but it was from who and where he had stolen the money, that was bothering me.

Unlike today when most churches lock their doors, and barricade their windows, the door on our local church was always open. It was just unthinkable that anyone would enter a Church, other than to seek the solace and comfort, which was offered there. I think most people had a genuine fear that to commit a crime, or wrongdoing in a sacred place, would bring terrible reprobation on the perpetrator. But Harry had no such feelings or fear.

I cannot remember the time or day when the theft took place, but I know I was with Harry in the park and we had wandered off up to the church. It was not a school day, so it must have been Saturday or even Sunday, after Sunday school. It was a warm sunny day I do remember, and we stood in the shade of the church outside the great oak doors, which was the main entrance. I was already beginning to feel very uneasy, as we should not have been in the Church grounds at all; I thought that Harry was as usual just being his belligerent self, being somewhere where he should not be, and dragging me along with him. He was showing his daring and devil-may-care attitude, and seemed to take a sadistic pleasure in seeing me squirm. Pushing things and people to the limit was Harry's speciality; but I could hardly believe my eyes when he leaned against the heavy door and pushing this open, squeezed half through. I should have run for home then; but I could feel his eyes transfixed on me threatening me to hold my ground. "Come on 'andel", he ordered, "you come on inside".

I hesitated at first but knew that it would be hopeless to object, and meekly followed him as he opened the door wider and we both slipped inside. The fear and dread already building up inside me became too much to bear, and I realised then that I was more fearful of God than I was of Harry. I pulled at the heavy door, I wanted to get out of the Church and run away, but strain as I did I failed to open it.

Being trapped inside the church was bad enough, but I was horror-struck as I turned around, and watched Harry as he broke open and rifled the contents of a small wooden charity box, that was on a table near the font. With the loot secure in his grubby little hand, he was soon back alongside me, and together we managed to prise open the heavy oak door and left the church. All he got for his troubles was 4d, a brass threepenny bit that he kept for himself, and one penny, which he insisted that I take; thus ensuring that I became his accomplice. But the crime that he had committed had far greater implications for me, when I discovered that the charity box was for the Life Boat. For years after, I suffered terrible feelings of guilt, especially when we sung the hymn "For those in peril on the sea"; when I had visions of sailors drowning, and no lifeboat there to save them.

## CHAPTER 20

# THE YANKS ARRIVE

It had to happen eventually; like Columbus setting off to discover a new route to the East Indies; one bright summer's we day finally encircled the Great Tip. The Expeditionary party consisted of my trusty lieutenant Dinky Miles, Brammer Davies, Tommy Thomas and me. We had discovered a new and more favourable route to that part of the tip known to us as the caves. These giant slabs or lumps of clinker, which I had come close to for the first time two years before when collecting firewood with Daniel; stretched from the taboo area near the Devil's Inn up-to and beyond the railway signal box. This new route which we had discovered was far safer, as we did not have to cross the railway line and property, and thereby avoiding an unwanted encounter with the dreaded Chinky. After that first reconnaissance we also found it to be a lot easier and quicker; and as with most great discoveries, we came upon this new path, which enabled us to complete the encirclement, out of the blue, or just plain lucky.

Now that I was seven years old and had proved to Mammy that I could be trusted to act responsibly; I was allowed to roam the immediate vicinity on my own, even to go foraging for firewood without Daniel or Harry. On this particular day, one Saturday in mid-July, we were risking life and limb by tobogganing down the lower part of the tip, below the path or swathe that had been cut into it by the Jones Brothers. We were using an old piece of corrugated iron, which was curved at one end, as the toboggan, and was probably part of a dismantled Anderson shelter. Over the years the Tip had become a depository for many unwanted or discarded household items, which in turn were scavenged by others who could find a need or some use for this. It could be described I suppose, as a bit messy and untidy primitive form of recycling. We had seen the older boys having great fun sliding down from much greater heights on their improvised sleds, and today we were trying to emulate them, but wisely started off on the lower more gentle slopes.

Acquiring the knack of handling the unruly and treacherous corrugated iron sled, with two small boys astride it, came at a price, particularly if we encountered a large, solid lump of clinker lying in wait for us just below the surface of the loose ash and cinder. Then we would be tossed off into the air like cowboys from bucking broncos, to be battered and bruised on hitting the rough surface. But we persevered and gradually managed to assert our authority and gain a modicum of control over the beast, and with our growing confidence and increased daring, so did the height from which we descended. To gain the increase in height meant that we had to move away from the road and into the higher slopes of the tip, which was uncharted territory for the four of us. We spent the next hour or so; becoming more and more engrossed in dragging the piece of metal up to a suitable launching site, then whooping with the thrill and delight of speeding:

sometimes almost flying down to the bottom again; inwardly praying that the landing would be a soft one.

We were getting closer to the railway line, where the ash and cinder content of the tip mixed with that of the soil. It was overgrown with dense scrub, which was one of the reasons why we had not penetrated into this area before. Now at the height of the summer; we could see the great blanket of green foliage massed around the lower perimeter of the tip with the dominant plant growing there being the dreaded Japanese Knotweed. This alien plant was I believe introduced into this country, and deliberately grown alongside the railway lines, to act as an agent in binding the track's foundations into the ground. It is a bamboo-like grass with a rapid growth rate and can reach heights of ten to fifteen feet, the stalks or poles are reddish green in colour; in fact, the same colouring as rhubarb. Because it was an alien plant and becoming a nuisance spreading out of control, it was known to all especially us children, as German rhubarb, as indeed was anything that was strange, artificial, or nasty. For instance woodlice were known as German Beetles, pom or dehydrated potato was German potato, and frogspawn was German jelly. It seems ironic that the land either side of the railway lines was completely free of the German rhubarb, no doubt kept in check by the railway company's maintenance crews, but allowed to run rampant elsewhere.

Most of the railway property was protected by eight ft high chain-link fencing, particularly near roads, paths, and rights of way. But at this particular part, beyond the area covered by the German rhubarb, there was just a line of wooden posts with wire strands forming a fence about four feet high. The Great Western Railway, the company who owned and operated the railways in our area, probably believed that this was all that was necessary at this particular spot. They believed wrongly as it happened, that this part of their property was impenetrable to wayward little boys.

So it was whilst resting and recovering from the joys, aches and pains, bumps and bruises, from our improvised tobogganing that we viewed the layout now before us. "Look 'andy mun, there's the railway", shouted Dinky. "We can get to the railway from by yer mun".

The railways always held a certain attraction to us; as they have to boys and men for generations, and we felt pleased and proud that we had discovered this new route, especially Dinky; but to me the greatest prize was the access now open to the caves. I had listened to Harry and some of the older boys telling stories of their journeys to the caves, which seemed to be a mysterious, frightening, and fascinating place. But for all its foreboding I knew that it was a chance that we could not pass up, the challenge and sense of adventure within us, would overcome our fear. But before that there was still one obstacle that we had yet to overcome, and that was to fight our way through the maze of German rhubarb and other scrub that blocked our way.

I knew that the final decision would be left to me, and that Dinky would follow without question, but I was not quite so sure of the other two. Brammer Davies was a sparky little lad not much bigger than Dinky, who lived next door but one to him; and everything that was big, funny, wonderful, or just good; he would describe as a Brammer, hence his nickname. He had most likely picked up this word from someone in his family, I had heard other people use it; but with Brammer Davies the word had almost become an addiction. Like Dinky he was an only child and lived in a house that seemed full of women, but that was not unusual in those times when most of the men were away fighting the war. Tommy Thomas was entirely the opposite, and like me was from a large family. He was a big lump of a lad, easy-going and always had a big open smile on his face, and was generally happy to let others take the lead. But unlike Dinky and me they were not frequent visitors to the tip, and although they appeared to have fun and helped in dragging the corrugated iron up the sides of the Tip earlier, they refused to ride it down again leaving that bit to Dinky and me.

If we kept to the higher slopes we could avoid having to cut our way through the maze of German rhubarb, and get to the caves that way. But that meant negotiating some rather dangerous looking overhangs and precipices, where my instinct and common sense told me, that I had to steer clear of these. Anyway it was going to be far more fun, now that there were four of us, to battle our way through the overgrown jungle that lay before us. So to give my troops courage I charged down the Tip shouting, "Follow me, we're going to find the Lost World", intermittently beating my chest and yelling Red Indian war cries, like a cross between Tarzan and Geronimo.

The others were soon close on my heels, Dinky and Brammer venting blood-curdling screams, and rib tickling-laughs coming from Tommy.

Mentioning the words "Lost World" I knew was inspirational, it fired the imaginations of my three companions, as it did mine; Sir Arthur Conan Doyle's wonderful story, of the trek through the South American jungle to find the Lost World, was being broadcast as a serial by the BBC for the past month. We were not fortunate enough to have a wireless in the Swain house-hold, but they had one in Dinky's house, and every Wednesday evening at 6.45 I was allowed to join him and listen in. The wireless provided a new and wonderful form of entertainment, and everyone who owned a set or had access to one would have been aware of the "Lost World". The talk in school the following day would be all about the previous night's episode, and the children would re-enact the story so far over and over again to keep them going until the next week. The four principal characters in the story are professor George Edward Challenger, Ed Malone a young reporter, Lord John Roxton the great white hunter, and the niggardly pessimistic Professor Summerlee.

Excited and exhilarated, we completed our descent of the tip and now standing before us was the densely packed wall of German rhubarb. We needed weapons, substitute machetes; with which to clear a path through the Brazilian jungle that the German rhubarb had now become. At the edge, the plant growth was small, averaging two or three feet in height, but the stalks got gradually bigger and thicker towards the centre. Physically Japanese Knotweed is rather fragile, and we could if we had wished to, kicked our way through using our hobnail boots; but that would be taking the fun out of it. We wished to emulate our heroes and hack our way through. After a quick search along the edges of the Tip and the undergrowth, we soon had a useful array of armaments. Dinky found an old rusted metal railing spike which after bending it couple of times broke in two, we shared this and as the expedition's leader I had the sharp end, Brammer found an old piece of wire cable, and Tommy an old workman's boot.

So now suitably armed, we were ready to begin our journey into the unknown. But before that, we had to be redefined and transformed into the characters in the story. "Right boys", I said in as a deliberate and sonorous tone as I could muster, trying to emulate the original, "I'm going to be Professor George Edward Challenger". Almost spelling out the words.

The others could sense that things were now getting serious, and quickly got into the mood of the game. Standing still with their weapons at the ready, they waited eagerly for my next command. "You", I said, pointing my finger into Dinky's chest, "are now Ed Malone".

I could see that this pleased him, as I knew he fancied himself as the dashing young reporter. Next was Brammer, and I appointed him as the great white hunter Lord John Roxton, and his face lit up as he said, "Great 'andy mun, u're a Brammer".

That only left Tommy who had no other option open to him, but to be that miserable and pessimistic Professor Summerlee. The mere mention of his name usually brought boos and scowls from most children so I just quickly said, "and you be the other professor, right Tommy".

Immediately his normal radiant and smiling features changed to a downcast expression of gloom, his arms went limp, and his body sagged and he gave a mock cry, "Heh! Heh! I'm the grumpy one".

He stood like that for all of two seconds, then burst out laughing and stamping about waving the old workman's boot in the air and kept repeating, "I'm the grumpy Professor, I'm the grumpy Professor".

I gathered from his reaction that Tommy was not at all concerned at getting to be the one man in the story that we all disliked, or if he did he certainly did not show it.

In high spirits now, we were ready to tackle the unknown jungle and the perils hidden within it. I led the way wielding the rusty piece of railing, slashing the stalks to waist-high; with Dinky on one side of me and Brammer on the other, and Tommy fetching up the rear completing the job by stamping and kicking down the remaining stumps. Imagining as we penetrated deeper into the maze of growth, that we were in the Brazilian jungle; but we had not bargained for what turned out to be closer to the real thing. What we could not see from the outside was that the ground covered by the German rhubarb, was in a small depression, the centre of which had become waterlogged. The deeper we went in the ground became damp and slippery, then soggy, and our boots began to stick in the glutinous peaty mud. At first all this added to the fun and excitement of our adventure, but things then began to turn nasty, as we began to encounter much stiffer opposition, in the shape of scrub willow and hawthorn. Tackling these with our improvised weapons was of little or no use at all. We avoided them where possible, and tried to continue by hacking a route through where we could find the more fragile German rhubarb. But this was towering over us now reaching heights of six to eight feet, which meant that we could not see where we would going. We were getting muddy, scratched, and extremely frustrated now; in our entanglement with the scrub hawthorn, and we began to yell and shout at each other as panic set in. All the grand and romantic thoughts of cutting our way through the Brazilian jungle, and discovering the Lost World were gone.

"Cowin' 'ell mun 'andy", Brammer screamed out, "where're 'u taking us".

He had stopped wielding his rusty piece of cable and stood motionless, his arms hanging loosely. I mused at the transformation of this figure now standing before me. In a matter of minutes he had changed from a reasonably tidy, clean, and spunky little lad, to a mud-splattered, badly scratched, frightened little waif. Then Dinky chipped in, "Come on mun 'andy, get us out of yer".

If anything he looked worse than Brammer, as like me

he was not too clean and tidy to begin with; after our antics of sliding down the tip earlier on. I was their leader and got them into this situation, and now they were looking to me to get them out of it. I was at a complete loss what to do next, so I just shouted back at them, "shuddup mun, an' let me think by yer a minute". Undoubtedly the worst sight of our lost battered and bruised little group, was Tommy Thomas; he was absolutely covered in the putrid cloying mud, with bits of twigs and leaves stuck all over him. Being taller and much heavier than the rest of us, he had found it difficult to keep on his feet, and had spent most of his time picking himself up from the churned up muddy ground as he followed in our wake.

Incredibly he was still smiling, as he said, "Let me 'ave a turn with the iron spike 'andy".

We were now deep inside the towering stalks of the German rhubarb, which the light summer breeze could not penetrate. The air was still, and the flies and mosquitoes angry with us for invading their territory, were gathering in ever growing numbers circling the air above and around us; then suddenly there was a blast from the siren of the twopenny train, the little diesel passenger carriage that ran regularly between Swansea and Llanelli. It probably got its nickname because at one time that was the fare for a single journey. The blast of the siren seemed to reverberate through the stands of German rhubarb, and shake the muddy ground beneath our feet. The panic that was already building up within us, suddenly exploded with the sound of the siren, into a frightening hysteria. The broad grin on Tommy Thomas's face changed in an instant, as he became gripped with fear. He snatched the iron spike from my hand and charged past me, slashing away at the vegetation, his bulky form clearing a path as he ploughed through, with me Brammer and Dinky close on his heels.

Unlike the previous attempts to extricate ourselves from the maze, which ended up with us going around in circles, Tommy's dash for freedom worked. He bolted like an arrow in a straight line, and we were soon clear of the jungle, and out in the open again. The additional bruises and scratches we got as we charged our way through, were a small price to pay to break out from the tangled mess we were in. We found ourselves in a clearing of a reasonably flat strip of land of about five yards wide, between the tip and the railway fence. The ground was strewn with ash and lumps of clinker that had rolled off the tip; but in the main was covered with clumps of long spiky couch grass. In the distance about 30 or 40 yards away we could see the signal box, and the start of the caves, where the line curved sharply to the right forming the Swansea loop. Exhausted but very much relieved, we each threw ourselves on to the nearest clump of grass, out of breath and panting; but still trying to laugh at the sight of Tommy Thomas his legs and arms flailing as he tore and hacked his way through the scrub and German rhubarb.

Brammer was the first to recover his breath and over-come his fear-driven laughter, as he said, "Did 'u see Tommy mun, he was like a mad bull", his words aptly describing Tommy's charge.

We all began laughing again, more relaxed now as we gradually overcame our panic and fear.

"He was better than a mad bull", I said. I was searching for the words trying to outdo Brammer and regain my leadership, which momentarily I had lost to Tommy, who had albeit unwittingly, rescued us. I knew that I had to be really daring in my description, "No mun", I said "he was like a mad elephant with a red 'ot poker up his bum".

We all shrieked with laughter, with Tommy laughing longer and louder than the rest of us. It was good for me that he was such a good-natured boy, for if he was aggressive or a bully he could have easily made mincemeat, out of me, Dinky, and Brammer put together. His natural broad smile was back on his face, as he handed me the iron spike, "Yer Andy, 'u better 'ave this", he said, "I'm too dangerous with it".

So we had made it, we had overcome the perils of the jungle and had discovered the lost world, this part of the tip that had previously been beyond our reach, was now part of our domain. The way before us led to the caves, with all their hidden treasures and mystery waiting to be explored and conquered. We did not give a thought then to the obvious, that having fought and negotiated our way through the German rhubarb and the swamp, we would have to return the same way, or find an alternative route if possible. "What do 'u think we'll find 'andy", Dinky asked.

I could only repeat what I had heard from Harry, "There's money 'idden there mun, and gold and jewellery, that's what our 'arry says". "Did he find some", asked Brammer, "maybe we'll find some sweets", he added. He was right about the sweets, but he would not find them at the caves.

They were wide-eyed again, and ready for the adventure that lay ahead, the earlier trials and hardships of the afternoon now completely banished from their bright minds. But the caves and their treasures would have to wait for another day, as Dinky who always seemed to hear and see things long before anyone else, called out, "Listen 'andy, listen mun, there's a train comin'".

Sure enough within a couple of seconds, we could hear the distinct sound of the steam railway engine chuffing and puffing, pulling its heavy load as it approached us. At first we thought that it must be a goods train pulling wagons of coal, steel, or tinplate, for they travelled normally at a slower pace. Passenger-carrying trains usually travelled at much higher speeds. We were surprised therefore when it came into view, to discover that it was in fact pulling passenger carriages. The railway line split here near the signal box, with the through traffic going East to Cardiff and London bearing left, and traffic to Swansea to the right. Slow-moving traffic at this point, on the Swansea line, would generally be goods trains carrying fruit and vegetables, or livestock to Hafod sidings.

It was late afternoon now but the mid-July sun was still fiercely beating down, its harsh glare reflecting sharply on the roofs and windows of the carriages. All the vents on the doors and windows were open, and as the train drew closer to where we were now standing by the wire fence; we could hear in the background behind the sound of the steam engine and the clatter of the carriage wheels, the distinct mass sound of great numbers of people. Then out of the jumble came the individual sounds of people talking and shouting; and music, swing and jazz music coming from radios or gramophones. We had never seen or heard a passenger train like this before, and we were in for a great surprise, and excitement; not only for this afternoon but for a long time to come. We were told that they were coming and coming soon, but the shock to our culture and way of life were going to be dramatically altered from now on, certainly until the war ended. The Yanks had arrived.

The steam engine came on, slowly grinding its way past us groaning under the tremendous weight of carriages and people it was pulling. Then as it drew level with the signal box, already on the Swansea track, it let out a great jet of steam, gasped, and shuddered to a halt. The sudden end to the train's movement seemed to jolt the soldiers from what ever preoccupied them, and almost in unison those on our side of the track turned and looked out of the windows. I felt a thousand eyes looking at me, warm and friendly eyes from our American cousins, for they were our allies and we were no longer on our own. I could only guess that they had docked at one of the West Wales ports; and from the track that they were now on I knew that their destination was Swansea. At first, I do not believe that they were quite sure just what they were looking at, four mucky, scruffy little urchins, standing behind the railway fence in amongst the long tussocks of couch grass, with the grim wasteland of the tip behind us. They could not be blamed for thinking, that the four small creatures that were wide-eyed and staring back at them, were not human at all, but some of the local fauna that lived amongst the great rocks of clinker in the background. Any doubts that they had about which species we belonged to, were soon dispelled as Brammer broke the momentary silence that had gripped both us and the soldiers when he shouted, "Are you Yankees mun".

His accent and the "mun" at the end of his sentence must have thrown them, as we were met by a row of puzzled looks and faces. Then one voice responded, its owner being a little sharper than the rest, "Hell man, they're kids" he yelled, and laughing now shouted back at us, "yeah, we're Yankies boy".

Of course his accent was not a problem to us; we had for many years, for as long as we had attended the local cinemas, been exposed to the various American dialects from the Hollywood films. It must have been a terrible shock to them though; when they discovered that the average British man, or woman, spoke with so many different accents and dialects, and not the perfect Oxford English that they may have expected. It was probably a greater shock to them if they believed; that standing there as we did, dirty, dishevelled, and unkempt little creatures, that we were a true representation of the local juvenile population. God only knows what they thought our parents looked like.

Then it came, hurled from one of the carriage compartments, the small cellophane wrapped package that hurtled towards us; the sun glinting on its shiny wrapper as it curved and twisted through the air and landed on the railway ground inside the fence. We had tracked the little package as it flew towards us and could see where it had landed, and our natural instinct was to run and pick it up; but it was the other side of the fence, on railway property, and very close to the signal box. The American soldiers did not understand our hesitation, and one of them shouted, "Go and get it kids, its candy".

We still did not move and he shouted again, but it was more of an order this time, "Jesus kids, go and get the candy".

The train almost erupted now as other soldiers began shouting, some standing at the open door vents waving their arms encouraging us to go and get the package. There were shouts of, "Go for it boys", and, "go get the candy kids".

With this sort of backing and encouragement, we lost all our fear of the man in the signal box, and even the thought of Chinky was banished from our minds, as we scrambled through the wire fence and raced to where the package lay. Great cheers and howls of laughter and delight emanated from the train, as the soldiers saw and realised that we had now conquered our fear. To them our enterprise and daring could not go un-rewarded, and suddenly we were being showered with other small packages, which were mainly candy, but included chewing-gum, biscuits, and even cigarettes. We were four very good friends; particularly Dinky and me who were almost soul mates; but with all these luxuries been strewn about the ground it was every man for himself. We hardly heard the steam engine whistle blowing, blasting out its warning that it was moving again, as we scrambled about gathering as in many of the packages as we could for ourselves.

The train was on the move again, and the soldiers were still waving and cheering with more shouts of, "So long kids, enjoy the candy". But it was only when we had found, and collected the packages of goodies, that we graciously stood and waved goodbye to the departing Yanks. We were very excited about our good fortune and did not have the words to shout back to show our appreciation; but our beaming faces would have meant more than words to the generous soldiers. As the train crawled past us, it was not far to the railway sidings where the soldiers would disembark, one of the young soldiers in the last carriage shouted words that I would hear time and time again during the Yanks stay in our neighbourhood. "Hey kid", he shouted, "You gotta a sister kid", he paused, then called again, "you gotta sister kid, you come looking for me ".

He was grinning; his white teeth gleamed in his red sun burnt face, he was very young, still a boy, trying to be a man, in his light brown uniform and short crew-cut hair. He waved and shouted once more, before the train disappeared around the bend of the Swansea loop, "You gotta sister kid, you can have all candy in the world".

That Saturday night, there were going to be four very happy households in the Hafod. Enjoying the unexpected, but very welcome gifts we had received that afternoon from the American soldiers. The day had ended much better than we thought, as we had to deal once more with the Swampy ground and the German rhubarb. But with the added incentive of wanting to get home with the goodies, we studied the lie of land more carefully. We discovered that if we took out time, we could skirt around the edges of the German rhubarb, and cut a way through on much firmer ground. We had learned a valuable lesson in life that a lot can be achieved, with a little bit of thought.

My share of the loot amounted to four packets of candy, two packets of biscuits, six packs of chewing gum, and one packet of Lucky Strike cigarettes. The candy was little sweets, which were soft and sugary and very fruity, and there were about eight sweets to each packet. The biscuits, Mammy said were butter biscuits, they were hard and brittle, and most were broken; when they were thrown from the train; but we did not mind that, as we dunked them in hot cups of tea after our weekly bath time. The funniest thing that night was the sight of Mammy, trying to come to terms with smoking one of the Lucky Strike cigarettes. American cigarettes were packed much looser than British ones, but they were much stronger. She did smoke occasionally, but never really mastered the art; more often than not the cigarette just dangled from the corner of her mouth burning away to a long fine ash. Thankfully she never inhaled, which was fortunate for her when trying the Lucky Strikes; when after trying the first one, which brought about a fit of bronchial coughing, and watering eyes, she decided that she would forgo the delights of American cigarettes and try and swap them for some Woodbines. Mammy rationed the chewing gum, doling out half a stick a time as a reward for good behaviour, or when she thought we deserved some. She was very uneasy about chewing gum, and would have preferred if the stuff had never been invented; honestly believing that if swallowed, irreparable damage would be done to your body, even resulting in death.

The American soldiers were almost addicted to what seemed their national pastime of chewing gum; they were rarely seen when their mouths were not in motion chewing away,and the addiction quickly spread to the town's local population, especially the children. The Yanks seemed to have a never-ending supply of the stuff, and would respond positively to the children's requests of, "got any gum chum".

CHAPTER 21

# COOKIES

It was the Monday following the Yanks arrival in the town, that the Jones brothers moved their mechanical shovel from the lower part of the tip, and were now working directly opposite our house. They regularly changed the site where they were working, probably choosing an area for its mix of ash or hard-core to suit the job in hand. As far as we children were concerned they were a grumpy old pair of spoilsports; who chased us away if we got too close to where they were operating. But if anybody knew the complex make-up of the tip it was the Jones brothers, they had been working it for many years, and probably regarded it as their own property. In all fairness they probably had good reason for being sharp with us children, to keep away from where they were working; not only for the security of their machines and vehicles, but for our safety as well. The tip could be a dangerous and treacherous place, but even more so when machines and vehicles were added.

From where they were operating now, it was not necessary for me to get too close to see them in action as they dug away at the tip with their mechanical shovel, then dropping its load on to their battered old tipper lorries. I had a splendid view, from the window of the upstairs front bedroom, where I would sometimes stand for hours watching them. Like all children, I loved watching and was fascinated by diggers, cranes, and mechanical shovels; and nowadays, if I wish to entertain my grandsons, I take them to the nearest building site, as I did with my sons before them. Although of course, I had the additional amusement of watching Ianto, the younger brother, who found great difficulty in operating the mechanical shovel and unloading it on to the tipper.

The area where they had begun working was behind the derelict white cottage and the sheds or garages, where they had cut out a path or rough road when they had worked this site on previous occasions. During the first couple of days, their work routine was no different to any other day and never altered. They worked the same hours as the building trade. For the summer months, starting at 7 o'clock in the morning, half-an-hour for breakfast at half-past nine, half-an-hour for dinner at one, and finishing work at half past four in the afternoon. In the winter they started at 8 o'clock in the morning, with 10 minutes' break for breakfast at 10 o'clock, an hour for dinner at one, and finishing for the day at 5. Each brother would drive his tipper on to the site, always Dai first with Ianto following, then mount the mechanical shovel, fill the lorry with its load of ash, and off they would drive in convoy.

But then on the Wednesday, their routine was to alter abruptly, along with the whole neighbourhood, as we were sharply and loudly woken up from our sleep. The noise and commotion was coming from the road in front of our house. I could hear the movement of heavy traffic, of engines running, and the banging and slamming of metal doors. It was a light, bright sunny morning that greeted us, as we woke up in the back bedroom, which I now shared with Daniel, Walter and Eddie. Harry still had his problem of bed-wetting, and was confined to the small bedroom on his own. We all dashed into the front room to see what was going on; to find Maggie and Molly who shared this bedroom with Mammy, already at the window very excited at the scene before them. Mammy was already up, she still rose at 6 o'clock every morning, we would never have burst into her bedroom like this if she were present. Normally Maggie would have sent us packing, but not today, as she too could hardly contain her excitement as she called.

"Come quick boys, look the Yanks are here, lots of them with great big lorries".

She got hold of Walter and held him up to the window, and Molly did the same with Eddie, so that they too could see out to the road and the amazing scene before us.

There stretching from the site on the tip where the Jones Brothers were now working, and parked along the rough road and on to Pentremawr Road; was a line of huge tipper trucks with metal bodies; very different, to the wooden tippers belonging to the Jones Brothers. These two small, battered, and scruffy looking lorries, looked totally out of place; as they took precedence and led the impressive line of American trucks now lined up behind them. They must have been delivered straight from the United States, and even though khaki in colour, they were gleaming brand spanking new. Each with a great white star on the cab doors, and numbered from 1to 50 also in white, painted on the sides. The young drivers most of them chomping away at the inevitable chewing-gum, were in their cabs waiting eagerly to start work; every now and then trying to speed things up by revving their engines. Other soldiers stood near the mechanical shovel, gathered around the Jones Brothers. But there was one who was undoubtedly an officer, and in charge. He stood out, a tall man with glasses, and was older than the rest of his men.

Dai and Ianto Jones must have felt very pleased with themselves, leading the line of Americans. This was their territory, and their mechanical shovel was to be used to load the trucks, and soon Dai was in the cab of the machine demonstrating just how it was done. His part of the demonstration went quite smoothly, as he could handle the monster and its array of complicated gears and levers reasonably well. God only knows what they thought next, when it came to Ianto's turn; as he started swinging the jib of the machine, with its shovel biting and snapping at the air, long before filling it, then unloading it half in and half out of the tipper. The soldiers who had been casually standing around watching his brother Dai earlier; now scattered away from the mechanical shovel, no doubt fearing for their lives. I am sure that they could not believe their eyes, as Ianto who as usual got completely carried away in trying to operate the machine, and was oblivious to anything else. Some of the young drivers got down from their lorries and raced towards the tip, wanting to get closer to the action, and have a good view of the madman that they believed was now in charge of the shovel.

Eventually the brothers Jones completed loading their tippers, and off they went to wherever the ash and clinker was required. They had shown the Yanks just how the job was to be done, and now they were leaving them to it. But there was no question that the Yanks were going to allow each driver to use the mechanical shovel to fill his own lorry; this part of the operation would be carried out by The Army Engineers; if they could find one old enough and familiar with the workings of this ancient machine. It was undoubtedly going to be a challenge, but there were probably several men amongst the Engineers present who were just itching to get their hands on this mechanical monster. First one and then another got into the cab, taking it in turns to demonstrate to the officer, that he was the boy for the job. There were various degrees of success, from not being able to start the thing, to over eagerness and enthusiasm resulting in the cab rocking on its tracks, with awful noises coming from the engine and gears surpassing any abuse that even Ianto Jones could do to it.Surprisingly, it turned out to be quite a young man who finally managed to handle the shovel at least to Dai Jones's standard, and he was awarded the job.

I had become so engrossed that morning in watching the goings-on between the Americans and the Jones Brothers; I had failed to respond to Mammy's shouts and eventual threats from downstairs, that I would not have any breakfast and would be late for school. This meant that she had to come looking for me, and I was rudely brought back from the world of diggers, tipper lorries and the tip, with a sharp rap from the palm of her hand across the back of my neck, accompanying the words.

"Handel, how many times have I got to call you, get downstairs you're going to be late for school".

I did not mind the cuff around my neck from Mammy, but I hated being late for school and being scolded by the headmistress. So I was quickly on my way tearing up the lane behind Odo Street, stuffing down my throat a doorstep of bread covered with margarine and jam; that was my breakfast. But my thoughts were still with the tremendous events going on at the tip, and I just could not wait to get home at dinnertime.

At playtime that morning I was quite a celebrity, as word of the Yanks arrival at the tip had spread like wildfire throughout the Hafod, and of course I had already got a first class view of what was going on. I had all the information of how many Yanks there were; about their gleaming new lorries; of how the Jones Brothers seemed to be in charge, and they all laughed when I told them of Ianto and some of the Yanks almost losing control of the mechanical shovel. I was becoming quite an authority on the Yanks and their movement in the district. Along with my three companions of Saturday's adventure, we had already told them on the Monday of our first encounter with the them at the railway line, and of the treats of candy, biscuits, and chewing gum, that we had. So it was no surprise that when dinnertime arrived and the school gates were opened, there was a general exodus of children from the entire school. The news had also reached the boys' and girls' schools, and all were heading in the direction of the Tip.

The American soldiers must have thought that it was an invasion of the starving and homeless, or to a neutral observer, he was watching the second coming. As hundreds of children, most of them running, poured out of the school and down Odo Street, finally spilling out into the broader space of Hafod Square. Nothing had changed much since I left the scene that morning, except that the line of tipper lorries stretched now from the tip, on to Pentremawr Road, and down the hill almost as far as the main road. It was comical to see the Jones Brothers battered little vehicles, in the middle of the line of the huge Yankee tippers. They looked more like toy trucks and so much out of place.

Probably the greatest attraction for the mass of children was merely the sight of the American soldiers, the Yanks. So much had been written and spoken about them, that to us, grown-ups and children alike, they were knights in shining armour coming to rescue us. For the children, the added incentive was the possibility of getting their hands on some candy or chewing gum.

There were children all over the place now; especially the older boys who began encroaching from the road on to the Tip, and many going into the derelict remains of the old white cottage to get a better view. Every one of the Yankee tipper lorries had its own cluster of children, with the driver being bombarded with shouts of, "Got any gum chum", or "give us some candy mister".

It was beginning to sound like, and take on the atmosphere of a pantomime, as the children kept up with their shouts and chorus of, "got any gum chum".

From the noise and din emanating from the tip and square; it was not long before the mothers of those children who lived close by, who had been patiently waiting for the offspring with their dinners cooked and waiting to be eaten; realised where their wayward sons and daughters were. Soon there were a dozen or so women, then joined by many more, searching and moving about amongst the melee of children, calling out names trying to locate their offspring.

This all added to the pandemonium, as children were warned by their friends, "Watch out Billy mun, u'er mother's comin'", or, "run Sam mun u'er mothers after 'u".

Then there followed the whackings and scoldings, as the mother's tracked down the ones they were after, and dragged them kicking and screaming back to their homes. One of those that I had been looking for, but could not find was Dinky. But it did not take his mother long to get him, and he pleaded with me as his mother hauled him past, "elp me 'andy mun 'elp me".

Throughout all this the American soldiers kept on with their work, the lorries slowly moving from the road to the tip, to be loaded up before driving off again. The young engineer was handling the mechanical shovel much better now, and the machine itself seemed to be smoother and less noisy than before. The Yanks had probably given it a quick overhaul, and applied the necessary oils and greased the moving parts the Jones Brothers had failed to do over the past years. But still the whole operation was slow and laborious, and they were working in an extremely confined area with only the one rough road in and out from the tip, with very little room to turn. This was their biggest problem, the lack of space in getting the lorries on and off the tip. The old derelict white cottage and the remains of its outbuildings were right in the centre, blocking easy access to where they were working. It was not a problem for the small operation, and slow pace that suited the Jones Brothers. But it was obvious that with the amount of huge trucks that the Yanks had brought with them, that they were involved in some major project, and clearly the pace of loading the vehicles would have to be speeded up.

The numbers of children hanging around the square and the tip were thinning out now; as more and more mothers turned up, and hunger getting the better of the children's enthusiasm of chanting for the chewing gum, were departing for home and their dinners. Then two of the masters from the boys' school appeared, and the numbers reduced dramatically to three, Daniel, Harry, and me, who were now watching the scene from behind the front wall of our house. We were lucky, fate had been kind to us, for we lived directly opposite where the Yanks were working and would be for many months to come.

That afternoon, there was an emergency assembly held in the school hall, as there were in the boys' and girls' schools. Stern warnings, were given by the respective heads regarding the dangers of hanging around the tip, now that the Americans were excavating there with their increasing numbers of machines and vehicles. We were told to keep off the tip and well away from the soldiers, and not pester them for candy and chewing gum. The message was rammed home of the seriousness of the situation, when we were told that the local bobby would be keeping an eye on the place; and any child, who was found to be creating a nuisance, would be warned then taken home for their mothers to deal with them. This was enough to frighten off most of the children, for the shame it would bring on the family, to be warned by the policeman and then reported to their mothers. So we were suitably chastised regarding our future behaviour. Of course this suited me, as I could watch the Yanks from our front garden, or for a better view from Mammy's bedroom, and what a view I did get when I got home from school that afternoon.

The American tipper lorries were gone, and all that was left was the mechanical shovel, the Jones Brothers lorries, and one incredible machine the like of which I had never seen before. At first I thought that it was an American tank, but I was soon discover that this machine was a bulldozer. In the next couple of days this bulldozer in the expert hands of the American engineers, was going to completely transform that area of the tip where they were working. They needed space in which to turn, to get their lorries on and off the tip much more speedily than they had earlier today.

They had already started to level the site, beginning with the remains of the old farm outbuildings. The bull-dozer was slicing away at these with its enormous blade, pushing the rubble into the many dips and holes in the uneven ground. The operator of the machine certainly knew his job. He was already beginning to widen the area where the work was taking place, and every so often cutting into the tip and bringing a load of the ash and clinker to cover the rubble, creating as flat and level a surface as possible.

The Jones Brothers who were standing near their mechanical shovel; must have been watching this operation with mixed feelings of admiration and envy. Although I dread to think what would happen if Ianto got his hands on one of these machines, I doubt whether there would be a building left standing in the entire neighbourhood. They continued watching the bulldozer in operation, but their fascination with the machine had its limits. At 4.30, knocking off time, they got in their tippers and drove off. Working times, habits, and practices, are difficult things to break with.

I had been watching all this from the vantage point of Mammy's bedroom. From here I could look down on the site without my view being blocked, as it would from the front garden, by the remains of the old white cottage. For most of the time I had been on my own, Harry and Daniel were with me to begin with; but Daniel soon got fed up and wandered off, and Harry had gone down to the square where some of the older boys had gathered. They had an old tennis ball, which they were kicking about; full of bravado, they were not frightened of any policeman. That was not the case however when the local bobby did appear, as the brave lads had second thoughts, including Harry, and had scattered in all directions. This had always been the case, playing football on the road was strictly forbidden, and there was never any question or contest about respect for the law, for as soon as the bobby appeared, the boys disappeared.

It was just after Dai and Ianto Jones had left the tip, that Mammy called me to run a message. "Here Handel bach", she said, "run down to Pops cafe, and get a large loaf".

She handed me a shilling piece, and as I ran out of the house she shouted after me, "and no nibbling mind". Her last remark was warning me not to bite the corners or "nibble" the bread, which I, or any other child during those years, would find extremely difficult not to do. It would have been a very well disciplined child, or one with an extreme loss of appetite, to arrive home from the shops or bakers, without great chunks of the bread being already consumed.

Pops cafe was in the Pentre, perhaps a couple of hundred yards from where we lived. Pop was a big barrel-chested man, and if he was not laughing he always wore the brightest of smiles on his face. He was either Italian, or of Italian descent, and bearing in mind the problems these people had during the war when a lot of his fellow countrymen were interned, it says a lot about his strength of character that he could laugh or smile at all. Although the cafe was the mainstay of the business; he had a good takeaway trade as well, selling hot pies, sandwiches and pastries, doughnuts, cream buns, and the aptly named starvers. These were really a compressed, heavy form of bread and butter pudding without the butter; about an inch thick they came in two-inch square slices, and as their name suggests one was usually enough to satisfy your hunger. They were cheap, and were a particular favourite with children. But even these were beyond the means of our family, and it was a rare treat indeed on the odd occasion when I did taste one. He also sold a lot of bread, and cigarettes, tobacco, and sweets, when he could get them. For long periods the only cigarettes he stocked were disgusting foul-smelling cigarettes called Pasha, and the only sweets, and even these were rare, would be Victory V's, hard, mouth and tongue burning lozenges, and tiny squares of liquorice called Nippits. Like a lot of corner shops and cafes in those days, he sold a little bit of everything. I expect you could say that Pop's cafe was a convenience store.

Then on my way back, I had my first meeting with Sergeant Nick. He was the soldier who expertly handled the bulldozer, I had been watching since getting home from school. Some other soldiers had arrived with a Jeep pulling a small caravan type trailer, which they were now unhitching. This I discovered later was sergeant Nick's home. He and his bulldozer were inseparable, and wherever the bulldozer was, so was Sergeant Nick. No one else was allowed to operate it or even go near it, "That machine", he would often say, "is like my wife, to get the best out of her she has to be treated firmly but with love".

He, like the officer in charge, was much older than most of the other soldiers. In the main they were fresh-faced lean, clean-cut young men with crew-cut hair, full of life with great enthusiasm and oozing confidence. But Sergeant Nick was a red-faced, pot bellied, scruffy individual, with greying black wispy hair, whose hands like his dungarees and forage cap were always covered in grease and oil.

He was standing near the wreck of the old white cottage, his hands on his hips, when he shouted across to me. "Hey kid, comeeah".

He startled me, it was one thing watching the Yanks from a distance, but I had not envisaged actually speaking to them. "Comeeah, comeeah", he repeated.

I stopped running. I took running messages literally, and slowly walked across the road, but stopped a good 10 yards short from where he was standing. I was wary of him and he knew it. From my experience with the Jones Brothers I did not expect to be invited for a chat with men working on the tip. "Relax boy, relax", he said, softening his tone of voice then thrusting his chin forward said, "where'd ya get da bread".

I understood perfectly what he said, but as yet, had not come to terms that he was actually speaking to me. "Cain you get me some bread like thet boy", he said slowly almost spelling out the words. "Yes mister", I replied, then quickly added so there was no misunderstanding, "but 'u will 'ave to gim'me some money first".

His hand was already in his pocket from where he pulled a roll of bank notes, he peeled off one ten shillings note and handed this to me, "There you go kid", he said, "is this okay".

I nodded my head knowing that he could buy 20 loaves of bread with this. Then as I turned, I had to take the family bread home to Mammy first, he added, "Get me some cookies too kid".

Now I had some idea of what he meant from Hollywood films, cookies were either cakes or biscuits, but I was not quite sure which. So I asked the question, "Biscuits or cakes mister", to which he replied, "Sure kid, biscuits and cakes".

I did not think it wise to continue the discussion any further, as Mammy would be wondering where I was with the bread. Well, I thought, I would just ask Pop for the bread and some cookies, and put the onus on him.

Ten minutes later I was back with Sergeant Nick with the bread, but no cookies. Pop said that if the sergeant wanted cookies, then I would have to get there early in the morning. I felt quite sure that he would reward me for running the message and getting his bread, and was hoping for at least two or three pennies. My hand was stuffed full of the change from the 10 shilling note, and as I opened my palm to give this to him, he just waved me away saying,

"You keep thet boy, but be sure to come in the morning to get me some cookies".

I felt light-headed and my heart was pounding, as I raced home, my hands still clutching the money. Mammy could hardly believe her eyes as I slammed this down on the kitchen table, at the same time babbling on, "Mammy, Mammy, look what the yank gave me for running 'is message, and I've got to go again early in the morning to get 'im some cookies".

Daniel, Molly, and Walter, were sitting at the table having tea, and we all just stared, almost shocked to disbelief at the amount of money; the windfall of three half crowns, a two shillings piece, and two pennies.

## CHAPTER 22

# LOVE AND WELSH CAKES

Over the next months, during the Yanks work on the tip, I became firm friends with Sergeant Nick. We both benefited from our relationship. I ran his messages which invariably meant getting fresh bread and cookies from Pop's cafe, whereas I and my family were rewarded with tinned meats, fruit, cigarettes and Candy, as well as the odd shilling or two.

Sergeant Nick had demolished most the remains of the old farm outbuildings, during the first day he and his bull-dozer had come on to the tip. That just left the wreck of the old farm cottage, and for this he required the help of the Jones Brothers mechanical shovel. This task was given to the young American engineer, who had handled the big shovel the day before, so much better than the Jones Brothers. This work was timed by the Yanks for the early morning, before the brothers arrived on site, to avoid any argument, as to who would operate the machine. So by the time they arrived, the American engineer was already in the process of rendering the derelict cottage to rubble. I had watched this from the safety of Mammy's bed room, and it was only when this part of the operation was complete, that I was able to carry out my promise of running to Pop's cafe to get Sergeant Nick's cookies.

It was the last day at school, before we once again broke up for the summer holidays. During the dinner break and after school that day, I watched fascinated as Sergeant Nick once again levelled that part of the ground, where once stood the old farm cottage. Some of the big Yankee tipper lorries had returned to be laboriously loaded with the ash and clinker, but it was quite clear that due to the length of time it was taking to fill each lorry not so many were required. They reduced the number from the original fifty down to about half a dozen, as by the time the sixth lorry was loaded, the first lorry had already returned.

At the end of the day's work when the tipper lorries had returned to their bases, and the Jones Brothers had gone home, the tall officer with glasses returned and got into what seemed to be a long and detailed discussion with Sergeant Nick. They wandered about the site where the work was taking place, but also paid long and particular attention to the area at the back of the garages; where the Jones Brothers had cut a swathe in the side of the tip, and where I, and the rest of my gang had been playing the previous week. That weekend I was to discover just what they were planning, and if it came off, the method of work was going to change dramatically, resulting in the turnover of traffic being greatly speeded up.

Saturday was a normal working day in those days, but at the start of that weekend the mechanical shovel was silent, and there was no sign of the Jones Brothers or the Yankee tippers. Instead I was surprised to see that Sergeant Nick had began cutting a path with the bulldozer at the back of the garages, to link up with the swathe or ledge which was already there. Then about an hour later, a squad of a dozen or so American engineers turned up with an assortment of heavy shoring timbers, stout metal girders, and heavy metal sheets. Whilst they got to work with metal burning equipment and chainsaws, Sergeant Nick was skilfully widening and lengthening the ledge into a rough road. It became evident after a couple of hours of just what he had in mind, as the road he was now shaping and forming was rising steadily upwards; cutting a curve into the side of the tip that would eventually take him and his bulldozer to the top. By working steadily and almost non-stop he achieved his goal late that evening.

The engineers, who were engaged at the work area, had constructed a raised platform of about 20 ft high. It was difficult to see the reasoning behind such a construction; but the following day Sergeant Nick who was now on the plateau of the tip began to shave off the surface with the bulldozer, extending his road downwards now towards the platform. He was cutting a wedge of about 20 ft wide out of the top edge of the tip, and pushing the ash down on an ever-increasing slant towards the work area. By the middle of the afternoon when I had arrive back from Sunday-school, the work was complete with the bulldozer now parked in the ravine that Sergeant Nick had carved out, just above the level of the platform.

Monday morning, the first day of the holiday, and once again with all the noise, hustle and bustle of the previous Monday, when the Yanks first arrived. The rest of my family were not at all as fussed or bothered as they had been then, but to me it was exciting and intriguing. I was dying to see just how they used the bulldozer and the raised platform, which were now both in place. I had taken up my station at the window of Mammy's bedroom, Maggie was already up and on her way to the Star Supply Stores, and Molly was still lying down basking in the enjoyment of having the bed all to herself. Mammy as ever had already been up since 6 o'clock. All of the big Yankee tipper lorries were back, parked in a line stretching the length of Pentremawr Road; and I was just in time to see the two small and battered tippers belonging to the Jones Brothers, cut in front of the first of the Yankee lorries to take their rightful place at the head of the queue.

Sergeant Nick was already seated on his bulldozer waiting to begin, as one of the young engineers who had constructed the platform, called the first of the Jones Brothers forward to begin loading. Now, in all previous work involving these two, Dai Jones, the older of the brothers was always first in line. But today surprisingly, it was Ianto who led the way. He was going to be honoured with having his tipper loaded first. The engineer, called him on cautiously and slowly, until his wagon was in the right place ready to be loaded. The Engineering Officer who conceived the idea of the new method of working, was nowhere in sight.

The Yanks had constructed the platform to be used in conjunction with the bulldozer, and of course they had strictly in mind; that the tippers they would be filling, would be the huge metal Yankee tippers. Not the puny little things that belonged to the Jones Brothers. As young as I was my commonsense told me that something was wrong. Sergeant Nick revved up the bulldozer behind the mound of ash and clinker that was soon to be deposited into Ianto's truck. After he had positioned it as instructed by the young engineer, Ianto had wisely got out of the cab and stood with the others, who were now going to witness this innovative operation, which was going to do away with the ancient and laborious mechanical shovel.

Now Sergeant Nick could drive that bulldozer through the eye of a needle, and knew exactly where the load had to be dropped to get the maximum effect. He slowly drove the machine forward, the blade gathering the mound of ash and clinker, sweeping it over the platform, and as it avalanched down, hit Ianto's tipper the full length and width of the body, including the cab. Its progress seemed relentless, as its weight simply crushed and shattered the timber body, before bursting through to the chassis below and finally burying the vehicle completely. All that remained to be seen, as evidence that Ianto's truck was ever there, was the front of the cab, which was now tilted up, and the rear wheels still attached to the axle squeezed out at the back.

After the initial shock, Ianto who had remained motionless during loading, or a better word would be attack on his tipper which was now smashed to smithereens, went berserk. He was jumping up and down, shouting and cursing, "Look what you've done to my cowin' vehicle", remonstrating mainly with the young engineer and Sergeant Nick.

He was almost in tears with rage, as he turned to his older brother shouting, "Look mun Dai, look what they've done to my cowin' lorry". Dai, just shrugged his shoulders, he seemed to be taking what was a disaster to Ianto, all in his stride.

He did not seem overly concerned, his vehicle, was still intact.

More and more of the drivers had gathered round the distraught Ianto, and the mound of ash, which had buried his truck, trying to console him. It was then that the jeep arrived carrying the tall bespectacled officer, who was no doubt going to sort everything out. As the officer ran forward, Dai Jones appeared now to be backing his brother up shouting. "Dew dew sir, just look what your men 'ave done to my brother's lorry, wrecked it they 'ave

Sir, wrecked it".

I could see that the officer was nodding his head in agreement, and full of sympathy for the damage his men had inflicted on the local hauliers. I could not hear what he said, but he had taken hold of Ianto by his arm and began leading him back to his jeep, with Dai Jones following. He was also barking out orders to his men, who had already started clearing away the mess. The young engineer was already in the cab of mechanical shovel, and began digging away at the mound from under the platform, and loading the ash and bits of Ianto's lorry into one of the Yankee tippers. The officer sped off in the jeep taking Dai and Ianto with him. He was probably taking them back to the base up at the old racecourse, where there was some serious talking and bargaining to be done.

Whether it was a conspiracy by the Yanks, to take the Jones Brothers out of the equation, I will never know. But I have a sneaky suspicion that if they had not done so, then the important and essential war work that they were engaged in, would have taken twice as long to complete. I also have the same feeling that Dai Jones was not the protesting innocent party that he made out to be, as no doubt generous compensation would be paid by the Yanks for the damage they had done. To them of course it was worth it.

Within a matter of a few days, the Yanks had flattened the old cottage and outbuildings, levelled the ground, got a bulldozer to the top of the tip, constructed the platform, and got rid of the Jones Brothers. Now the real job of removing the ash and clinker would begin in earnest. Rumour had it that they were building roads, and extending the airport to the north-west of the town, whether this was true or not I never found out.

For the remainder of the summer the Yankee tipper

lorries rumbled on and off the tip, as Sergeant Nick cut deeper and deeper into the plateau. It was uncanny, but he had worked out just how much ash was needed to fill one of the tippers with one sweep of the bulldozer's blade. Compared with the old mechanical shovel, the bulldozer and the platform had speeded up the work tenfold.

Once the initial excitement and impact of the Yanks working at the tip wore off, our lives went on pretty much as normal. Several times we cut our way through the jungle of German rhubarb, exploring in some depth the maze of giant clinker that formed the caves; but alas, once again Harry's tales of finding treasures of money, gold, and jewellery, proved to be worthless. The only thing of value we did find was the rim of an old bicycle wheel, which Dinky insisted on dragging back home to be used as a hoop. A hoop could be anything from an old car tyre to a bicycle wheel, as long as it could be driven along and guided either with a stick or the palm of your hand. But we did have fun exploring the caves, and even though we did not find anything of value, they still held a certain air of wonder and mystery for me, and still do.

I continued foraging the tip for firewood and anything else that would burn; but I had one extra duty now, which was collecting dried grass and chickweed. Mammy was determined that we would not have a repeat of last year, when she was unable to obtain a chicken for our Christmas dinner. So earlier in the summer she had bought some White Leghorn day-old chicks. Where she got these from I do not know; but I seem to remember that they came in the post, in a large cardboard box. I believe we started out with a dozen, but through illness or perhaps injury, this number was gradually reduced over the next few weeks to four. They were now a couple of months old, and had recently been transferred from the kitchen to a makeshift chicken coop that Mammy had knocked up in the back garden. She had scrounged some old corrugated iron sheets and some chicken wire from somewhere. The plan was that we should at least have a proper chicken dinner at Christmas, and the remaining three if they survived, would be sold to provide some sorely needed cash for the festive season.

They were fed mainly on boiled up potato and other vegetables peelings, mashed up with bread so stale that even we would not eat it. Many of our neighbours, who perhaps had their reservations about us when we first moved into the neighbourhood; I think now were beginning to have a grudging sense of admiration for Mammy. Many people kept chickens in those days, but not in the posh part of the Hafod where we now lived. Under normal circumstances, I believe they would have strongly objected at the very idea; but they rightly understood, Mammy's need to use every avenue open to her, to provide sufficient food for her family. In fact they shared our interest in the welfare of the chicks, and our anguish and dismay as the weaker ones died off, then our joy with the survival of the four stronger ones. They also contributed their kitchen waste; without which I am sure, not one of the chickens would have made it to Christmas, certainly not on the meagre leftovers from our table. This diet of scraps was supplemented by fresh chickweed, and collecting this was another one of my daily duties. I discovered that this grew quickly on any freshly cultivated soil, and a good source was the flowerbeds and borders of the shrubs in the park. If the chickweed was scarce or unobtainable, grass was the next best thing, particularly grass with seed heads. In the summer and early autumn, I also collected dried grass, which was used as bedding for the chickens.

There were so many things going on now, that the

arrival of Florrie seemed to pass almost unnoticed. How or why she became a fixture in the Swain household I do not know, but she appeared to grow on us. I remember her coming to visit us at irregular times at first, chatting and having a cup of tea with Mammy; but then after a couple of weeks she seemed to be in and around the house most days. I think the idea was that she was to become a home help, someone to help Mammy, now that Maggie had started work. The initial visits were simply a testing or proving period, to see if she and Mammy got along with each other. It had parallels with Puss the cat all over again, as another waif and stray found a niche in the Swain household.

Florrie had been orphaned at an early age, and although now a woman in her forties, she had remained at the orphanage. She was a tiny, bird like creature, timid, and underdeveloped in mind and body. Therefore, it was no wonder that she took to Mammy, who was the complete opposite; with her strength of body and character, which would have been like a magnet to this poor defenceless and dispirited woman. She liked being with Mammy, to do her bidding, trying to help and assist with the daily chores; I believe that some of Mammy's strength rubbed off on her, and she derived a certain amount of security from this.

Whether it was the local council or the Church that instigated the idea of Florrie becoming our home help, I never found out; but they probably believed that she would benefit as much if not more from the relationship than Mammy. Because we were at school most of the time, we did not see a lot of Florrie, only at dinnertime or for an hour or so in the afternoon when school had finished for the day. She never came to work at weekends, but she sometimes came for tea on Saturday or Sunday. It must have been a big treat for her to visit her friend, as she came to look upon Mammy. Traditionally teatime on Sunday was a bit special, and Mammy always tried to get that little extra such as a jelly, stewed apple or rhubarb and custard, or at least some Welsh cakes. There was not much to spare, but Florrie was always welcome, as squeezing nine out of eight did not entail a great deal of hardship.

We could not help but like Florrie, she was so open and innocent that even the most malicious of people, even Harry, would find it difficult to harm her; but we used to tease her sometimes and play tricks on her. One of her tasks in the afternoon was to fill the coal bucket ready for the evening. We would wait for her to do this; then when her back was turned, we would quickly take the bucket back to the coal shed, empty it, and put it back by the fireside. Invariably Mammy would notice the empty bucket as the afternoon wore on, and would shout to her, "Don't forget to fill the coal bucket Florrie love".

Although she had only filled it up minutes before, she never questioned or argued the fact, but just blithely filled the bucket up once more. Our undoing with this trick finally came when we tried it on twice on the same day, not knowing that Mammy had actually witnessed Florrie filling it for the second time. So Harry and I received a good whacking with the threat of more to come if we did it again. Another trick we would play on her was at the dinner table when I would distract her, and Harry would help himself from her plate. This would generally be a potato; she liked potatoes and always kept these until last. Once again there was never any protest or question, just sometimes a puzzled look, had she eaten the potato or not? This trick was far more difficult to do, as generally Mammy was in much closer proximity when we were eating.

It is highly doubtful whether Mammy benefited in time

saving and energy, by having Florrie around. Instead of supervising her, she could have done the job quicker herself, but having her for company probably more than offset this. However, there was one area where their relationship proved beneficial to Mammy, and that was looking after my two younger brothers. During the day when the rest of us were at school she would play with Eddie and keep him occupied, whilst allowing Mammy to get on with the housework. She was very good too at handling Walter, who was still missing a lot of school. She played with him and sympathetically nursed him, which was a great boon to Mammy and the rest of us, as the amount of time and volume level of grizzling reduced dramatically when she was around. Having Florrie, as our home help, was another one of the good things that happened in the summer of 1943.

I continued running messages for Sergeant Nick, mainly for his cookies in the morning, which in English turned out to be cream buns and jam doughnuts. I also got to know the Major, who if he did not come to the site during the day, would pop down in the evening to discuss things with the Sergeant. Often they would sit outside Sergeant Nick's mobile cabin, and open a huge tin of pineapple chunks, and would proceed in turn to spoon out its contents. They never finished the whole tin; it must have contained at least five or six pounds of fruit, and if I was near, one of them would call me over, and give the remaining chunks to me. Then, I would take them home to Mammy; but not before first draining off most of the syrup, and stuffing myself sick with some of the pineapple chunks. It did not take me long to savvy that when the Major was on an evening visit to the sergeant, there was a strong possibility that there would be some pineapple chunks on offer.

My craving for the sweet canned fruit led to other things, one of which was to bring a little romance into Mammy's harsh and austere life. I used to get the odd packet of candy and some biscuits from the sergeant, and he was still generous with his tips for running his messages; but never gave me anything like the amount of money that I received the first time. Sergeant Nick soon learned the value of sterling against the dollar. So after the second or third time I had taken home the pineapple chunks, Mammy reciprocated their generosity with a few of her precious Welsh cakes. The Major was absolutely delighted with this gesture from Mammy, knowing full well that the ingredients for the cakes were all on ration, and that there was really none to spare; especially for the well paid, well fed, American troops.

Then that evening as I was waiting around outside the house, hoping for the call that there were some pineapple chunks on offer; I was disappointed to see that the Major had finished his business with Sergeant Nick and was leaving. He had climbed into his jeep, and was slowly driving over the rough ground of the site and down to the road. But instead of turning right, as he would normally do to take him back to the base, he drove across the road, waving with one hand to me as he came. To my amazement, he turned sharply and parked right in front of me, immediately outside our house.

"Hi sonny", he called, "is your Mom at home".

His sudden arrival outside the house, and asking me if Mammy was at home, threw me into a state of confusion.

He called me again, "Come here sonny, you go and take this to your mom", and holding his hand out produced a small tin of corned beef.

I moved the couple of steps forward that was necessary, and took the small tin from him. I was literally at a loss for words at having the Major, this powerful man who was in charge of all the American soldiers, right here outside my house.

"Relax sonny", he smiled and said, "now you run along inside and thank your mom for those delicious Welsh cakes, and ask her please could I have the recipe".

I managed to squeeze out, "Thank 'u Major", as I turned and ran into the house.

Mammy was sitting at the table with Maggie, who had not long got in from work, and was having her tea.

"Mammy, look mun Mammy", I said proudly, putting the small tin of corned beef on the table.

"Oh that's nice Handel", she said, "is that from the sergeant?

"No mun Mammy", I replied, "it's from the Major, 'e's out the front and 'e said thank-u for the Welsh cakes".

"Oh I am glad he liked my Welsh cakes", she said, but not moving from the table.

I was sure that the Major was still outside the house, but I was unsure of just what he wanted from Mammy, as the word recipe then was not in my vocabulary.

"He wants something Mammy", I went on, "something to do with the Welsh cakes. Go and see Mammy, go and see the Major out the front", I pleaded.

Mammy looked as confused as I felt, as she said, "No Handel bach, the Major doesn't want to speak to me, does he?

Maggie, as sharp as ever, was already on her way into the front room and looking through the window, she yelled at first, "Mammy", but then had second thoughts about shouting and rushed back into the kitchen where in a forced whisper said, "Mammy, the yank is outside in his Jeep".

Mammy stood up with a jolt, looking embarrassed, not

really knowing what to do, and once again it was Maggie who took control of the situation.

"You'd better go and see him Mammy, find out what he wants".

She hesitated, straightening her pinafore that she almost permanently wore, and smoothing her hair in an attempt to gain some courage and smarten up.

"Do I look alright Maggie"? she asked still hesitating.

"Yes Mammy", my sister almost shouted at her.

Then getting hold of her arm-she was slightly taller than Mammy now-and gently guided her to the back door and out into the back yard.

I wanted to go as well, and was about to follow Mammy when Maggie grabbed me by the shoulder saying, "No Handel, you stay by yer boy".

She was bursting with curiosity, and wanted to see Mammy talking to the Major, but she still did not want to risk me sneaking out. So pushing me in front of her, we made our way into the front room and stood peeping behind the net curtains. I should imagine that the Major's presence outside the front of our house, had attracted a lot of attention from our neighbours, and you can bet on it that Maggie and I were not the only ones spying on Mammy and the Major from behind net curtains.

It was obvious that there was a mutual attraction between Mammy and the Major from that very first meeting, which must have lasted for half an hour or more; for the next day when I arrived home for dinner, the Major's Jeep was parked outside the front of our house again. When I got near to the back door he was just leaving, and he ruffled my hair as he passed me saying, "Goodbye now Mrs Swain, looking forward to this evening".

Inside the house, on the kitchen table, there were a

couple of bags of flour, a bag of currants, a packet of sugar, and some lard. These I recognised as the ingredients necessary for making Welsh cakes, so amidst all the talk of the previous evening, Mammy had at least given him the recipe.

That evening, there was an abundance of Welsh cakes for tea, and later on, after the Major had discussed the day's work with Sergeant Nick, he too experienced the delights of hot fresh Welsh cakes, straight from Mammy's frying pan.

CHAPTER 23

# ANGELS IN HOBNAIL BOOTS

September 1943 was the start of a new school term, which was to be my last in the Infants School. I realised that I would be leaving its cosy, gentle regime, and joining the more robust and stricter discipline of the boys' school. But this did not worry me in the least, since I was quite looking forward to it. Anyway this final term, I was going to be without the comforting presence of Maggie and Molly in the school playground. Maggie had long gone, since the end of last year, but now Molly too had finished at Hafod Girls School. The new term for her was to be at a new school, as Mammy had ambitious plans for Molly. She had seen how our neighbours', the Evans' girl had attended the Greggs College, and was now a qualified shorthand typist working at one of the banks in Swansea.

Greggs College was a fee-paying school, so how Mammy managed to get Molly a place there I do not really know. With our meagre resources, we certainly could not afford the fees. So I can only guess that she must have received help from somewhere. The only possible source, or people that I can think of, that could be in a position to help financially would be the British Legion. This splendid organisation came to my rescue later on in life; they provided funds to enable me to purchase tools, when I was apprenticed to a firm of wood workers. As the widow of an ex-serviceman Mammy probably approached them for help, and I do not think they let her down. But then it was not only the school fees that she had to find, there was the additional costs of bus fares, books, and although there was no school uniform; there was a need for Molly to be dressed in better clothes than when she attended Hafod school. Apart from all these changes, we were horrified to learn that Molly was even to have a new name. Apparently Molly was not a suitable name for a girl attending Greggs College, and she was now to be known as Margaret; or at least when she attended class, and in the future when she was seeking employment in one of the town's professional offices.

Whether the same opportunity of acquiring office skills was offered to Maggie I doubt it. I should think that it was almost certain that Mammy only managed doing something for Molly, now that she had the added income provided by Maggie. I would also very much doubt she would have wanted the opportunity anyway; I do not think that she would have fitted in, and put up with a lot of the pretentious nonsense that Molly had to contend with. One thing is for certain she would not have changed her name for the King, let alone the Head Mistress of Greggs College.

Our family was moving on and up in the world, with Maggie working and Molly aspiring to be an office worker, Mammy must have quietly felt very pleased with herself. Then with the advent of autumn and the shorter days, she felt at that it was time now to introduce electric light into the household; so she bought one light bulb, which was to be used in the kitchen come living room only. Candles would still be the main source of lighting for the remainder of the house. The electricity was switched on by inserting a shilling piece into a meter, which was read periodically; every three months I think, by a man from the electricity board. There was always a rebate of three or four shillings, and the meter reader would hand this back to Mammy, which she looked on as a bonus to help with that week's funds. After the war ended; the returning soldiers brought back with them many foreign coins, and it was not long before people discovered, which of these coins would be accepted by the meter in place of the shilling piece. On the whole people realised that it would be foolish to use too many of these coins, and generally kept within the limit of what ever their rebate would be. But there were always some who exceeded this, who then had to beg, borrow, or steal, what ever the balance was required to make up the charge of that quarters electricity. If this could not be found, then their supply of electricity would automatically be switched off.

With the passing of summer and the onset of autumn, I was saddened to discover when I got home from school one dinnertime, Sergeant Nick, together with his bulldozer and cabin had gone. There were no tipper lorries coming and going, being loaded, and the young noisy Yankee drivers calling and shouting at each other. The gruff, scruffy old Sergeant who seemed to live only so that he could drive and operate his bulldozer; had said nothing to me the previous day when I had run down to Pop's cafe for his cookies. But perhaps I should have guessed that there was something not right, as like the first time we met many weeks before, he waved me away when I offered him his change, "You keep it kid", he growled, "you keep it".

I wondered whether we had seen the last of the Major

too, as he and the sergeant belonged to the same unit, so I naturally thought that he would be going as well. After that first meeting with Mammy during the summer holidays, when she first made him some Welsh cakes; the Major became a regular visitor, and although there were no outward signs of a blossoming romance to me at least, I do believe that they became close to each other. Because of his appearance, he was tall, fair-haired, and wore spectacles; Maggie and Molly at first thought that he was Glenn Miller the great American bandleader that he bore a striking resemblance to. He kept on calling for several weeks after Sergeant Nick left, and what I didn't know then; but discovered years later from Maggie and Molly, was that he was ardently courting Mammy. He was a middle-aged bachelor with no relatives, and he saw in Mammy and her children a ready-made family for him to settle down with, and that we would be more than welcome in the USA. I cannot remember him mentioning it to me, but Maggie, Molly, and Daniel, all agreed that he very often asked them.

"How would you all like to come and live with me, I'll be your father, and tell your mother she'll love it in America".

But Mammy was a pragmatic woman, she could not live in dreams or rely on the whims of others, however true and genuine they may be. She must have felt flattered, and enjoyed being courted by such a person as the Major, but her feet were firmly on the ground. For the time being at least she had to settle for what she had, her seven children all in good health; even Walter was getting stronger, and a roof over our heads. She may have told him to return after the war if he was still in the same frame of mind, but he never did. By late October he had gone, and we never saw or heard of him again. Of course what we did not know then that he like millions of his countrymen, along with our own men, were preparing for D-Day and operation Overlord; when the allies would have to fight the bloody battles against the Nazis in the re-conquest of Europe. Did the Major survive and live to return to America, or did he die on some battlefield in France or Germany?

Everyone agreed that the time was also right, for me to join Daniel and Harry in the Church choir. Much to my amazement, Harry had managed to survive not only the wrath of God for stealing the money from the charity box, but also the rigid discipline imposed on the boys by the church organist who was also the choir master. Every Wednesday evening we had to attend choir practice for which we were rewarded with two or three pennies, the amount usually depending on length of service and age. Any boy who did not attend, or had misbehaved the previous Sunday, would have part if not all of this withheld. I shall never forget the first time I donned the surplice and cassock and as the newest, youngest, and smallest addition to the choir, I had the privilege of leading the procession from the vestry down the aisle and into the choir pews. The number of boys in the choir was about a dozen, with four elderly men. There were no women or girls.

Mammy, who did not attend Church very often, made a special visit on that first Sunday to witness the event of having her three oldest sons singing in the choir. The tiled floor of the church seemed to resonate with the sound of small boys marching in their customary boots. Even though I had seen the choir do this twice every Sunday for the past two years, being there marching with the rest of the choristers, the sound as the hobnails hit the tiles and being close to the vibrating Church organ, was almost deafening. Then just above the din I heard a voice, a lady's voice with a lovely Celtic lilt, saying, "Dew, they are angels. Angels in Hobnail Boots."

The pace of life quickens, as you grow older, even for a seven-year-old going on eight. That final term in the Infants School passed by quickly, and soon it was Christmas once more. The autumn and winter nights were much more tolerable, as there were no more infuriating dashes from your warm bed to the air raid shelter; now that we had our permanent construction in the parlour. There were several false alarms, but thankfully no German bombers ever materialised. We were looking forward to Christmas in eager anticipation, as there was more produce in the shops and although in short supply and still on ration, there were some sweets and chocolates about. Money was still tight; but with Maggie's wages coming in we were hoping for a return to much fuller Christmas stockings than the last couple of years, and maybe a Christmas gift. But the biggest Christmas treat was waiting for us, still strutting about in Mammy's makeshift chicken coop in the back garden. Unless we were overtaken by a disaster such as a stray bomb or a strike of lightning hitting it, there would be no repeat of last year when we had to make do with rabbit for our Christmas dinner. The best of the four chickens that had survived was reserved for us, and Mammy had already taken orders for the three remaining chickens; which were to be plucked, dressed, and delivered to her three lucky customers on Christmas Eve.

The gruesome deed, the slaughter, took place one grey, cold, and damp morning, three days before Christmas. Mammy, and I to a lesser degree, were about to be rewarded for the hard work we had put in, rearing and nurturing the chickens. As there was no school that day we had been allowed to stay that little bit longer in bed, but

Mammy rose at her usual hour of 6 o'clock. We were allowed to get up when and how we pleased during the school holidays; well at least up until 9 o'clock, when Mammy would begin to get a bit impatient and start banging things around, and entering the bedrooms and opening the windows. So by the time that I got up and went downstairs to the bathroom to wash, the four chickens were already suspended over the bath, with the last drops of blood slowly oozing out of their lifeless bodies. Mammy had spared us the horrors of the slaughter itself, which had been carried out in the early hours, in a swift and competent manner. How she had silenced them, for there had been no noise or protest put up by the chickens, I'll never know. The only evidence to show that they had been killed was two cuts on the neck, high up behind their' ears. Mammy was not at all squeamish, killing chickens, skinning rabbits, cleaning and gutting fish, or drowning kittens, it was all in a day's work. If a job had to be done, then she would do it.

Removing the chickens' feathers was probably the messiest job of the whole operation, as Mammy had to do this in the overcrowded, confined space of our kitchen cum living room. For the next couple of days, there seemed to be feathers and down wafting about throughout the house; in your hair, your mouth, and up your nose; but we did not mind, we were too excited with the prospect of a happy Christmas. Then the chickens were gutted and cleaned, with the giblets of each one placed back inside the cavity, as the customers would expect, and delivered in time for Christmas Eve.

In contrast to the year before, the Christmas of 1943 lived up to all our expectations; each stocking containing an apple, an orange, a small bag of hard boiled sweets, and plenty of hazelnuts, with a few walnuts, and Brazils, or horseshoe nuts as we called them. I had a Christmas present too, a small box of watercolour paints. The chicken was certainly the freshest and tastiest I ever had, before then or since, and we had Christmas pudding for afters. In the afternoon Mammy brought out a couple of large bars of chocolate, and shared these out. By the time we got to bed that night, and Christmas was over; I think that we were all feeling pretty well pleased and satisfied with ourselves if not a little bit sick. The following day, Boxing Day, we had a visit from Florrie. She told us what a wonderful time they had at the orphanage on Christmas Day, and for dinner she had the Parson's nose; it must have been a very small chicken that was on offer, or that the number of people sharing it was unduly large. But still she did not seem to care that she had been awarded the poorest piece of meat on the chicken, and just laughed when Mammy pointed out just what part of the chicken's anatomy the Parson's nose was. Her response covered a stark message to us children, that here was a middle-aged woman who had lived all of her life in an orphanage, and was quite happy to receive such a meagre offering for the main meal of the year. Could we have ended up like this poor creature; if it were not for the sheer courage and fortitude shown by Mammy, in her determination, to keep the family together.

## CHAPTER 24

# BRAMMER
# AND THE BALLOON SHED

The most impressive image and memory I have of joining Hafod Boys School, was being introduced to the school at assembly at the start of the school year in 1944, by the headmaster, the colossal Mr Joe Morgan. As the titular head of the whole school, no man or woman could be better in representing all those in his charge, teachers and pupils. He will always remain the embodiment, of what the boys' school meant to me: trust and solidarity.

Standard one, the first rung on the ladder at the boys' school, was in the charge of Miss Noyle. She was the boys' school only woman teacher. It was her job really to break the barrier, or soften the blow; for those children when first joining the boys' schools from the Infants. She did the job superbly; introducing a stricter form of work and routine, and of course that other form of discipline used only in the boys' school, the cane. Many lurid tales had been told to little boys in the Infants by older brothers, of the cane, and the different methods and pain that could be inflicted with this weapon, on any miscreant who fell foul of the teachers. Miss Noyle's cane, the smallest of those wielded by the teaching staff, was always kept at the front of her desk in clear view for all to see; but I can honestly say that I never saw her use it. The other teachers, all men, had their own preferences for the lengths of the cane they used, and where it was kept. Some like Miss Noyle kept it in full view, but others preferred to keep it out of sight, on the floor under the desk, or behind the blackboard.

Unlike the Infants School where all of the desks were on one level, the boys' school classrooms were stepped sloping up towards the back of the room; so that all children were in full view of the teacher. Even the tiniest child could not hide behind the boy in front of him. We sat two to each desk, with five desks to each row, and four or five rows per class. The average classroom size was between 40 and 50 pupils. The learning of the three R's was stepped up, and we now had to learn the new art of double writing, or joined-up letters, instead of the printing used in the Infants. Great emphasis was placed on the art of double writing, and special lessons on penmanship were frequent. Children who had mastered the art with well-formed rounded letters; would have those classmates who were not so fortunate, placed next to them, so that they could copy from their written work. It was a fact that the cleverer teachers, used their brighter pupils as examples, and encouraged the not-so-bright children to copy from them, especially in forming letters, words, and numbers. Children learn quicker when they can mimic or copy, particularly from other children.

I was eight years old in January, and I felt very grown-up now that I was in the boys' school. Over the coming months I was to increase greatly the size and range of the territory I would cover; along with Dinky and the rest of my gang, in pursuit of further adventures away from the familiar grounds of the square, the tip, and the park. Sergeant Nick and the Major were gone, but other Yankee soldiers had replaced them in the large tented city up on the old racecourse. Another regiment of American soldiers were stationed up in the Morriston area, near the golf course and the cemetery where my father was buried. The significant difference here was that these soldiers were all black. This was in keeping with the then American philosophy of life, of segregation between black soldiers and white soldiers. It was a harsh lesson that we learnt, that when intolerance and lack of understanding take charge; which resulted in terrible scenes that took place on the streets of Swansea, with the inevitable clashes between these men. Both camps were strictly out-of-bounds to people other than American service personnel, and were well guarded. The old racecourse where the white soldiers were based was within easy reach; but the black soldiers' camp at Morrison, I only saw on a few occasions in the spring and early summer of 1944. That was when Mammy instructed Daniel to take the rest of us boys, giving him a brown paper bag containing five pieces of rock cake, repeating the words, "Go and see your Father".

We began to explore the area around the Hafod railway sidings; where the trucks bringing in coal, livestock, fruit and vegetables, were shunted off the main lines, to be emptied of their goods and distributed by lorry, van, or horse and cart, throughout the town. It was a busy commercial area, the heart of the Hafod, there were many shops lining the main road, with warehouses and small industrial units clustered around the sidings and along the canal and river-banks. Of all the works there I must give special mention to one in particular; an old works carrying out an ancient craft, that at least once a week inflicted a nauseating, disgusting stench, on the residents of the Hafod and indeed anyone up wind from the prevailing south-westerlys. This was the Mosdall bone, skin, and hide, company, or known to us and commonly referred to by everyone as the Pong Works. It was probably a tannery producing leather, and manufacturing glue; and every so often, about once a week, they would render down the bones and other offal, releasing its offensive by-product in dark billowing clouds, which could lie over the surrounding district for hours. At the first signs, or rather smell of the cloud of nauseating fumes, people groaned with despair, knowing that there was no escape from the sickening stench. Some people I knew swore that the gas masks were issued not as protection from Hitler and the Germans gas attacks, but to protect us from the terror of the Pong Works.

Further along, past the railways and the canal, flows the River Tawe, which gives its name to Abertawe, the Welsh name for Swansea. It is wide at this point, with a strong current, as it meets and flows into the tidal waters of Swansea Bay. The only means of crossing the river was here, by the Hafod ferry; where an old man with a rowing boat, would row you across the river for a penny, or three halfpence return. Heaven only knows why people would want to risk such a precarious crossing, as the land on the other side, which was dominated by the treeless, wind driven rocky terrain, known as Kilvey Hill, was sparsely populated.

*********************************

I only made the ferry crossing once, with Dinky. It was about a year after the war had ended, when we heard reports that sparrow hawks, or falcons, that used to raid the birds of the town's pigeon fanciers, had their nests high up on Kilvey Hill. It was one adventure too far, and we got into serious trouble that day. We did not set out on the journey until the afternoon, and with only a penny each, we could not return by the ferry; but would have to travel the long way round via the town centre. After a long hard struggle, we did not even make it half way up the hill, and with the light of the day beginning to fade; we decided to abandon our quest for the birds of prey and start our journey home. It was Saturday evening and almost dark by the time we got to the town-centre, where the streets were filled with Saturday-night revellers thronging the pavements, coming and going amongst the numerous pubs that lined both sides of the High Street.

We were ten years old then but it was still a frightening experience to be caught up in that hedonistic atmosphere; where the crowds of people, which were mostly men, were hell-bent on achieving one thing, which was getting blind drunk. It was turning into a nightmare as we tried to weave our way through the crowds, dodging the wobbly legs that their owners' brains were slowly losing control over, and the cars and buses that filled the road. Luckily, we were rescued by one of our neighbours. He put us on to a bus near High Street station, and paid the penny fares to get us home. That night before my bath; I got the hardest whacking that Mammy had ever doled out in my young life, such was the stress, and worry, she had suffered when I had not returned home much earlier. I am sorry to relate that Dinky fared even worse than me, as his father, who was home from the war, had meted out a terrible thrashing to the little lad.

\*\*\*\*\*\*\*\*\*\*\*\*\*\*\*\*\*\*\*\*\*\*\*\*\*\*\*\*\*\*\*\*\*\*\*\*

We were to have many a scrape and times of mischief,

down at the railway sidings and its surrounding area. But it was Brammer who suggested at first that we should go down there, not to see the goings-on at the sidings particularly, but to visit what he called the balloon shed.

"U gottoo come and see the balloon shed 'andy mun", he pleaded with me one morning in the early spring.

The days were getting longer, and the weather a little brighter, which enabled us to carry out little expeditions in the late afternoons and early evenings; that is, running messages and other chores permitting. Apparently he had discovered an old shed in a back street near the sidings, where there was an abundance of balloons. Now, toy balloons were a rare commodity indeed, I do not think I had had one in my whole life.

After school that afternoon Dinky, Tommy Thomas, and me, with Brammer leading the way, ran down to the main road. We crossed this, and entered one of the streets on the opposite side, which led to the embankment over-looking the sidings. It had been a fine dry day, and the late afternoon was surprisingly warm for the middle of March. We stood with faces pressed against the railings, which lined the embankment, and watched the activity going on below. Even at this hour of day the sidings were bustling with activity, with the small shunting steam engines huffing and puffing as they worked the maze of railway lines, shunting and separating the rows of coal and cattle trucks, fruit and vegetable wagons. Men with long handled hooks, were hurrying about unhitching and dodging the shunted trucks and wagons. Ordinary railway lines are dangerous places for children at the best of times; but I could see that this place, the sidings, was probably the most dangerous place of all; even for those men who worked there. I watched fascinated by the skills of the engine drivers, and the shunters, who so deftly and quickly hitched and unhitched the wagons. Then suddenly, the afternoon, which was bright and sunny, felt a lot colder. Like a bolt of lightning, I was struck with the chilling thought that I was now right at the centre, in the heart of the domain of Chinky, that spectre who could materialise out of the shadows and pounce on un-suspecting boys.

I was on unfamiliar territory and although I was on the right side of the railways, I felt that even now Chinky was watching and waiting to ensnare me. I felt uneasy, being high up there on the embankment in full view of the workmen below. I shouted to Brammer.

"Come-on mun Brammer, where's this cowin' balloon shed". I was in the boys' school now, and felt that I could use the Hafod's favourite expletive, by right.

Like me, the others too were fascinated by the workings of the sidings, and they also had momentarily forgotten why we were there.

"Aye come on mun Brammer", Dinky echoed my words, "where's the cowin' balloon shed"?

He needed no further prompting from the rest of us, he was off running along the path between the railings and the garden walls of the houses that backed on to the embankment, calling as he ran, "Follow me, follow me, it's a Brammer mun".

The three of us rushed after him, in a line along the narrow path, until he stopped in a clearing where the long narrow gardens of some of the houses had been removed. Here stood an old dilapidated corrugated iron shed, with one door gone and the other just about hanging on. There was an opening between the houses, which gave access to the clearing from the main road. Inside the old corrugated iron building were the remains of an old motorcar, which had been stripped of most of its removable parts such as the doors, wheels, and engine, leaving just the shell. It looked as though the place had once been used, as a motor garage workshop.

Whether Brammer had opened his mouth prematurely or they had discovered it for themselves, but running about, and inside and out of his "balloon shed", were half-a-dozen little boys and girls. Some of them, I recognised from the infants school, had beaten us to it. Then to my horror and disgust, I knew exactly what Brammer had mistakenly taken for balloons, as I saw some of the little tots putting the long white sheathes to their mouths, trying to inflate them.

"You cowin' fool Brammer", I yelled at him, "they're not balloons mun, they're Spunk Bags. It's what the Yanks use when they are doing the girls. Harry told me".

There were many pubs dotted along the main road between Swansea and Morriston, and this reasonably secluded spot with its old shed and wreck of a motorcar, would prove to be a convenient stopping place for those seeking the pleasures of the flesh. I am not sure if the other three fully understood just what the so-called balloons were, as they did not have a streetwise brother called Harry. But I think they got the gist of it when I mentioned, "doing the girls" for they certainly knew what this meant.

They looked stunned, especially Brammer, as Dinky asked, "why do they use 'um 'andy"?

I was on shaky ground now, but I knew it was something to do with babies. "Oh, they are for making babies", I said, "the Yanks use 'um when they want to 'ave babies".

Brammer tried to put on a brave face, but Dinky quick as a flash, pushed his finger into Brammer's stomach and in a jeering voice asked, "Did 'u touch one Brammer"?

He hesitated, a split second, then shouted back firmly,

"No I didn't touchum, I didn't touchum 'onest.

Not to be outdone, Tommy Thomas chipped in "Yes 'u did mun, yes 'u did", then in chorus, we all sang out, "Brammer's having a baby, Brammer's having a baby".

Like a lot of extravert children Brammer was a very sensitive boy, as the tears welled up in his eyes he fled from the balloon shed. It must have taken a lot of convincing talk, from his mother and aunts that night, that it was only girls who had babies, and not little boys like Brammer.

A lot of myths and legends were built up around the Yanks at this time, and most alleged acts of infidelity were attributed to the presence of these young American soldiers. They were awash with money, and could court the young women and girls with luxury items such as silk stockings, scented soaps and perfumes, sweets and chocolates. Probably there was a lot of truth in this, which led to one of the notorious clichés of the times, that the Yankees soldiers were; overpaid, oversexed, and over here. This was even taken up by the Nazi propaganda machine. They tried to destroy the morale of the British troops, who had been fighting since September 1939, and drive a wedge between them and the Yanks. It would have been totally understandable, human, and natural, if they had felt a certain amount of resentment to their American allies.

But there were many well-heeled fat cats, local businessmen and tradesmen, who also profited from the war, at the expense of the majority who had to rely solely on their meagre rations. These men like the Yanks were able to woo and exploit the great numbers of young women, whose husbands and boyfriends had been conscripted into the armed forces, and were absent in some cases for years. Some of these men and women were blatant and arrogant in the way they behaved, as we children can bear witness; having often observed from a suitable distance, many an adulterous act in the bushes of the park, behind the sheds and garages near the tip, and the areas around the railway lines and the canal banks. Some were local girls and women we recognised, and yes sometimes with American soldiers, but equally as often with local men. Babies were born to some of these unfortunates, and often the child would then be passed off as a sibling. Many a young soldier returning from the war, would be greeted with the news that his wife or girlfriend had a new baby brother or sister. I distinctly remember one black child being born, which no doubt proved difficult or impossible to explain.

But life, and making love was not all sordid, and furtive. I remember several young girls finding romance with the young American soldiers, and many of the marriages took place at our local church. When the war ended they sailed off across the sea, to their new homes in America as GI brides.

Like a million wartime liaisons the brief romance between the Major and Mammy was over, and no doubt eyebrows were raised and disapproval expressed in certain quarters, with his frequent visits to our house. But Mammy was an honourable widow, and a free woman, who could make her own choices in life, and did not hurt or betray anyone else. I will not sit in judgment on other people, as the time of war is a cruel time, and many people behave, as they would never do under ordinary circumstances. Young men and women married and celebrated their brief union, knowing and believing that their first acts of intimacy could also be their last. They lived entirely for the present, in an uncertain world, where there was a strong possibility that they would have no future together.

## CHAPTER 25

# MORE TROUBLE
# WITH THE LAW, AND
# CHICKENS

With the coming of late spring and early summer 1944, the last of the American soldiers had left Swansea, and were soon to be involved in the greatest invasion upon land from the sea the world has ever seen. Soon millions of British and American troops would be fighting their way across Western Europe, to meet up with the Russian onslaught on Germany, and so end the war. That was the state of things on a world stage, but for our family, especially Mammy, we could only concentrate on the daily grind of ensuring that we had sufficient food, clothing, and warmth. The basic needs of life.

Things had greatly improved in the last year. Mammy had added some more furniture, a couple of kitchen chairs, a couch, and some more curtains. She also got another single bed for the third bedroom, for Daniel. Eddie, who was now four, could move in with Walter and me. My youngest brother Eddie, the baby of the family, which he hated being called; found this very strange and unnerving. Out of necessity, we did not have the room; he had remained being nursed at night by Mammy, Maggie, or Molly, in the bed, which they shared. I was the oldest in the bed now and slept on the outside, with Walter on the inside nearest the wall, and Eddie in the middle. At least we did not have to sleep head to toe, as in the early days.

Eddie missed the warmth and comfort of Mammy's bed, and must have felt very insecure in being removed from it after so long. To help settle him, I would read stories to him and Walter every night by candlelight. The candle would be stuck onto the wooden headboard, using some of the hot wax that formed around the wick when it was lit. Their favourite, was Treasure Island, which I seemed to read forever. They mostly fell asleep before I had completed reading one page, and Eddie would always plead with me, as he was tiring, "Put 'u arm around me 'andel".

I would cradle his head and shoulders in my left-arm, whilst holding the book in my right hand, straining to read the words of the tattered old book by the faint candlelight. It was only after I was certain that he had fallen into a deep sleep, that I would dare to remove my arm from around him. Very often my arm and hand would be numb, before I could relax.

Things had been going well for me that summer, and our family. But then something happened, that was so reminiscent of a previous time in our lives, when we got entangled with the police and the juvenile courts. This time the offence was deadly serious. We could have, or at least Harry because it was his second recorded offence, been sent to an approved school or even Borstal. Heaven only knows what sort of lives we would have led if this had happened, and where we would have ended up.

Why on earth did Harry want to steal a railway lamp; but that is what he did, and getting me to help him in the process. It should never have happened on such a day, which was a beautiful high summer's afternoon, with not a cloud in the sky. The long August holiday was drawing to an end, and within a week I should have been looking forward to resuming my first year in the boys' school. We had finished dinner, and I was mucking about on the square, probably waiting for Dinky and the rest of my gang. For some reason, Harry seemed to be at a loose end, which was unlike him. Normally he would have been out much further afield, seeking kindred spirits and looking for mischief. But today, he too was hanging around. It was as if the heat of the afternoon sun had quelled his spirit to wander, and he decided to amuse himself with my company. He persuaded me to venture on to the tip, up on to the level where the previous year Sergeant Nick had gouged out a huge portion with his bulldozer, reducing the height on one side by approximately half. Harry was so much quicker and stronger than me, and he was at the top of the tip when I was only halfway up.

He kept shouting at me, "Come on 'mun andel, 'urry up "urry up".

I did my best to keep up with him, but he always kept a distance between us, calling and shouting at me leading me on like a lamb to the slaughter. When I finally got to the top, he was already on his way down the other side, heading in the direction of the railway line.

I had a fair idea of where he was going, and he confirmed this when he shouted, "Come on, we'll go down to the caves".

It was much easier going, now that the height of the tip had been reduced. But we would still have to negotiate our way around the German rhubarb, which was once again in full bloom, before we could get to the caves. He slowed up as he approached the great swathe of Japanese Knotweed, and waited for me to catch up with him.

Now Harry always carried with him in his pocket, what we called a bull knife. This was a folding knife, bigger than a penknife, with a blade on one side, and a curved pointed dagger on the other. It was a formidable weapon, and I am sure that today it would be classed as dangerous, and be prohibited to carry on your person. It was hot, I felt tired and thirsty, and was glad to sit down in the shade of the German Rhubarb when we got there.

We sat there in silence for a couple of minutes, then he jumped up and surprised me by saying, "Would 'u like a drink 'andel".

I thought for a moment that he was teasing me, but this was not so, he got hold of one of the big sticks of knotweed, and with the blade of his bull knife cut this down. Just like its close relative the bamboo, the stem of German Rhubarb is mainly hollow, and Harry proceeded to slice off sections, then tipping these into his mouth drinking the water they contained. Harry liked to show off, but I must admit I was glad that he had his knife with him, and was able to provide me with the drink that I so badly needed.

Until then, I do not think he had in mind, what he intended doing. We easily skirted around the margins of the German rhubarb, and very soon we were in the open space where a year earlier I had witnessed the Yanks arrival by train. Harry stood near the fence; staring intently at the track below, then turned his attention to the signal box and studied this at some length, before switching once again to the track scrutinising the scene below him. The early afternoon sun beat down relentlessly, reflecting its harsh bright light on the steel railway lines, the air was still and silence prevailed, even the Cwmfellyn Works magnetic crane was strangely quiet. It must have been the workmen's dinnertime. The summer heat seemed to imbue a state of lethargy, over the normally busy, bustling, railway line. I was certainly gripped, by the sluggish mood that was cast over us, and would have been willing to sit there calmly for the rest of the day. But not Harry, his mind like his eyes was in over-drive, working out just what his next move would be.

It happened so quickly it was just like a dream, one minute I was sitting quietly, then, I was being yanked to my feet by Harry, and bundled through the fence on to the railway cutting. Still grabbing my arm, he pulled me along as he ran down towards the line.

"Don't be afraid 'andel", he shouted, "no one can see us, they're all 'aving their dinners, even Chinky".

I knew that it was quiet, but we were in full view of the signal box, which was only about 50 yards away. The man in the signal box might be having his dinner, but he was certainly in there.

My first thoughts were, that we were simply dashing across the lines to the other side, but that was not his plan. There was a double track of lines here, and in between the tracks there was a fixed oil lamp. Harry was heading straight for it. He had let go my arm now, but was encouraging me to follow him.

"Come and look at this 'andel", he yelled, "let's see what this is".

He had reached the lamp now, which was about three feet high, nearly as tall as me, and began to examine it.

There was no backing out for me. I was so scared that I would not know which way to run, or what to do. I had no other choice but to stay with him, hoping that he would soon come to his senses and get us away from there. But it was too late. The plot was set. He had discovered that the top of the lamp had a hinged lid, which he now opened, revealing the inner workings.

" 'ey 'andel, come and 'ave a look mun", he said excitedly, "its just what I want mun, I've always wanted something like this".

I stood beside him and looked inside, the lamp was not lit. The signalman, must light it at night, and I could see the burner with the wick, and below that the container which held the paraffin. Above the burner there were two metal rods about six inches long, and it did not take Harry long to work out, that these were used to lift out the whole contraption for cleaning and maintenance.

He gripped one of the rods, then said, "Go round 'andel, and do the same as me".

I would do anything now to get away from there, as I could feel eyes burning into my neck. I looked up, and saw the man at the window of the signal box. I grabbed the rod, and simultaneously we yanked the lamp out of its container. It was bigger and heavier than I thought, and we struggled, as together we carried the lamp back across the line, up the embankment, under the wire fence, and on to the tip.

As we ran, I could hear the signalman shouting, "Stop, stop, stop", whilst Harry kept yelling, "Keep going, keep going".

I did, and kept going until we reached the safe haven of the German rhubarb, and quickly disappeared into its sprawling mass. Once inside there, and hidden away from the outside world, we dropped the lamp. As it hit the ground, it spewed out its contents of paraffin, its sour acrid odour increasing the sickness and nausea I was already beginning to feel. I stumbled to the ground on my knees, not caring now whether the signalman caught us or not; but Harry, with one thought in mind, self-preservation, was already planning his next move.

He stood above me and pointing his right forefinger at me, said quietly, almost in a whisper, "Right 'andel, you stay by yer with the lamp, no one can see 'u, and I'll go and get 'elp, right".

The speed of his recovery was remarkable, he was only slightly out of breath, and he spoke in a tone of voice that somehow reminded me of the vicar giving his sermon on a Sunday evening. His facial expression too was serene, so calm and righteous. There was nothing to fear. But there was still a hint of a threat in his voice, as he turned to leave, he looked back at me and said, "Don't u say anything to our Mammy mind, or to anyone else, right".

After he had gone, I stayed within the cover of the German rhubarb for perhaps ten or fifteen minutes, but I got well away from the lamp and the pool of paraffin that was slowly being sucked into the peaty ground. I was glad of the rest, and the shade from the relentless sun. As I sat there, recovering my breath, and courage, I reflected on the afternoon's events, completely baffled by Harry's action in stealing the lamp for no reason at all other than sheer vandalism.

There was no sign of Harry when I got home later that afternoon, it was nearly four o'clock and soon we would be having our tea. Mammy reminded me, that I was going to visit the Central Library, where I had joined the junior section. They had promised, that they would keep a copy of the Lost World for me. I was still apprehensive, and worried about the theft of the railway lamp; but these feelings eased after tea when I took the bus to the library, and the anticipation of having the book of the Lost World. I was so thrilled with the BBC serial, that I wanted to read it to Walter and Eddie. But the elation I felt as I returned from the library, with the book clutched in my hands, soon faded, when I saw the two burly policemen standing at the gate in conversation with Mammy. I realised immediately that they were there in connection with the stolen railway lamb, but my hopes were momentarily raised when the older of the two policemen smiled at me and asked me about the Lost World. He seemed surprised, that I wished to read the book, and even more so when he learned that I had joined the library. My hopes were, however, short lived, when I saw the look on Mammy's face, which was a combination of anger and despair.

I readily confessed to the crime when the policeman asked me about the stolen lamp, and confirmed that my accomplice was my brother Harry. There was no use denying it, we were so close to the signal box that the Railway man must have given a pretty good description of us to the police, and they soon tracked us down. The interview with the police, which took place in the kitchen, lasted probably less than 30 seconds. It was the older of the two policemen who asked the questions, and was directly to the point.

"Have you been up on the railway lines son".

"Yes sir", I replied.

"Did you steal a railway lamp".

"Yes sir", I said once again.

"Right son, now who was with you"?

"My brother 'arry sir", I confirmed.

That was it, as soon as the words were out of my mouth, Mammy could contain herself no longer, as she got hold of me and hit me from the kitchen, and through the parlour to the bottom of the stairs, where I broke free from her grip and ran crying to the bed room. When Harry returned much later that evening, I almost felt sorry for him, as

Mammy laid into him, holding him by the scruff of his neck with one hand, and lampooning him, on his head, back, and shoulders, with the other.

We had to attend the central police station in Swansea the following day with Mammy, where I assume we were charged with trespass on railway property, and criminal damage to the railway lamp. There would be a summons issued in due course, for us to appear before the juvenile court, when our fate would become known. Thankfully we did not have to wait long for this, which came just after the new school term had started. But before then there was another summons to be dealt with, and that was appearing before the school headmaster Mr Joe Morgan. This was the second time for Harry to come up before him, but the first time for me. He was very angry for the disgrace that we had brought upon the school; but was genuinely more concerned for the distress and worry that we had brought upon Mammy. Her struggle and determination to keep us all together as a family, and for us to grow up to be decent law-abiding citizens, had won great admiration from many people, and Joe Morgan was one of them. I am convinced, that his report to the juvenile court asking for leniency in dealing with us, proved successful in the punishment that was eventually meted out. I was given a severe warning with regard to my future conduct, and Harry, who Mammy feared might be taken away from the family, was placed on probation for two years. We had been dealt with quickly, and I must admit fairly. The thought that Harry, had come close to being sent to an approved school, got the message firmly home to both of us. I am glad to say that was the last time we fell foul of the law.

Although the court case, and Harry being put on probation threw a dark cloud over the end of the summer and the start of the new school term, we quickly recovered and got on with life. One of the success stories, of the previous year, was the rearing of the White Leghorn chickens. This year she decided to do the same again, with the programme becoming a little bit more ambitious, she decided to go for day old Rhode Island Red pullets, which would serve the dual purpose of meat for Christmas dinner, with the additional bonus of fresh eggs every day. Well that was the plan. But after a matter of just a few weeks, disaster had struck, and out of the dozen chicks we started out with just one remained. We prayed for the best but expected the worst, as this lonely pitiful survivor clung on to life, and eventually won through.

As spring turned to summer, the little creature grew bigger and stronger, and by September when it was five to six months old, it had developed into a fine looking specimen. Then Mammy said that it should soon start laying eggs, and to encourage this she bought a small packet of Karswood Poultry Spice. This was a branded product that we had seen advertised in the national press, which it was claimed, produced miraculous results for chickens and eggs. She thought that the extra outlay; the cost of this wonder product, would be more than offset if the net result, was an extra three to four eggs a week. So once a day, a measure of the Poultry Spice, would be added to the chicken's mash, which it seemed to eat with relish. Several weeks passed by, and I would look in the little nest box that Mammy had made, countless times every day. But not one egg materialised. The only change that occurred concerning the chicken, which was clear for all to see, was a sudden increase in the amount of chicken dung covering the floor of the coup. If it did nothing else, the Karswood Poultry Spice was proving to be a damn good laxative.

Then came the day of reckoning, the moment of revelation when the chicken revealed its true self. It was on one of those mid October dawns, a blue grey sky and a weakening sun beginning to rise, with the first chill of winter in the air. The bedroom I shared with my two younger brothers, was at the back of the house overlooking the chicken coup, and at first, I thought the first stifled cry I heard, was the call of one of the local tomcats seeking Puss the cat. In my drowsy state, I did not pay particular attention to this, as it was a common occurrence for the backyards and gardens to be taken over at night by the prowling cats. Then, it could have been minutes or an hour later, I was still in a state of half sleep, I heard the cry again, but this time it was stronger. As the dawn broke into morning, the intervals got shorter, and the sound grew stronger, until finally with the break of day, there rang out a full throttled cry off "Cock a doodle doo".

My state of drowsiness was shattered, as I sat bolt upright, my mind refusing to believe my ears. I sat still, waiting, and thinking it was a dream, then it came again "Cock a doodle doo".

It was not a dream, and the cockerel's cry was emanating from right beneath my bedroom window.

Walter and Eddie were already stirring, disturbed not only by the shrill cry, but by me as I jumped out of bed, quickly put on my trousers socks and boots, and ran downstairs. I knew that Mammy would already be up, and Maggie would be awake preparing herself for work. I was surprised to see not only them, but Molly, Daniel, and Harry as well, all out in the back garden staring in bewilderment at our Rhode Island Red pullet, that was now a cockerel. The puzzled look on Mammy's face said it all, she did not know whether to laugh or cry. Gone were all the hopes of having fresh eggs, along with the cash expended on the Karswood Poultry Spice. The thought crossed my mind, that it would have been indeed, a more

329

wondrous product than its makers claimed, if it could have got this chicken to produce eggs. In the end we all burst out laughing, led by Mammy, who stuck to her philosophy of life "of getting on with it", though, it must have been highly embarrassing for her, with her farming background to have made such a mistake as this.

Shortly after, like an omen, the rickety old chicken coup that Mammy had knocked up, collapsed in a heap of decaying rusty metal, and we never kept chickens again. But the chicken that was now a cockerel, spent most of its time pecking around the garden, and in and out of the House. Harry christened him Archie, after some ne'er-do-well acquaintance of his, and he gradually became the family pet, which was more than Puss the cat had ever been. Walter and Eddie became very fond of him, and they would follow him around absolutely fascinated by him.

As we no longer had a chicken coup, there was only one suitable place for Archie to roost at nights, and that was the coalhouse. This was an integral part of the main house, and his rousing crowing at dawn, was not welcomed by all, particularly by Daniel and Harry, whose bedroom was immediately above it. Anyway, his days were numbered. He had been bought originally for the dual purpose of providing fresh eggs, and our Christmas dinner. He had dramatically failed on the first count, so as the festive season approached it was time for him to redeem himself, and return with interest all the care and attention devoted to him. So a couple of days before Christmas, with all the excitement building up for the big day, Archie quietly disappeared, only to re-appear for his final act at noon on Christmas Day. Nothing was said, he was not referred to by name, but we all knew the true identity of the bird that now adorned, the Swain family Christmas table. All that is except Walter and Eddie, who were blissfully unaware that the perky cockerel that they had watched with fascination, and had kept them amused for hours, was soon to be carved up and placed before them. I was sorry for Archie and his demise, but soon banished all such thoughts when I tasted just how good he was with a bit of gravy. Walter, and Eddie, were quite happy too, until Harry, who timed his intervention perfectly, when they had both eaten about half their portions asked them, "Did 'u enjoy eatin' Archie then".

The shocking reality of the truth, told bluntly by Harry, hit home savagely to their young impressive minds, as first Eddie, and then Walter, their spoons clattering on to their plates, began bawling and wailing, "Archee-ah, Archee-ah".

Mammy stepped in quickly, dashing from the head of the table where she always sat, and gave Harry a couple of thumps between his shoulder blades, at the same time reassuring the two little ones that the chicken was not Archie.

"No, no, bach", she said soothingly, "Archie's gone to stay with Father Christmas".

She patted and fussed over them for a minute whilst still glaring at Harry, who despite the hiding he just had, continued eating his dinner as if nothing had happened. Quickly Mammy had got the situation under control, and soon everyone was eating purposefully once more. Even Walter, and Eddie, calmer now, eating their potatoes, carrots, and cabbage, but carefully avoiding the bits of chicken and bread and thyme stuffing. They might, have had an inkling that it was Archie that Mammy pulled out of the oven that day, but suppressed that thought in favour of the succulent meat. It was only the truth blatantly told that made it unpalatable.

CHAPTER 26

# CUB SCOUTS AND FOOTBALL

January 1945, and the year got off to a bad start for me. It began with Dinky, or rather his mother, who suggested that he should join the cub Scouts. The idea did not appeal to him at all, the general consensus being that all cubs were sissies, but he thought that he could put up with it as long as I was with him.

"Will 'u join the cubs 'andel, if I do", he said, that first day back at school after the Christmas holidays.

"Mammy says I've gottoo join the cubs, and she said 'u should join to".

He was almost pleading with me, when he said this, adding weight to his case that his mother was press-ganging the two of us. It was not an argument he should have used really, as the year before I similarly tried to get him to join the Church choir, but his mother had come out firmly against the idea. They were not churchgoers. He did sometimes attend the Sunday school, but somehow I do not think his mother thought of this in the same way as attending Church.

At first I firmly declined his offer, but Dinky was a

persistent little imp, and over the next couple of days he gradually wore my resistance down by constantly harping, "Oh come on mun 'andel, it'll be great mun, you an' me in the cubs", and, "we won't be sissies 'onest mun, we won't be sissies".

So eventually, I gave in to shut him up if nothing else, and agreed to meet him at the Old Parish Hall that Wednesday evening, when the new cubs were to be enrolled.

Now I had already seen some of the existing cubs, and was aware of just what their uniform consisted of, which was mainly a green jersey, black or grey trousers and socks, which were adorned with two little garter-like, green tassels. But the one essential item it seemed, was the green jersey, this was the key, the passport to becoming a cub scout. The colours of the rest of the apparel I thought, did not really matter, except perhaps for the little green tassels. Luck was on my side, for as it happened my main school upper garment at that time was a green jersey. I had it made, I was in the cub scouts. I had black trousers, grey socks, and with some blacking on my boots I would be as smart as any of them. But, I thought, I would not take any chances and directly after school, I raced home and nagged Mammy to help me make the little green tassels. Unfortunately the family rag box was right out of green material, and the nearest we could come up with was light blue. This would have to do we thought; they would be better than nothing, so in no time at all Mammy had cut four three inch strips about an inch wide, cut the all-important inverted V, then looped and stitched the strips over two pieces of string. So just before 6 o'clock that evening, the time the meeting was being held, Mammy tied the tassels on to my legs, slicked my hair, and off to the Parish Hall I went.

Dinky and his mother were waiting for me, and soon we were sitting in a semi-circle around this imposing figure known as Akela. She wore a green shirt that was covered in insignia and badges, and a green pleated skirt, with light brown socks and shoes. Her long dark hair was curled over and clipped together like a big horseshoe shaped sausage, which I think was called the Victory roll, and she wore glasses. But I thought she looked very smart and beautiful. She had a note pad and pencil, and wrote down the names and addresses, of all six of us who were aspiring to join her troop. Then, she outlined the rules and regulations; the do's and don'ts for all good cub scouts. This is where I met my downfall. The uniform was as I thought, with the green jersey being the main part of the dress; but it was not essential to have the little green tassels. Then came the bombshell. She said that the green jersey had to be kept solely for use when attending cub-scout meetings, and must not be used on any other occasion. Certainly not for every day wear.

Then, she looked directly at me, and with no emotion said, "Any boy who has to wear his green jersey to school cannot join, and must leave now".

She had probably guessed that I fitted into this category, as my jersey was not as new, or not quite as shiny as those worn by the other boys. I felt a terrible sense of shame, as I sat there with everyone's eyes on me. My hopes dashed, knowing I had no argument. But then I felt angry, as I thought of Mammy and the work she had put in to make me as presentable as possible, and I stood up, turned my back on the Akela and marched, my arms swinging, out of the room.

That was how the New Year started for me, in disaster. But there was an even bigger disaster waiting for Daniel, who like Molly, had now left Hafod school to join Greggs

College. Daniel was not a delicate child physically, and could hold his own with any one; but it was his almost saintly presence or attitude to life, that probably prompted Mammy to send him to Greggs, to study bookkeeping. She probably thought that he was not suitable for factory or shop work, and would be better off working as a clerk in an office. I think her ambitions for him to become a minister of religion had faded. He must have felt it strange, moving from a boys' only school, to Greggs, whose pupils were more than 90 per cent girls. For the first week or so, he appeared to be irritable, and not at all his usual helpful and caring self; which we thought was probably because of his change of school. It is odd that what would be innocuous to one person, can prove to be so irksome to another. The root of his problem, or what was disturbing him; was the fact that he was the only boy at the college who wore boots, albeit, that they were brand spanking new boots, and you could not see them anyway, because he was now wearing long trousers.

He must have given the matter considerable thought, since he was not a boy who would rush into anything, before working out the pitfalls of any action he would take. What he eventually decided on was to cut the boots down, and shape them into a pair of shoes. It was a bold decision he made, and without the consent of Mammy, but he did have the added safeguard of his old boots, which he intended to experiment with first. If the result was satisfactory; then he would hopefully have Mammy's approval, to complete the job on his new boots. He planned his move carefully, waiting for the weekend, one Saturday afternoon when he knew that Mammy would be in town shopping. We had one, good, strong, sharp knife in the house. Mammy used this, for cutting and boning meat, gutting fish, and cutting bread, and it was this deadly tool that he intended to use. I was the only one present that afternoon to witness just what Daniel did, which was to end in disaster for the boots, and Daniel.

I can picture him now as he set out the two pairs of boots, the old ones, and new ones; side by side on the coconut matting on the kitchen floor, and placing the knife beside them like a surgeon preparing for a major operation. He even had a piece of white chalk, to draw the curve on the welt of the boot that was necessary to get the right shape. This he had to do from memory, as there was not a shoe in the house that he could copy from. But undeterred, he pressed ahead; marking the left foot boot with the chalk, until he was finally satisfied that he had the correct curve in the correct place. Then the operation began, he had to be careful, as there was not much room between the eyelets or lace-holes on the boots, where the cutting would begin. I thought that he had done an excellent job, as he sliced into the thick leather, carefully following the curved outline of the chalk. There was a tremendous beaming smile on his face when he had finished, for the end result did not look so bad at all. Now it certainly looked like a shoe, well more like a shoe than a boot. He was well pleased with himself, and I felt very proud of him, that he would have the thought and nerve to do such a thing, and do it so success-fully. After admiring his handiwork for a moment, he quickly got hold of the right boot, marked this with his chalk, and with confidence now, sliced through the leather with ease. Then he placed it next to the left foot boot-cum-shoe, and stood back studying them with a great look of satisfaction on his face. He was so taken up, with the elation and joy of what he had accomplished, that he failed to notice just what he had done. I did not mean to spoil his moment of triumph, but I could not help myself as I blurted out, "Look mun Daniel, look what u've done".

He refused to believe that there was anything wrong, until I pointed my finger, touching each boot-cum-shoe, and said in a whisper to soften the blow, "Look mun Daniel, u've cut one old boot, and one new one".

The shock to his system was sudden, and I thought for a moment almost fatal, as he slumped to the floor on his knees, holding his head in his hands, the tears welled up in his eyes as he cried, "Mammy will kill me when she gets home, she'll kill me mun, she will, she'll kill me".

But to this day I do not think that Mammy ever found out about the calamity with the shoes, or should I say boots-cum-shoes. After he had calmed down and regained his composure, and taken stock of the situation, he thought that it would be best for all concerned, especially for himself if he said nothing to Mammy at all. He knew that I would keep quiet about it, unless I was asked directly by Mammy. If she suspected something, he understood then, that I would spill the beans. Initially he had not taken into account the fact that he was now wearing long trousers, the style of which then was quite baggy, and without close scrutiny you could not tell whether he was wearing boots or shoes. The only giveaway for any discerning person would be the sound of the hobnails striking the ground, and of course Mammy would be expecting this sound anyway. After a couple of weeks, he cut down the remaining old boot, showed the pair of boots-cum-shoes to Mammy who did not seem to mind, and a week later he cut down the other new boot. He had got away with it.

\*\*\*\*\*\*\*\*\*\*\*\*\*\*\*\*\*\*\*\*\*\*\*\*\*\*\*\*\*\*\*\*\*\*\*\*

That episode with the boots proved to me that "necessity is the mother of invention", not only with Daniel's efforts to turn his boots into shoes, but also the way he overcame the problem. It showed that he could be as devious and shrewd as anyone, even Maggie or Harry, when it was essential to preserve the status quo. But that was just one instance, and not the way I prefer to think of and remember Daniel. A better example would be what happened some years later, when Daniel was working as a clerk to a firm of auctioneers, and I was picked to play football for the school. The one problem was, that I did not possess a pair of football boots, and it was not possible to turn out and represent the school without them. Wearing and playing in ordinary boots, which we did at playtimes and in practice matches, would not do. But the schoolmaster who is in charge of the football team, believed that he could overcome this. There was one lad in the class, about the same height and build as me who did have a pair of football boots, but had no chance of playing for the school. So when the team was announced on Friday afternoon, all matches were played on Saturday morning, he asked the lad if he would lend his boots to me. The answer was a categorical NO, his mother would not permit it. The teacher said he was sorry, and gave my place in the team to the first reserve. Once again, this was done in front of the full class, and like the similar experience of being rejected by the cub Scouts a couple of years earlier, I felt angry and humiliated.

Thankfully the announcement of the football team was the last item on the school agenda for the day, and I was soon able to hurry away. I managed to contain my anger and disappointment, until I reached the quiet back lane that ran parallel with Odo Street; I just wanted to avoid people and be on my own, and then burst into tears. It must have taken me a quarter of an hour, to cover the distance, which I would normally do in two to three minutes. When I eventually got home, Mammy could see that I was very upset, the tell-tale tear stains around my eyes did not help, when she asked, "dew, dew, Handel bach, what's the matter boy?"

Her words of concern set me off again, as I burst into tears and ran out of the house. I needed more time on my own, to come to terms with the problem to which I knew there was no solution, and to get a grip on myself. I was competitive by nature, and desperately wanted to play in the school football team, I had earned that privilege and felt that it was my right. But there was no way that Mammy could afford to buy such luxury items as football boots, and I would just have to accept the situation.

That was in September 1947 and I was 11 years old, and over the months that followed I banished from my mind any thought of playing football for the school. I had to adopt Mammy's philosophy in life and just had to "get on with it"; but it was very hard to bear as every Friday afternoon I had a sharp reminder of what could have been, when the school football team was announced. Then at Christmas time something happened that was for me, the nearest thing to a miracle, when I had the greatest Christmas present I have ever had in my life. At the bottom of the bed that Christmas morning, was a large brown paper parcel, which to my amazement, when I opened it up contained a junior size full Arsenal strip of jersey, red with white sleeves, white shorts, red and white socks, and one pair of football boots. I ran down the stairs carrying the precious gift in my arms, to express my delight and thanks to Mammy.

She was sitting at the table, and opposite her sat Daniel, both of them with enormous smiles on their faces. I put the parcel on the table then quickly took it off again one of Mammy superstitions, putting boots on the table was unlucky.

But there was nothing unlucky about today, "Oh thank 'u Mammy", I said, "this is the best present I've ever 'ad".

The smile on her face changed into a great big beam, and almost giggling like a little girl, she shook her head and pointed across the table at Daniel.

"No, no, bach, it's your brother Daniel, it's him you want to thank, he got you your lovely Christmas present".

I could hardly believe it, how did the he managed to pay for it, for a family like ours the cost must have been a small fortune. Daniel just smiled, and said nothing, we found it difficult as a family to respond to any show of gratitude or appreciation, and Mammy sensed this when she said.

"Well, come on bach try them on, let's see how they look on you".

Fortunately the entire outfit was a little on the large size for me; but out of choice that is just what Mammy would have chosen, as she helped me into the jersey and shorts she said.

"Oh you do look great Handel, and they are a good size too, you'll grow into these lovely, boy".

The same thing applied to the football boots, they were a bit on the large size to, but that was not a problem that Mammy could not solve with a ball of newspaper rammed into the toe ends.

Before that day, the weather on all previous Christmases seemed dark, cold, and gloomy, and we rarely ventured outside, preferring the cosy warmth of the fireside. But the morning of Christmas Day in 1947 was crisp, sunny, and bright, and all of my brothers and sisters accompanied me to the park, where I was paraded in the full glory of my Arsenal strip. If my memory serves me well, I think I wore the jersey and shorts for the whole of the Christmas holidays, even sleeping in them. The football boots I treasured, and they lasted me for at least two seasons. Mr Evans, our next door neighbour; gave me a small tin of dubbing to rub on the leather uppers, but not the heels or toes, to keep them soft and supple. And at the start of the new school year, I proudly walked to school with the football boots tied together by their laces; slung around my neck, as was the fashion for all aspiring young footballers in those days, and the following Saturday, I took my rightful place at left half in the school's football team.

The puzzle of how Daniel, had managed to get such a wonderful Christmas present for me, was explained later by Mammy. She said that he was so upset and angry; when he had heard about me not being able to play football for the school, he was determined to do something about it. As luck would have it part of his job at the auctioneers where he worked, was to list or write itineraries for the various lots brought in to the firm for auction. Amongst one lot was a bag containing the second hand football kit. He told his immediate superior, the managing clerk of my problem, and how he would dearly love to get the kit for me. The man must have been a kind hearted soul and came to an agreement with Daniel, that he could have the kit for a price that he could afford. He knew that Mammy could not help with the payment, but there was one source of income that Daniel had control of, and that was his bus fares to and from work every day. This amounted to tuppence a day, which he gave to his boss, and walked the round trip of four miles a day, every working day from September until Christmas.

\*\*\*\*\*\*\*\*\*\*\*\*\*\*\*\*\*\*\*\*\*\*\*\*\*\*\*\*\*\*\*\*\*\*\*

January 1945, I had completed my first year in the boys' school. I was moving up a class, and was now in perhaps what could be termed the real boys' school. Now for the first time in my life, I had a male teacher. Mr Harris, or Wiggy; as he was known to the children, was in charge of standard two. All of the teachers had nicknames, such as Baldy, Beaky, Bouncer, Charlie, Titus, and Pet. I never fathomed out, why Miss Noyle did not have a nickname, like her male counterparts; perhaps it was some form of chivalry that prevailed, even amongst rough working-class boys that prevented us from doing so. It was even more of a mystery as to why Mr Harris was christened Wiggy, as there was no apparent sign or evidence that he did in fact wear a wig. It still amazes me of what legends and myths can evolve, not only amongst impressionable children, but mature and otherwise intelligent adults.

March 1st, St David's Day was the first big event of the year, and it was normal for each class to create something special; to put on a show with a welsh theme, to celebrate the day. There would be no ordinary schoolwork that day; we would all assemble in the hall in the morning, to watch each class make its presentation, and there was a half-day holiday in the afternoon. Standard two, our class, were going to re-enact the Battle of Bosworth; where the future Tudor King, Henry the 7th defeated Richard the Third. Norman Lloyd, who seemed to be growing by the foot rather than inches, was awarded the part of Henry, probably because of his size, and I was cast as his trusty lieutenant. We all had to dress up as best we could, making our own costumes, but most essential was acquiring a weapon such as a sword, pike, or pikestaff. Always up for a challenge, I decided that I would have a sword.

Mr Harris said these were only toy weapons, so they could be made out of wood or cardboard, and they did not have to be too fancy, and I knew precisely, where I could get the raw material. There were several bomb-damaged houses near my house, and most had been made safe and secure, but some were still open to the elements. If you could get up on to the first floor, then it was quite easy to hack away at the lath and plaster ceiling and extract some of the timber. This, which came lengths of about 3 ft long, an inch wide, and a quarter of an inch-thick, I thought, was workable, and I could easily fashion into a sword, with a simple kitchen knife. So getting the timber was easy, and I got several lengths of the lath to work and experiment on. I had an idea of just what the final length and shape of the sword would be, but somehow it did not quite work out like that, and I ended up with something entirely different.

That evening, working on the concrete area between the back door and the garden, I tried my hand in the skill of woodwork. The wood was dry and brittle and difficult to work, with bits breaking off as I hacked away with one of Mammy's kitchen knives, which was not all that sharp. But I did eventually manage to shape a length about a foot long into a blade, which was really a piece of wood with a pointed end, and cut a smaller piece about six inches long for the hilt. Now came the tricky bit, I had to nail these two bits of wood together. The hatchet we used for chopping firewood; the blunt end of which also served as a hammer, was the tool for the job, and I also knew where to get some nails. We had boxes for everything, rags in the rag box, bits of string in the string box, buttons in the button box, and nails in the nail box. Nothing was thrown away that might come in handy. So with the hatchet and what I thought were two suitable nails, I proceeded to attach the hilt to the blade. I was lucky, the wood split but the nails held. Whether it would hold up to the rigours of a mock battle in the school hall I had my doubts, and the size and shape of the thing resembled more of a dagger than sword.

I soon found out the following day, when we had a

rehearsal, or practise run of our historic spectacular. There were about a dozen of us taking part, six on each side, with very few words spoken, the main emphasis being placed on the battle. Naturally the big scene was between Henry and Richard, with the rest of us skirmishing about on the perimeter. As Henry's trusty lieutenant, it was my duty to engage in battle, my counterpart on the opposite side, a boy that we called Batty. He was much bigger than me, as were most of the boys in my class anyway, but what's more he was equipped with a well fashioned sword, which looked a lot firmer and stouter than mine. It was only supposed to be a pretend battle, really just going through the motions, waving our weapons in the air, and prancing about whilst the rest of the class cheered us on. We took up our positions, Henry against Richard, both holding their swords aloft, and as they advanced towards each other I to marched towards my adversary Batty. The whole class was getting excited, shouting and whistling, as the two main protagonists threatened and gesticulated. I closed on my opponent, holding my sword high before me, and stopped about one pace away from him. I stood there pulling faces, threatening him and pointing my puny, fragile, and pathetic sword directly at his heart. Then, this was not supposed to happen, with one mighty swipe he brought his formidable weapon down upon mine, smashing it into smithereens. This brought a great cheer from the onlookers, and some wag shouted out, "Lay down mun 'andel, 'u are dead".

So I collapsed in a heap on the floor, everyone was laughing, the battle continued for a few more seconds, until everybody except Henry was dead and lying on the floor. We all agreed that it was a tremendous battle, and that the real thing on St David's Day would be a great success.

I did not feel embarrassed or humiliated, that my sword failed so miserably and disintegrated so quickly. In fact I felt rather pleased with myself in the way that I reacted, and the applause I got from the class when I did my dying act. There was only one problem now, the following day was St David's Day, and I had to get myself a new sword. I needed help, as I only had the rest of the afternoon and evening, so I turned to Daniel. The way he saw it, the cause of my problem was my flimsy sword, against the much stouter weapon of my opponent. The answer was simple, I needed a much stronger weapon, and for this he produced from the coal shed, where we kept all manner of things that might come in handy, part of an old broom handle. It was about two and a half feet long, and using the hatchet he soon sharpened one end to a point, then he rummaged in the stock of firewood and produced a suitable piece for the hilt. With the kitchen knife he gouged out a groove in the broom handle, and slotted this in and secured it with a nail. It was a grand and formidable looking weapon, the only problem was, that it was so heavy, I needed two hands to hold it.

Still, I was undeterred, and on St David's Day I marched to school with a piece of rope tied around my waist, my sword stuck in this, dangling on the ground, with a cocked hat made of paper on my head. Unlike the previous day when we held the rehearsal in the classroom, today we were on the big stage, in the main hall in front of the whole school. Standard one, Miss Noyle's class were on first, and they sang a couple of welsh songs. Then it was our turn, the Battle of Bosworth. As at rehearsal the day before, we lined up; the respective armies facing each other; and to great cheers, started by our class, but now picked up by the whole school we closed upon the opposing force. This time I was prepared for my opponent, and holding my sword in both hands I advanced upon him, grim and determined yelling "Come-on by yer now boy, come-on mun, come by yer".

It was almost an exact repeat of the previous encounter, as I stopped before him, he brought down his sword upon mine with a grand flourish; but this time the broom handle proved to be more than a match for his weapon. A shudder shot through me, as with a crunch and a crack the blade of his sword snapped at the hilt, and all he was left standing with was the stump. Our class leading the others chanted, "'u are dead Batty, 'u are dead, lie down Batty 'u are dead".

Then the whole school took up the chant, "lie-down Batty 'u are dead, lie down Batty 'u are dead".

I think he was overwhelmed by the noise, and so shocked he was at a loss just what to do. So instead of lying down, as he should have, he took up a defensive stance, with the stump of his sword held out in front of him. My blood was up now, and I began to wield the broom handle, which I clutched in both my hands. But unfortunately it was so heavy that I had little or no control over it, and started laying into both friend and foe alike. All mayhem broke loose as the participants scattered to avoid the swinging broom handle, and near hysteria broke out among the rest of the screaming, cheering children. Fortunately there were no heads cracked, as Mr Harris and some of the other teachers dived in, with one of them ripping the broom handle from my hands. Order was restored quickly, with the dead and dying soldiers helped to their feet, and cheered as we left the front of the hall and rejoined our classmates. What ever happened to the sword made from a broom handle, I do not know. Perhaps one of the teachers kept it as a memento. It was never returned to me, but ever since, on St David's Day, I think back to the

Battle of Bosworth that I won with a broom handle, and smile.

## CHAPTER 27

# THE BATTLE WON

May 8th 1945, VE-Day, the war in Europe was over. World War II still had several months to run before Japan was defeated; but the war that we the civilians, women and children, had been directly involved in was ended. Soon the young men would be coming back home, some had already returned, and street parties were quickly organized to celebrate this wondrous event. Bonfires were lit to symbolise the lifting of the blackout, and the materials used to put this into effect were to be burnt. Some people had special black blinds made that could be quickly and easily drawn at night. But that did not apply to us, and indeed most other people, who used dark blankets, paper, or anything else they could lay their hands on that was suitable. Still, each street had their bonfires. Mounds of anything that could be spared, and was combustible, were piled high in the middle of the roads and burnt. We had our party in the middle of Hafod Square, with trestle tables that we borrowed from the Church, lined in a long row. We had blancmange and jelly, some people made sandwiches, Mammy made rock cakes and Welsh cakes, and we had large bottles of gassy pop to drink.

Games were organised for the children, mainly races, and prizes were awarded, 6d for the winner, 3d for second, and a penny for third. The groups for each race were made up according to age, and I conserved my energy, having great hopes of securing one of the prizes. The races were over short distances, great for the sprinters, but not for the likes of me who excelled over the longer distances where stamina was required. Out of the six of us who started the race, I was last but one to finish. I took the whole thing very personally, that I had been hard done by, and that the whole concept was most unfair. I was very competitive as a child, and probably still am, and hated losing. The party went on long into the night, on that glorious summer's evening, when we could rejoice and celebrate that we had come through and survived total war. Although unfortunately not for all, for some wives in particular, their troubles were yet to come.

After the initial euphoria of the men returning, and being reunited with their wives and families, the camaraderie and togetherness that united people in the time of war began to lessen. Then doubts, and suspicion, of how their wives behaved while they were away, began to fester in some men. Sadly, one of those that suffered was my pal Dinky, and even more his poor mother. Since that night in the air-raid shelter, when I first met Dinky and his mother, I spent many happy hours playing in their house, and was always welcome to listen to their radio. His grand-mother also lived with them during the war, but once Mr Miles, Dinky's father returned, then the old lady left and went to live elsewhere. I don't know whether this was a voluntary move on her part or not. I continued playing with Dinky, and our friendship blossomed, as before, but over the coming months I was gradually discouraged from entering his house, which I had freely done in the past.

Violence in the home, physical abuse by a man, upon his wife and children, was not an uncommon feature of life in those days. Spare the rod and spoil the child, was regrettably a golden rule for most families, where both husband and wife would physically chastise their children from one degree to another. Having a "good hiding" would vary from a couple of sharp slaps on the child's bottom or legs, to what could only be correctly termed as grievous bodily harm. Society accepted and even demanded that children, particularly boys, should be subjected to physical discipline from an early age to prevent unruly behaviour. Many parents honestly believing, the old adage of "this is for your own good", whilst laying into and knocking the child senseless.

Wife-beating if not openly accepted was tolerated by society and even the authorities would turn a blind eye using the excuse that it was part of life, and what a man did behind closed doors was his business. Sometimes, as in my father's case, the physical attacks upon Mammy occurred only when fuelled by drink. But the beatings inflicted on us children, could come at any time, as punishment, if he thought that we were guilty of wrongdoing. As with anything else in life, there are markers or guidelines, that would be considered to be the norm, and it was only when the violence exceeded these that the family, particularly the woman, would feel a sense of shame. Many women suffered terrible abuse, and often these attacks were witnessed by their terrified children; but to avoid that phoney word shame, they suffered in silence, whereas they should have cried out to the world to have it stopped.

These things are not easily apparent at first, even more so for a child, and sometimes even adults that are close to a family, are shocked when they discover that the pleasant, courteous, and smiling man, think they know, is a wife beater. So it was with Dinky, whose personality gradually changed from a self-assured impish spirit, to a quieter more timid soul, when his father returned after the war. It was only with the passing of time, that I came to realise that the cause for this, was the suffering his mother endured at the hands of his father.

There were many rumours of attempted suicide amongst women, who could no longer cope and driven to despair by their husbands, and no longer prepared to suffer in silence. The most common and favoured method of these poor women was an overdose of pills mixed with alcohol, or if they were privileged enough to have one, was putting her head in the gas oven. Physical abuse was not always the cause of these desperate women's attempts at suicide; the mental abuse of silence and suspicion can sometimes be harder to bear. I got to hear of one poor man who refused to speak to his wife, who would wander the streets after his working day had finished, and only return to his home late at night. He would often come and watch the children playing in the park, or I would see him trudging the wastelands of the tip, his haversack, in which he used to carry his sandwiches to work, still slung over his shoulder. What was he thinking of, what was on this man's mind, that after a full day's work he refused to go home to his wife, preferring to pace the streets in solitude. Could this be put down entirely to the war; that a man would behave in such a strange way, or would it have happened anyway, resulting finally in his wife taking her own life?

Contrary to what most people expected, the ending of the war did not bring an end to rationing, and indeed as some things became more plentiful other things like bread and potatoes became scarce. The combined efforts of the miners' strike and the terrible winter of 1947, proved to be the most difficult period for our family, even accounting for what the war threw at us, apart from the bombs. There were many more people scouring the tip that winter, to top up their dwindling coal supplies with cinders, than I ever saw during the whole of the war.

On the plus side we now had a wireless set of our own. We did not own it, but rented it from Dan Morgan's shop in High Street. This worked off a battery, which would be about half the size of a modern car battery, and had to be recharged at least once every week. A spare battery was essential, as you could never tell when the one in use would run out; the only warning would be a crackle and a splutter, and seconds later the radio would die on us. This always seemed to happen at one of the exciting bits, or the climax to a Dick Barton serial or episode of Appointment with Fear. Then there would be a frantic unscrewing of the leads from the spent battery, and re-connecting them to the spare as quickly as you could, and pray that you had not missed some vital part of the plot. The spare battery was always kept near the fire to keep it warm and charged up, which I realise now, but unbeknown to us then was a very dangerous practice indeed. We were lucky, as there was no resultant explosion experienced by us; but as this practice was carried out in thousands of houses throughout the land, I should imagine that there must have been some horrendous accidents in other homes.

Over the coming years slowly but surely the evidence of the war, like the air-raid shelters, and emergency water supply tanks, was removed. The Anderson shelters, which had been sunk in people's gardens, were either disposed of, or were raised to the surface and used as garden sheds, or chicken coups. Our massive indoor shelter was thankfully taken away, and our front room, the parlour as we called it, was restored to once more, giving our family much needed space. The communal brick air raid shelters were demolished by the novel use of a huge iron ball attached to a chain, which was in turn hooked on to a mechanical shovel, and repeatedly smashed into the shelter's brick-work. I spent many happy hours watching this deafening spectacle of destruction.

The tip remained for many years after the war had ended. Slowly diminishing from the colossus it once was, as other more efficient contractors than the Jones Brothers attacked and removed its wealth. To the great majority it was an unsightly giant slagheap; only fit to be used as hard core, with the increasing demand for new roads and buildings. Until finally it disappeared, and lives on now only in the memories of those, whose young lives were influenced by and fashioned around it.

Mammy continued with her struggle of keeping our family together, and succeeded, living to the great age of 88 years. She kept her promise of the early years, and made a nice home for us with a carpet on the stairs, and even acquiring that greatest of status symbols a brand-new piano. But, sadly none of us ever mastered the art of playing it. The only tune I can ever recall being played on its pristine keys was vamped out by Maggie, and called "In the Chapel in the Moonlight. She had the pleasure and I believe her just reward, in seeing all of her children prosper and carve out worthwhile careers for themselves. We all became house-owners, having learned the vital and important lesson, that half the battle was won, by having a roof over our heads.

THE END